Richard III and
the Princes in the Tower

ALSO BY GERALD PRENDERGHAST

*Britain and the Wars in Vietnam:
The Supply of Troops, Arms
and Intelligence, 1945–1975* (McFarland, 2015)

Richard III and the Princes in the Tower

The Possible Fates of Edward V and Richard of York

GERALD PRENDERGHAST

McFarland & Company, Inc., Publishers
Jefferson, North Carolina

LIBRARY OF CONGRESS CATALOGUING-IN-PUBLICATION DATA

Names: Prenderghast, Gerald, 1954– author.
Title: Richard III and the princes in the Tower : the possible fates of Edward V and Richard of York / Gerald Prenderghast.
Description: Jefferson, North Carolina : McFarland & Company, Inc., Publishers, 2017. | Includes bibliographical references and index.
Identifiers: LCCN 2016051548 | ISBN 9781476666655 (softcover : acid free paper) ∞
Subjects: LCSH: Richard III, King of England, 1452–1485. | Edward V, King of England, 1470–1483—Death and burial. | Richard, Duke of York, 1472–1483—Death and burial. | Great Britain—History—Richard III, 1483–1485. | Great Britain—History—House of York, 1461–1485. | Great Britain—Kings and rulers—Biography. | Princes—Great Britain—Biography.
Classification: LCC DA260 .P74 2017 | DDC 942.04/60922—dc23
LC record available at https://lccn.loc.gov/2016051548

BRITISH LIBRARY CATALOGUING DATA ARE AVAILABLE

ISBN (print) 978-1-4766-6665-5
ISBN (ebook) 978-1-4766-2590-4

© 2017 Gerald Prenderghast. All rights reserved

No part of this book may be reproduced or transmitted in any form or by any means, electronic or mechanical, including photocopying or recording, or by any information storage and retrieval system, without permission in writing from the publisher.

Cover image of "Princes in the Tower" © 2017 duncan1890/iStock

Printed in the United States of America

McFarland & Company, Inc., Publishers
Box 611, Jefferson, North Carolina 28640
www.mcfarlandpub.com

Table of Contents

Preface: Why Another Book About Richard's Nephews?   1
Introduction   3

Section I: The Reign of Richard III   7
One. "Usurpation" and the Tower   8
Two. The October Rebellion   20
Three. The Road to Bosworth Field   32

Section II: Life for Edward and Richard   49
Four. Life in Fifteenth Century England   50
Five. Edward and Richard: The Princes in the Tower   60
Six. Sojourn in the Tower   74

Section III: Which Road from the Tower? What Might Have Happened to Edward and Richard?   89
Seven. The First Solution: Did They Simply Die?   91
Eight. The Second Solution: Was It Murder?   96
Nine. The Third Solution: Did They Escape?   102

Section IV: Witnesses   115
Ten. Who Might Have Known?   116
Eleven. The Family of Edward and Richard   122
Twelve. Edward's Council and Servants   135
Thirteen. Richard's associates.   150
Fourteen. Henry Tudor and His Early Associates   165

Fifteen. The October Rebellion	175
Sixteen. The July Rescuers	183
Seventeen. Where from Here?	196
Appendix 1: Chronology of Edward and Richard, 1470–1483	209
Appendix 2: Chronology of Richard III and the Princes	211
Appendix 3: The Titulus Regius	222
Appendix 4: Sir Thomas More's Account of the Princes' Deaths	226
Appendix 5: Perkin Warbeck's Confession	229
Glossary	231
Chapter Notes	233
Bibliography	239
Index	241

"Take nothing on its looks; take everything on evidence. There is no better rule."
　—Mr. Jaggers, in Charles Dickens' *Great Expectations*

Preface: Why Another Book About Richard's Nephews?

From its original basis in Sir Thomas More's account and Shakespeare's subsequent historical fiction, Richard's alleged murder of his nephews in the Tower during the summer or autumn of 1483 has become one of the generally accepted "facts" of history. This is unfortunate because the facts, such as they are, fully support neither Richard's guilt nor the later theories claiming him to be an innocent victim of Tudor propaganda, although the very sparsity of the facts means that they can be presented to serve any particular turn an author chooses to take.

Books about the fate of Richard's nephews are plentiful, and although many of these publications are well argued, albeit from a variety of viewpoints, they all have one unavoidable failing: the facts upon which the authors are obliged to base their speculations are too few on which to base a firm conclusion. Their texts, by virtue of the available subject matter, are forced to be mainly speculative and, unfortunately, in some of the more sensational publications, this sort of speculation has been presented as incontrovertible fact. Moreover, despite the large number of books about the boys and their uncle, the most basic questions about them still require definitive answers.

If the boys died:

- Was it murder or might they have died of natural causes, such as accident or disease?
- How likely would death by natural causes have been?
- If it was murder, where and when was it done, and who did the actual killing?
- Who might have known what happened to them?
- Why is there no record of *anyone* coming forward after Richard's death

to say what happened to Edward and his little brother, when they would certainly have been well rewarded for such information?

- And finally, although this is something of a side issue, why did the former friends, servants and allies of Edward IV rebel in the autumn of 1483, when they could expect no possible advantage from doing so?
- Even more significantly, why did Henry Stafford, Duke of Buckingham, commit what was virtually political suicide by siding with Henry Tudor and the rebels?

If Edward and Richard did not die:

- Where *did* they go after leaving or escaping from the Tower?
- What eventually happened to them?

Clearly, it would be of little use to try to erect yet another theoretical framework based on currently available information. So this book is not of that type and consequently does not include extensive detail or discussion about the nature of Richard III or events during his reign, nor does it really set out to explain what happened to the boys, although one possible answer is suggested and discussed. Rather, its main purpose is to look at a number of different directions new research might follow and that may help to move the investigation into the boys' fate forward because it is investigation and a few hard facts that are required here and not more speculation. While these events occurred over 500 years ago and many would consider a search for new material pointless, anyone who takes that view might want to consider that Mancini's manuscript, one of the main sources about the boys during the summer of 1483, was found only by the purest accident in the Lille Bibliotheque in 1934, and Richard's body had to wait until 2013 before being located under a car park in Leicester.

Reference material is included here, but original sources are avoided except where they are readily available, because most of them are included in full in the standard works of reference about the period.

A final word: Fresh information does not come from a reexamination of old facts; it depends upon taking different directions. This book was written to suggest some of those directions and, as such, it is intended to serve as a point of departure for further argument and discussion, in the hope of finally providing a definitive answer to this question:

Which road did Edward and Richard take from the Tower?

Introduction

On 9 April 1483, Edward IV, king of England, died, leaving behind a twelve-year-old son, Edward V, as heir to the throne. Edward, however, was never crowned, and after being joined in the Tower by his brother Richard on 16 June 1483, neither boy was ever seen in public again. The throne was subsequently occupied by their uncle, Richard, Duke of Gloucester, who was crowned as Richard III. What really happened to his nephews has become the subject of debate, often acrimonious, since Richard's death at Bosworth on that summer's day in 1485.

Historians are divided into three fairly distinct factions in their opinions about Richard. There are the traditionalists, who believe everything Sir Thomas More and William Shakespeare had to say about Richard, accepting the story of the twisted, murderous hunchback who had his nephews killed to protect his own theft of the throne. Some go even further, claiming Richard intended to gain the throne even before his brother's death and that he was responsible for not only the death of Edward IV but also the deaths of both his brother, George, Duke of Clarence, and the former Lancastrian king, Henry VI.

Then there are the revisionists for whom Richard was the victim of beastly Tudor propaganda, an honorable man forced against his better nature to accept the throne to protect England from the ravages of a yet another civil war between Lancastrians and Yorkists. They further maintain that he has been unjustly blamed for the murder of the two little princes, whom he was unable to protect from his host of villainous rivals, the identity of their murderer depending upon which twist in the plot one happens to favor.

Finally, there is a group who adopt a significantly less dramatic and more balanced approach, accepting Richard as a man of his times, overly ambitious perhaps, certainly skilled in propaganda and coercion, but in truth, morally no better or worse than those who surrounded him, just more unlucky and perhaps a little too trusting.

The main feature of Richard's reign, and the one that has set him apart from every other English monarch, is the controversy surrounding the fate of his nephews: the never-to-be-crowned king, Edward V, and his little brother Richard. In fact, it became much more than a simple controversy, since Richard came to be seen by many in the Tudor period, as well as by a number of later writers, as the archetypal wicked uncle, and a whole mythology subsequently grew up to justify this view, including stories about his unnatural birth, misshapen body and unnatural lusts, whose potential victims included his niece.

Later opinion divides itself, some believing that Richard murdered the boys, while others see him, perhaps inevitably, as the innocent victim of the Tudor political machine, suggesting Henry Tudor, Buckingham or even Margaret Beaufort, Henry's mother, as more likely, even more realistic, candidates. Of course, if the boys were murdered, Richard is the obvious—in truth, really the only—choice. He had means, motive, and opportunity in his favor, and any except his closest associates would have found arranging the deaths of the boys during his reign impossibly difficult.

However, no evidence of any sort exists to confirm what really happened to Edward and Richard. What all the information gleaned from each of the contemporary accounts, such as Mancini, Fabyan and Rous, amounts to is as follows:

> Edward and Richard were together in the Tower of London, on the evening of 16 June 1483, after Richard, Duke of York, had been removed from his mother's care at Westminster that day and conveyed there, where he joined his brother. After that date they were both seen daily by Edward's physician, John Argentine, until an unspecified date some time before 6 July, when Mancini says the doctor's visits were discontinued, despite Edward's feeling that his death was imminent. Edward may have attended his uncle's coronation, and after that event, it was claimed that they were seen occasionally, shooting and playing in one of the gardens of the Tower, although this is strictly hearsay, second-hand evidence from Robert Fabyan, the writer of the "London Chronicle" of the period, recording something he was told. They certainly never appeared again in public after the coronation, and there is no record of their whereabouts after the end of July, when an abortive attempt was made to remove them from the Tower and their sisters from Westminster, for which four commoners were executed. There is, however, no evidence to show that the boys were still alive when this botched rescue attempt was made, although their sisters certainly were.

Despite such a lack of evidence, an answer to the question of their fate has had to be found, and most professional historians quite reasonably prefer the view that Richard murdered them, because the timing of their disappearance makes him the most obvious candidate. Sir Winston Churchill was adamant, saying, "Indeed, no fact stands forth more unchallengeable than that the overwhelming majority of the nation was convinced that Richard had used his power as protector to usurp the crown and that the princes had disappeared in the Tower. It will take many books to raise this issue to the dignity of a historical controversy."[1]

However, despite Richard's obvious credentials as the murderer of his nephews, other explanations are not impossible. One or both of the boys may have escaped; they may have been removed for their own safety; or they may have died of other causes; and despite all of the conflicting reports, rumors and speculation to the contrary, it is quite clear that the real answer to the question of what happened to the princes in the Tower is that no one has ever been able to claim to know for certain; not even Sir Winston.

Section I
The Reign of Richard III

CHAPTER ONE

"Usurpation" and the Tower

The Death of Edward IV

Edward IV, father of Edward and Richard, died on 9 April 1483 at the Palace of Westminster, as the result of a cold caught on a fishing trip and exacerbated by longstanding ill health brought on by overeating and sexual excess. Although it is now generally agreed that there was nothing suspicious about the king's death, opinions differ over what happened just prior to it and whether Edward IV did appoint his brother, then Richard, Duke of Gloucester, to the post of protector of his son Edward V.

Prince Edward, now the new king-designate Edward V, received the news of his father's death and his own succession on 14 April 1483 while at his usual residence, Ludlow Castle. This letter, from the Royal Council, also set the coronation date for 4 May and informed Earl Rivers, the new king's governor, that he should bring Edward to London, accompanied by a large escort, which, after much debate in council, was finally ordered not to exceed 2,000 men.[1] According to the council, now dominated by its Wydeville faction led by Elizabeth Wydeville (alternative spelling: Wydville, Woodville, or Widvile), Edward's queen, there was to be no protectorate but rather a regency council, headed but not dominated by Richard, Duke of Gloucester, whatever the late king's stipulation. Once Edward, aged twelve, was crowned, his minority would end and he would be fit to rule with the help of councilors, who would be of his choosing.[2]

When Richard heard about his brother's death is unknown but it was certainly some days after 14 April, probably in a series of letter from Edward's chamberlain, Lord Hastings. No notification appears to have been sent from the council, *possibly* by the connivance of the Wydeville faction, so the family's power could be consolidated and Edward's place on the throne secured before his uncle could act, although Mancini claims that Richard wrote to the council, putting his case for his own appointment as protector and professing his loyalty to the queen.³ At this point, the queen's family held the advantage. They could bring the king to London and have him crowned; then, with Edward surrounded by Wydevilles and their followers as councilors, his uncle Richard would be powerless, the role of protector being solely concerned with protection of both king and realm and usually lasting only until the coronation. It conferred no *right* to rule, either on behalf of or in place of the king.

Richard later claimed that it was the potential danger of his position that necessitated the ruthless action he took, especially given the hostility between himself and the Wydevilles. Opposed as he was to the queen and her family, after the coronation he would lack the necessary authority to protect himself and would therefore be dependent upon the good offices of his nephew, who had been reared, almost from birth, by the Wydevilles and their adherents.⁴ Such being the case, Richard implied, control of the king—or at least his person—seemed, for him, to have become imperative; except that Richard had previously always been of good terms with the Wydeville family, even acting as agent for several of them in a number of business transactions. There had never been any marked hostility between the king's brother and the queen's family, even after the death of the Duke of Clarence.⁵

Edward IV, king of England from 1461 until October 1470 and then from April 1471 until his death on 9 April 1483, from a portrait painted in 1470. Scholarly, erudite and a confirmed and practiced lecher, Edward was also an able soldier and financial administrator. Despite his ability to accumulate wealth, when he died his exchequer contained hardly sufficient ready money to pay for his funeral (Wikipedia).

Stony Stratford

Richard rode south from York, intent upon intercepting his nephew and removing him from Wydeville influence. The city's records, however, show that before leaving York, he had masses sung for his dead brother, and afterwards led the local magnates in taking a solemn oath to his nephew.[6]

Both Richard's piety and loyalty are a matter of record, so, for him, enclosed in an environment of fifteenth century religious conformity, this oath would have had immense significance, and breaking it would have been seen by his contemporaries as almost unthinkable. Whatever his real motivation, Richard

Elizabeth Wydeville (aka Wydville, Woodville, or Widvile) was queen consort of England as the wife of Edward IV from 1463 until his death in 1483. Beautiful and ambitious, she proved no match for her brother-in-law, Richard of Gloucester (Wikipedia).

was observing all the proprieties, thus showing himself in the best possible light. He finally caught up with Edward's party at Stony Stratford on 30 April. Once the boy was in bed, there followed a night of carousing during which Richard, Rivers and the rest of Edward's escort were joined by Henry Stafford, Duke of Buckingham, an unwavering opponent of the Wydevilles.[7]

Next morning, Richard had Edward's companions, Earl Rivers, Sir Richard Grey, Sir Thomas Vaughn, Edward's elderly chamberlain, and Sir Richard Haute arrested and imprisoned while he and Buckingham conducted the boy to London themselves, having first also dismissed Edward's remaining long-time servants and the soldiers guarding him. Richard justified both the arrest of Rivers, Grey and Vaughn and the dismissal of the boy's original retainers by claiming that the Wydevilles' influence was corrupting the boy and that he was only safe with his paternal uncle.[8] The relationship between the two dukes at this point is difficult to define. Buckingham's right to the throne was second only to Richard's, and debate continues as to which of the

The Guildhall in York, where Richard swore the oath of fealty to his nephew, Edward, in April 1483, in a photograph taken in 2001 (Wikimedia Commons/CC-BY-SA 3.0).

two men was the instigator of the events at Stony Stratford, although Richard is said to have always continued to claim that all his actions during the period April–July 1483 were prompted by his dead brother's wishes and the need to defend himself from the Wydeville faction surrounding the young king.[9]

Entry into London

Hearing the news of Richard's maneuverings and the arrest of her adherents, Elizabeth Wydeville and her son, the Marquess of Dorset, first attempted to raise a force to counter Richard's actions. However, she quickly found that the loyalty of those about her was wavering and, in consequence, the queen sought sanctuary in Westminster Abbey on 1 May, accompanied by Prince Richard, Dorset and her five daughters. At this stage she cannot have been unduly alarmed by Richard's actions because her transition to the abbey was fairly considered, so many of her possessions going with her, in fact, that part of a wall of the abbey had to be demolished to allow access for her property.[10] Dorset did not remain with his mother for very long and escaped soon after, intent upon stirring up opposition to the new regime, if his subsequent actions are any indicator of his original intentions.[11] Meanwhile, Edward's party continued their journey and, after entering London with his nephew on 4 May, Richard once again behaved with due propriety. He had previously written to the city authorities, promising an early coronation. To bolster this assertion, Edward now received all the ceremonial observances a new king had a right to expect, the soon-to-be protector ordering all the lords "spiritual and temporal," as well as the mayor and aldermen, to swear the customary oath of fealty to his nephew.[12] At the same time, Richard displayed a collection of weapons bearing Wydeville insignia, which he claimed had been intended to be used by men intent upon ambushing his party, although it seems to have been generally known that these weapons had been cached outside London so as to be available for use in the Scottish war.[13] Public opinion seems to have been on the side of the new protector, however, since both nobles and ordinary people were fearful of the results of a Wydeville-dominated monarchy, with a minor occupying the throne, perhaps remembering the avarice of the queen's family during her husband's reign. More importantly, the majority saw the activities of the two dukes as aimed against the Wydevilles, not against the young king.[14] Croyland even stated that those whose support was sought by the queen were "not only irresolute, but altogether hostile to themselves. Some even said openly that it was more just and profitable that the youthful sovereign should be with his paternal uncle than with his maternal uncles and uterine brothers."[15]

Richard exploited this ill-feeling towards the former queen's family in a continuing campaign of misdirection against the Wydevilles, even before he and Edward arrived in the capital. One of the surviving letters he sent during that period, although it was in Edward's name, was to Thomas Bourchier, Archbishop of Canterbury, expressing his concern about the safety of the Great Seal, the custodianship of the Tower and the king's treasure. In this letter, sent on 2 May 1483,[16] Richard claimed that the Marquis of Dorset, one of Elizabeth Wydeville's sons, had seized the royal treasury, apportioning half to equip a fleet to defend the coast (the fleet was commanded by his brother, Sir Edward Wydeville), and dividing the remainder between himself and his mother. This letter is of considerable interest because it is the only document that makes any reference to treasure left by the late king or to Wydeville involvement in its supposed removal. Doubly significant is that the letter's origin was the Duke of Gloucester, most particularly because it was well known in royal circles that there was no treasure; the royal accounts showed that Edward IV did not even leave enough hard cash to pay for his own funeral. The truth of the matter was that Dorset and Sir Edward Wydeville had received this money from the Royal Council quite legitimately, for the purposes of "foreign defense," but the rumor, started by Richard, worked once again in his favor, striking yet another blow at the reeling Wydeville political machine.[17] He finalized the matter by offering free pardons to all in Sir Edward Wydeville's fleet except the leaders, and this resulted in a wholesale desertion, forcing Wydeville to escape to Brittany with only two ships.[18]

Richard as Protector and the Reign of Edward V

Richard's appointment as protector was confirmed by the Royal Council on 10 May, with the almost universal support of the citizens of London,[19] and plans for Edward's coronation, now put back to 22 June, were approved at the same council meeting.[20] Having rid himself of most of the Wydeville faction on the Royal Council, Richard immediately began replacing many of the great officers of state with men more sympathetic to his own cause, although grants and proclamations were still being issued in the new king's name.[21] In particular, he replaced Lord Rotherham as chancellor with John Russell, Bishop of Lincoln, although Rotherham still retained his place on the Royal Council. At this point, however, the council refused Richard's request to execute Rivers, Grey and Vaughn as traitors, because their alleged actions at the time had not been directed against a formally recognized protector but rather against the Duke of Gloucester, who was then a private citizen.[22]

By now, the situation in London seems to have been approaching normality, and although they refused his request for the executions of Rivers and his companions, the council appears to have been ready to accept that Richard intended his protectorship to be a temporary arrangement undertaken to stabilize the country and protect him from the Wydevilles, only intended to remain in place until Edward took his rightful place on the throne.[23] At the same council meeting on 10 May that proclaimed Richard protector, the decision was also made, based upon a suggestion by the Duke of Buckingham, to move Edward to the Tower. The prince was taken there some time between 16 and 19 May. This is less sinister than it may appear, however, conforming as it does to ancestral precedent whereby the prospective king was accustomed to spend the weeks before his coronation in what was then simply one of the principal royal palaces. Up to this point, Richard appeared to be fulfilling his role as protector responsibly, but in the period after 8 June 1483, the whole complexion of events in London changed.

Baynard's Castle, the London home of the York family, as seen from the river. Although this is a picture drawn some two centuries after Richard's reign, its appearance would have changed little in the intervening period (Wikipedia).

It is this period, the transition from protector to king, which has caused most of the controversy about Richard's motives and, consequently, about the eventual fate of the boys. Based on the available evidence, it has been difficult for writers about these events, even his contemporaries, to decide if Richard was a victim of circumstance or was making a premeditated attempt on the throne, possibly from before the time of his brother's death. Certainly, what he wrote in the days before the beginning of June, in particular the letter about the Wydeville theft of the king's treasury, seems to show that he was attempting to manipulate both official and public opinion towards a general acceptance of himself as, at the very least, the young king's most influential councilor and to defame the Wydeville family as a whole. Moreover, his activities up to this point could equally well have masked a preconceived plan to gain the throne that may have dated from shortly after his brother's death.[24] Whatever his motivation, certain events are clearly recorded.

Around 8 or 9 June, an informal council meeting—or a gathering of some sort—is thought to have taken place at Westminster attended by "all Lords spiritual and temporal."[25] No record of the meeting or what was discussed exists, but some change in the status quo must have occurred because on 10 June, Richard wrote to his supporters in the north asking for reinforcements and claiming that the queen intended to murder him, Buckingham and what he called the "old Royal blood of the realm," although how she could have achieved this is difficult to understand, since she was trapped in Westminster Abbey and her most important adherents were imprisoned.[26] It has been suggested that these troops were, in fact, sent for to oppose Hastings, Morton, Stanley and Rotherham, who had been conducting informal meetings without officially informing Richard. In particular, it may have been at one of these meetings that Hastings and his cronies decided that their best interests lay in opposing Richard as either protector or king and had let it be known that some or all of them were intent upon acting on that decision.

Stained glass window in Cardiff Cathedral with a stylized depiction of Richard III and his queen, Anne Neville. Even in this stained glass representation, Richard is depicted as thin and haggard, reflecting the strains that were known to have been imposed by his eventful, two-year reign (Wikimedia Commons/CC-BY-SA 3.0).

It is claimed that three days later, at another council meeting on 13 June and before his northern reinforcements had arrived, Richard charged Lord Hastings, John Morton, Bishop of Ely, Lord Stanley and Lord Rotherham, the former chancellor, of plotting with the queen and Jane Shore, one of Edward IV's mistresses, against his authority and life. Hastings had been a close friend and confidant of Edward IV and Richard's enthusiastic supporter during the late king's reign, as well as being privy to the myriad plots and factionalism that pervaded English medieval government. Considerable doubt exists about the truth of Richard's accusations, and it has been convincingly argued that he may have had good reasons for ridding himself of his brother's devious chamberlain, whose loyalty to the family of Edward IV was well established and who may have made it clear to Richard privately that he would support Edward's son rather than the protector in any attempt upon the throne.[27] Hastings is thought to have been immediately executed, although such an act by one having only a protector's authority would have been unprecedented. No contemporary record of the 13 June meeting exists, the only accounts being those of later historians (Mancini, Croyland, and Sir Thomas More). To prevent any further panic in a city already on edge from the events of the past weeks, a proclamation was also immediately issued explaining that Hastings and his associates had been planning to assassinate Richard and Buckingham during the council meeting and giving this as the reason for the immediate execution of the plotter's leader. Stanley and Rotherham were subsequently pardoned, John Morton alone continuing to be held in prison.

Events now began to move quickly to a conclusion. On 16 June, Elizabeth Wydeville was persuaded to relinquish her son Richard, Edward's younger brother, who was then removed from sanctuary in Westminster Abbey and sent to live with his brother in the Tower. Next day, 17 June, in response to the protector's orders, Edward's coronation was postponed again until November, and a meeting of Parliament convened on Edward's behalf by his uncle and arranged for 25 June was canceled. On the 22 June, a sermon was preached at St. Paul's Cross by a Dr. Ralph Shaa (or Shaw), brother of the Lord Mayor, Sir Edmund Shaa, in which he is said to have claimed that both the boys and their sisters were illegitimate, because of a precontract of marriage that their father had entered into before his marriage to Elizabeth Wydeville. The authority for this bigamy is quoted as Robert Stillington, the elderly Bishop of Bath and Wells and Edward's former chancellor, who is said to have claimed at the meeting on 9–10 June that prior to Edward IV's marriage to Elizabeth Wydeville, Edward had entered into a precontract with a noblewoman called Eleanor Butler, for the sole purpose of having sexual intercourse with her. Edward had used this device before, and Stillington himself even claimed to have performed what amounted to a marriage or betrothal ceremony between this lady and the king. If such a ceremony took place, canon law decreed that Edward's marriage to Elizabeth Wydeville was bigamous and their children illegitimate, although it is not absolutely certain that the precontract was not a complete fabrication on Richard's part. However, although no details of the June meeting exist, there is a record of a conversation between Buckingham and John Morton, Bishop of Ely, recorded in *Hall's Chronicle*, written some time in the sixteenth century, which describes Stillington as bringing in "instruments, authentic doctors, proctors, and notaries of law with depositions of divers witnesses."

Whatever its truth or otherwise, the consequences of Stillington's assertion, if accepted, were clear. Illegitimate children who had not come of age could be barred from the throne, although bastardy was not in itself a disqualification and had certainly not stood in the way of previous monarchs, such as William the Conqueror. Shaa, in his sermon, may also have suggested that Edward IV was not the son of his father, although since Edward had ascended to the throne by right of conquest, not birth, his origins would seem to be immaterial.[28]

Picture from an early version of the Rous Rolle depicting, from left to right, Anne Neville, Richard (crowned) and their only son, Edward, standing on the white boar of Gloucester (Wikipedia).

The Rolle

On 25 June in London, an assembly of the Lords Spiritual and Temporal and other notables previously summoned in Edward's name was convened, under Buckingham's chairmanship. This group, for which Richard later incorrectly claimed Parliamentary status, decided to offer him the crown, in the form of a petition or "Rolle," which gave the assembly's reasons, in detail, for taking such action.[29] These reasons included his brother's incompetence and avarice while king; his nephews' illegitimacy; and the disqualification of his brother George's children because of Clarence's attainder in 1478,[30] although the main grounds given in the Rolle for Richard's ascent to the throne were his brother Edward's disqualification because of his marriage, immoral behavior and subsequent manipulation by the Wydevilles, rather than the boys' illegitimacy, which is mentioned almost in passing. At some point after Shaa's sermon, Buckingham had also addressed the mayor and leading citizens of London at the Guildhall, persuading them of Richard's suitability, and subsequently, on 26 June, these notables, together with the "Parliamentary" group, proceeded to Baynard's Castle, the York family's London home, where he was staying. Once at the castle, Buckingham presented Richard with the petition offering him the crown, the group apparently stating that they would not have Edward's sons to rule over them and that if Richard refused, they would choose another king (possibly Buckingham). The circumstances outlined in the Rolle left Richard as the only possible candidate; and although he showed a certain initial reluctance to supplant his nephew, witnesses record that he finally accepted without too much delay and formally succeeded to the throne later that day, in a ceremony at Westminster Hall.[31] The finishing touch had been added to Richard's schemes in Pontefract, on the previous day (25 June), with the deaths of Anthony, Earl Rivers; Richard Grey; and Thomas Vaughn; all three executed for treason under the supervision of Sir Richard Ratcliffe and the Earl of Northumberland.

Even if Richard had not wanted the crown, which seems unlikely, circumstances and the stability of the country meant he had a certain amount of justification for accepting. Rival candidates for the throne included Buckingham himself, Henry Tudor, and the young Earl of Lincoln, all of whom could claim at least superficially valid title and were only too ready to prove their claims with the sword, even if it led to another civil war. Moreover, many of the council may have honestly felt that the last thing England needed then was a Wydeville-controlled minor on the throne, king's son or not; although the presence in London of overwhelming numbers of troops loyal to Richard and Buckingham gave them little choice except passive agreement.

Incidentally, it is of interest to note here that, when he came to power, Henry Tudor called in and destroyed almost every copy of the Rolle and its accompanying Act of Parliament, the "Titulus Regius" which referred to it, in order to establish the legitimacy of his wife, Elizabeth of York, and so strengthen, by association, his own claim to the throne.

Richard was crowned king on the 6 July, all of Edwards' children having been formally declared illegitimate before the coronation. Significantly, in light of Buckingham's subsequent treachery, Bishop John Morton, who later became chancellor to Henry VII, had by now been turned over to the duke for safekeeping and was imprisoned in Brecon Castle, one of Buckingham's Welsh residences.

CHAPTER TWO

The October Rebellion

After his cornation, some time between 18 and 20 July, Richard began a royal progress through northern England and the Midlands, accompanied by a considerable entourage that initially included Henry Stafford, Duke of Buckingham. This period was to be the most peaceful of his reign, the leisurely journey beginning at Windsor around 20 July and visiting Reading (23 July), Oxford, Woodstock, Minster Lovell (home of Francis, Lord Lovell), Tewksbury, Gloucester (2 August), Warwick (8 August), where he was joined by his wife Anne Neville, before proceeding to Coventry, Leicester, Nottingham, Pontefract (27 August) and York. In York, where he stayed from 29 August until 19 or 21 September, he was joined by his son, Edward of Middleham, who was created Prince of Wales in York Minster, before Richard continued on his way to Gainsborough and then Lincoln, which he reached on 11 October. The progress was stopped at Lincoln by news of the October Rebellion and Richard's urgent need to move south to deal with Buckingham's treachery.[1]

Soon after he began this tour and sometime before 29 July 1483, an attempt was made to liberate both the princes from the Tower and the princesses from their Westminster sanctuary. The plot failed and the four men who (it was claimed) were immediately involved were tried and executed, although it was clear that they were only the servants of a group of more highly placed individuals, which may have included Margaret Beaufort, the mother of Henry Tudor.[2] Buckingham had left Richard at Gloucester on 2 August, returning to Brecknock and his Welsh estates, where the wily John Morton awaited him.[3] Although Richard appears to have been complacent about conditions in the country, he does seem to have been aware that trouble was brewing, although not where its real source was, because on 28 August he appointed a commission of "oyer and terminer," headed by Buckingham, to enquire into "treasons and felonies" in a number of southern counties. Areas specifically named were London, Surrey, Sussex, Kent, Middlesex, Oxfordshire, Berkshire, Essex and Hertfordshire, all of which were home to

York Minster, where Richard's son, Edward of Middleham, was created Prince of Wales (Wikimedia Commons/CC-BY-SA 3.0).

The nave of York Minster, looking towards the altar (photograph by David Iliff/CC-BY-SA 3.0).

officials and crown servants who were later to be heavily involved in the October Rebellion.[4]

Murdered Princes: Sir Thomas More's Account

According to Sir Thomas More's account of events, which he claimed was based on the confession extracted from Sir James Tyrell in 1502 before he was executed, Richard decided to kill his nephews, Edward and Richard, soon after he arrived at Warwick on 8 August. Having reached this decision, he sent Tyrell south with orders to obtain the keys to the Tower from the new constable, Sir Robert Brackenbury, and murder the boys. Brackenbury was a man widely known for his integrity, and More claims he had previously refused to kill the boys despite having been given Richard's direct order. Would a man ruthless enough to murder his nephews have allowed Brackenbury to escape alive after disobeying such an order, especially when, by issuing the order, Richard had made his intent public? Besides, Brackenbury died fighting for Richard at Bosworth, hardly the action of such a man, if he knew the king had murdered his nephews. Tyrell, however, so More's story goes, was not so punctilious. According to More, he obtained the keys and then employed John Dighton, his horse keeper, and Miles Forest, one of the princes' servants, to suffocate the boys in their bed clothes. More then claims that the bodies were then buried at the "Foote of some Stairs," although no mention is made of exactly where. Subsequently, Richard is supposed to have had a change of heart and had them removed to a more fitting spot.[5] This is the version of events that was accepted by Shakespeare as the basis for his play *Richard III* and has since passed into history as confirmation of Richard's guilt. Its basis is Sir Thomas More's account, which is thought to have been given him by Henry's chancellor, John Morton, although it is not known whether Morton had ever seen or read Tyrell's confession.

Rebellion

Although Richard's seizure of the throne took many by surprise, his reign had barely begun before the first stirrings of rebellion were manifested.

Barnard Castle, a property Richard of Gloucester received as part of his wife's dowry when they married in 1472 (Wikimedia Commons/CC-BY-SA 3.0).

What is perhaps most surprising about this enterprise is that its inception seems to have been the work of the old, well-established servants of Edward IV.[6] Almost without exception these rebels were prominent figures in the social, economic and judicial hierarchy of the southern counties of Kent, Hampshire, Wiltshire, Devon and Cornwall, and it is difficult to see what they could have hoped to gain from what turned out to be an ill-prepared and ultimately disastrous attempt to depose the new king. Self-interest was the usual guiding principal among landowners in the fifteenth century, and it has been suggested that many of these men feared losing the positions, influence and land they had acquired under Edward IV. This cannot have been the whole answer because it is a matter of record that, with the exception of some members of the former king's household, those of Edward's former retainers who remained loyal retained their places in Richard's regime. Moreover, Richard seems to have courted many of the most important southern magnates who rebelled later, in the months from August to December 1483.[7] It has also been suggested that the real cause of the rebellion was Richard's treatment, or rather alleged treatment, of his nephews and that the former Yorkists were so incensed at the murderous uncle that they were willing to leave all their carefully accrued land and titles and risk everything to throw in with a Tudor nobody, after news of the boys' deaths became common knowledge, simply because anybody was better than Richard.[8] This also seems difficult to accept fully, because if the southern magnates were incensed about the boys' murder, why did all the northern landowners, with the exception of Sir Reginald Bray, stand quietly by? Murdered children, whatever their original loyalty to Richard, would surely be as good an incentive for rebellion north of the Thames as south of the river.

Participants and Motives

Buckingham's original role in this scenario was as go-between, liaising with Henry and his mother on one hand and the Yorkist rebels and Elizabeth Wydeville on the other. John Morton was probably orchestrating arrangements in the background, once he had convinced Buckingham to assume the role of kingmaker and matchmaker between Henry and Elizabeth of York.[9] The duke, however, may have had a different outcome in mind; and it is certainly possible that he could have been using Elizabeth of York and Tudor to further his own plans for an attempt at the throne.[10] Whether he would have succeeded in deposing Tudor, when Henry was backed by his formidable mother and the devious intelligence of supporters such as Bray and Morton, remains to be seen.

The Original Plan

The rebels' original plan seems to have been to launch a three-pronged attack, probably centering on London. In the southeast, the Kentish rebels were to cross the Thames, turn west and proceed up the north bank of the river, finally seizing and occupying the capital. The men of Wiltshire, Hampshire, Somerset and Dorset were to meet Henry Tudor and his small, token force when they landed at one of the south coast ports (Poole seems most probable), presumably also then advancing towards London, while Buckingham was to raise a force in Wales. He would then cross the Severn into England and this concerted rising of most of the southern gentry would sweep Richard and his northern supporters away. Henry Tudor, or more probably, Henry Stafford, Duke of Buckingham, would then become the new king, a rumor having circulated soon after Buckingham became involved in the rebellion that Edward and Richard "had died a violent death." Alternatively, the southern Yorkist rebels may have forced the coronation of Elizabeth of York with Henry Tudor as her consort and consequently a king in name only, which seems the most probable scenario. Both Tudor and his mother were virtually penniless during this period, and the future king had no forces of his own he could rely on, unlike the 1485 expedition, when he was in command of troops supplied and paid for by the French king.

The story of the boys' demise and the subsequent change in direction of the rebellion began, according to Croyland, early in the revolt when "a rumour was spread" that Edward and Richard had been killed, with the veiled implication that this rumor had been deliberately circulated. Immediately after the story became current, according to Croyland again, a message was sent to "Henry, Earl of Richmond" by Buckingham, on the advice of John Morton, telling him to come to England, marry Elizabeth of York and "together with her, take possession of the throne." This description of events lends a certain credence to the idea that Henry Tudor was seen by most of the rebels, especially Buckingham, as a convenience that would allow a return to the former Yorkist rule by a child of Edward IV, rather than as a monarch in his own right. Possible sources for the rumor of the boys' death include Buckingham, who could have been using Henry Tudor as a diversion in his own attempt at the crown and the hand of Elizabeth of York, and Richard himself, who, it has been suggested, may have felt this story would weaken the resolve of those who wanted Edward restored to his rightful place.[11] It is not impossible either that John Morton had a hand in circulating the story, even possibly suggesting such a plan to Buckingham.

The Course of the Rebellion

Henry Stafford had returned to his Welsh estates by the end of September 1483, and in October, he began his attempt to rally support.[12] Unfortunately, he was so unpopular that few men would join him of their own free will and those he did manage to recruit were only a small force, consisting mostly of tenants coerced into the ranks, who would be easily discouraged if the revolt looked like failing. Undaunted by his troops' reluctance, he set off for the crossings of the Severn, probably convinced that some early successes would soon bring men flocking to his cause.[13]

Despite the duke's optimism, the whole business was a disaster almost from the start. The Kentish rising began prematurely, some ten days too soon, beginning in Maidstone on 18 October, Rochester on 20 October, and finally Gravesend from 22 to 25 October.[14] Almost immediately, the rebels found themselves opposed by John Howard, Duke of Norfolk, who had been touring Surrey and Sussex, inspecting his recently acquired Mowbray inheritance. Howard acted decisively, fortifying the Thames crossings at Gravesend before sending troops to protect London and informing Richard, then in Lincoln, of what was happening, although the king's own agents seem to have kept him well informed.[15] Buckingham and his army were caught when the river Severn flooded, and he was subsequently betrayed and captured, the Vaughans and Sir Humphrey Stafford of Grafton being instrumental in his downfall.[16]

Richard had already begun reviewing the troops he had summoned in Leicester on 21 October, and having left London in Norfolk's care and executed Buckingham at Salisbury on 2 November, he continued to move his army south, passing Bridport and reaching Exeter on 8 November, where he found that most of the remaining rebel leaders, principally those from Wiltshire, Hampshire and the other southern counties, had fled to France. One exception was Richard's brother-in-law, Thomas St. Leger, who was captured and subsequently executed in Exeter on 13 November.[17] Although Henry Tudor did bring a small number of men and ships from Brittany to support the revolt, a storm scattered his fleet and he arrived outside Poole harbor with only two ships, with which he soon wisely returned to Brittany.[18] By early November, Richard was back in London, faced with a new set of problems, this time associated with his empty treasury.

Table 1. Main Participants in the October Rebellion
In Kent and the southeast

Individuals	Location	Role	Literacy
Sir George Brown	Betchworth, Surrey	• 1472: MP for Guildford • 1478: MP for Surrey • 1480–81: Sheriff of Kent. • Only man executed for his part in the rebellion.	Not known
Sir John Fogge (1417–1490), married to Alice Haute (d. 1462). 66 at time of rebellion	Ashford, Kent	• 1461–68: Treasurer of king's household • Royal councilor to Edward IV • Royal councilor to Edward V • Administrator of Duchy of Cornwall	Not known
Nicholas Gaynesford	Carshalton, Surrey	Personal friend of Edward and Elizabeth Woodville	Not known
John Gaynesford	Alyngton	Squire	
Sir Thomas Bourchier	Barnes, Richmond	Constable of Windsor Castle	Not known
Thomas Fiennes	Herstmonceux, Sussex	1480–81: Sheriff of Surrey & Sussex	Not known
Sir William Haute (?–1497)		• Sheriff of Kent, 1465, 1474, 1482. • Constable of Swansea. • Steward of Richard's Gower lordship.	Gifted musician, so may also have been literate
Sir John Guildford	Cranbrook, near Rolvenden	Leader of the Kentish rebels, 1483	Not known
Sir Richard Guildford, son of Sir John	Cranbrook, near Rolvenden	Leader of the Kentish rebels, 1483	
Richard Haute (1450?–1487)	Ightham Mote, Kent	Kentish Justice of the Peace under Henry VII	Not known
John Pympe	Nettlestead Court, Kent	Squire	Not known
Reginald Pympe	Nettlestead Court, Kent	Gentleman, brother of John	

Individuals	Location	Role	Literacy
Edward Poynings	Marsham	Squire	Not known
Sir Thomas Lewkenor	Tratton		Not known
William Clifford	Iwade	Squire	Not known
John Darrel	Calehill	Squire	Not known
Anthony Kene	Woolwich, London	Squire	Not known
Thomas Ryder	Lynstede, Kent	Squire	Not known
William Brandon	London	Squire	Not known
John Wyngfeld	London	Squire	Not known
Alexander Culpeper	Goudhurst, Kent	Squire	Not known
James Horne	Westwell	Gentleman	Not known
Robert Brewis	London	Gentleman	Not known
John Boutayne	London	Yeoman of the Crown	
Roger Long	Southwark, London	Yeoman	
Richard Potter	London	Yeoman of the Crown	
Richard Fissher	Lye	Yeoman of the Crown	
William Loveday	London	Yeoman of the Crown	
William Strode	London	Yeoman of the Crown	
John Hooe	London	Yeoman	

In Wiltshire, Berkshire, Hampshire, Dorset and Somerset

Individuals	Location	Role	Literacy
Sir Richard Woodville	3rd Earl Rivers	Leader of the southern rebels	Not known
Lionel Woodville	Bishop of Salisbury	Leader of the southern rebels	Literate
Sir Roger Tocotes	Bromham, Wiltshire	Steward duke of Clarence's lands: 1470	Not known
John Harcourt	Stanton Harcourt, Oxfordshire	Clarence's receiver in southwest	Not known
Sir William Norris	Yattendon	• Clarence's steward in Caversham • 1474: One of Edward's Knights of the Body	Not known
Sir John St. Loo	Somerset	Fee'd retainer	Not known
Sir William Berkeley	Beverstone, Gloucestershire	Constable of Southhampton & Winchester	Not known
Sir John Cheyne	Falston Cheyne, Wiltshire	1479–83: Master of the King's Horse	Not known

Two. The October Rebellion

Individuals	Location	Role	Literacy
Sir Giles Daubney	Barrington, Somerset	Sheriff of Somerset, Dorset & Devon	Not known
Sir William Stonor	Stonor, Oxfordshire	1478: MP for Oxfordshire	Literate: letters between Sir William and his wife
Sir Walter Hungerford	Heytesbury, Wiltshire Farleigh Hungerford, Somerset		Not known
Richard Hill (1489–1496)		Bishop of London	Literate, an educated churchman

In Wales and the southwest

Individuals	Location	Role	Literacy
Henry Stafford, Duke of Buckingham	Brecon, Wales	Suggested to be prime mover in the revolt.	Not known
Thomas Grey, Marquis of Dorset		Constable of the Tower for Edward V until forced into sanctuary at Westminster with his mother, Elizabeth Wydeville.	Not known
Sir Thomas St. Leger; executed 13 October 1483 for his role in the rebellion	Exeter	• Controller of the Royal Mint: 1461–1483 • Esquire and Knight of the Body • Master of the king's hart hounds: 1478–1483 • Married to Anne, Duchess of Exeter (sister of Edward IV)	Not known
Sir Robert Willoughby	Brooke, Wiltshire	• Sheriff of Cornwall: 1478–1479 • Sheriff of Devon: 1480–1481	Not known

Individuals	Location	Role	Literacy
Sir John Willoughby		• Father of Sir Robert • Administrator in Wiltshire and Somerset.	Not known
Sir Thomas Arundel	Lanherne Cornwall		Not known
Richard Nanfan		Sheriff of Cornwall: 1479–1480	Not known
Sir Edward Courtenay	Boconnoc, Cornwall		Not known
Peter Courtenay	Powderham	• Secretary to Edward IV • Bishop of Exeter: 1478	Literate and probably numerate; degrees in both theology and law
Walter Courtenay	Powderham		Not known
John Treelyan			Not known
Thomas Pyne	Exeter	Edward IV last esceator of Devon, reappointed by Richard	Not known

*Source: Ross, 1981.

In the north

Individuals	Location	Role	Literacy
Sir Reginald Bray		Servant to Margaret Beaufort	Not known
John Morton	Brecon, as a prisoner of the Duke of Buckingham, then France, with Henry Tudor	Organizer	Literate
Margaret Beaufort	France, with Henry Tudor	Organizer	Not known

Table 2. Statistics Relating to Participants in the October Rebellion: Noblemen[19]

Original role	Total	Rebelled in 1483	Activity of remainder
Squires of the Body under Edward IV; those with southern origins	24	11	5 lost their peace commissions 2 rebelled in 1484 6 remained loyal

Original role	Total	Rebelled in 1483	Activity of remainder
Squires of the Body under Edward IV; those with northern origins	16	0	All remained loyal
Knights of the Body under Edward IV; those with southern origins	10	6	All remained loyal
Knights of the Body under Edward IV; those with northern origins	14	0	All remained loyal

Table 3. Statistics Relating to Participants in the October Rebellion: Government Officials[20]

Official role	Percentage involved in 1483 rebellion
Sheriffs in post 1478–1482	48%
Sheriffs in post from 1482	40%
Peace commissioners selected by Richard	35% Another 26% "stood down" after the rebellion
Principal southern officers replaced	40%

CHAPTER THREE

The Road to Bosworth Field

Securing a Power Base, and Financial Problems

Richard's immediate major problems in November 1483 were threefold. He needed to effect changes in his regime to initially control and ultimately secure the dissident southern counties previously controlled by the rebels. He also needed to convince his subjects that he was entitled to the crown he had usurped. Most importantly, he had to destroy or nullify Henry Tudor, together with his rebel following, and so dispose of the threat presented by their activities.[1]

The king began his attempt to control the southern counties by confiscating the estates of the men attainted for treason in the Parliament of January 1484, subsequently redistributing this property to his own trusted followers, who were mainly, but not exclusively, northerners.[2] This alleged "plantation" of Richard's northern followers throughout the south was never as extensive as has been suggested, and many of the minor southern gentry were quite content to collaborate with the new Yorkist regime. Nor did Richard face insurmountable political resistance from the more senior noble elements of that area. These rich, powerful landowners were, first and foremost, political realists and proved unwilling to take unnecessary risks, at least until they were shown that it would be to their advantage to wholly support either Richard or Henry Tudor. Many of them certainly cooperated with Richard's regime, even if they were to deny this later when Tudor became king.[3] Richard's problems in the south were not completely solved by his redistribution of rebel lands, however. Many longstanding tenants of the October rebels who had been on these lands for generations were uncomfortable with a northern newcomer administering their counties, in place of the families who, like them, were long-term occupants.[4] This rumbling discontent resulted in a lack of material support for the new regime in the summer of 1485, before the events at Bosworth brought most of the surviving representatives of the old, southern county families back into power on their former landholdings.

Control in the north was an easier matter because of Richard's former connections in that area, and it was exercised principally by the Council of the North as it had been during Edward's reign. Then it had been the responsibility of Richard himself, although now it came under the presidency of the king's nephew, the Earl of Lincoln.[5] Richard still retained tight political control over this region, however; being especially careful to subtly curb the influence of the two most powerful landowners, the Earls of Northumberland and Westmorland, although he did increase their landholdings as encouragement for their continued loyalty. East Anglia, Lincolnshire and parts of Surrey and Sussex were secured by the loyal Howards, both father and son, while Wales came under the sway of William Herbert, Earl of Huntingdon, who was married to Richard's illegitimate daughter, Katherine. Ostensibly, this looked like having the makings of a secure power-base, except that a major and significant part of the north was controlled by William, Lord Stanley, husband to Tudor's mother Margaret Beaufort, who was finally to betray Richard at Bosworth. Even in the winter of 1483, Richard seems to have been concerned that Stanley could not to be trusted.[6]

Uneasy Lies the Crown

Despite these maneuverings, which were intended to establish him politically, Richard remained unsure of the security of his position. His peace of mind cannot have been helped by the indifferent success he achieved in confirming his right to the crown. The Titulus Regius confirming the illegitimacy of Edward's children was passed by Richard's parliament of January 1484, but he must have felt insecure still because during the term of this, his only parliament, he felt it necessary to call together all the Lords Spiritual and Temporal, making them swear to adhere to his son Edward, if anything should happen to his father. He also reaffirmed the stipulations of the Titulus Regius before the London livery companies at Westminster.[7] Certainly, in that winter of 1483–84, he was a worried man, and it may have been concern for his public image that provoked the beneficent legislation enacted during this period, Richard claiming that "the kings' highness is fully determined to see due administration of justice throughout his realm." However, although many have described Richard as a reformer, the various acts and provisions dealing with the inadequacies of aspects of commercial and civil law enacted during this period may have been orchestrated by members of the House of Commons more competent and interested in such matters, rather than by the king himself.[8]

Financial problems also plagued Richard throughout his reign. He had inherited an empty treasury from his brother, and the costs incurred in putting down the October Rebellion, fighting the Scots in 1484 and defending the coastline from the expected invasion by Henry Tudor and his adherents meant that by the spring of 1485 he was so short of money that he was obliged to resort to a system of loans from his chief barons. These were, however, real loans, with a repayment date set for 1487, not a return to the hated beneficences—little more than kingly extortion—that Edward IV had introduced in the last years of his reign. The need to neutralize the threat of Henry Tudor and defeat the Scots also dominated Richard's foreign policy, although his early intention to continue the war north of the border seems to have been abandoned after the death of his son in April 1484. He concluded a three-year truce with the Scottish king on 14 September 1484 and at the same time arranged a marriage between his niece, Anne de la Pole, and the heir to the Scottish throne.[9] By November 1484, he was back in Westminster where he spent the winter, except for a brief visit to Canterbury.

Penny minted for the king during the reign of Richard III. Richard was well aware of the necessity for a stable fiscal system, reflected in the production of this currency that could be identified with him and his administration (courtesy Rasiel Suarez).

Family Problems

While Richard had his hands full dealing with rebellion in the West Country, Elizabeth Wydeville had begun marshaling the few resources remaining to her to strike back at him. She began her campaign against Richard in the autumn of 1483, when it is claimed by Croyland that correspondence began between Elizabeth Woodville and Henry's mother, Margaret Beaufort. This correspondence or negotiation eventually led to Henry Tudor's promising, on Christmas Day, 1483, in Rheims Cathedral, that he would marry Elizabeth of York as soon as he became king.[10] Many saw this as a severe blow against Richard's regime, because with the eldest daughter of the previous king as his wife, Tudor's claim to the throne was considerably strengthened. This was especially important because most of Richard's subjects seem to have been assured that what was being proposed was not Tudor as king to govern alone, but some sort of joint rule, similar to that of Isobel and Ferdinand in Castille, and popular feeling might have enthusiastically supported the return of one of Edward's children to the throne, even if it was a daughter.

Despite her plotting with Margaret Beaufort and the subsequent betrothal of her eldest daughter to an obscure distant relative of John o' Gaunt, when Elizabeth Wydeville was persuaded to leave sanctuary in March 1484 she entrusted the future well-being of her daughters to Richard, who promised to care for them and ensure they were well married, which he did for at least one of them. If she believed the rumors that said her brother-in-law had murdered her boys, this action would have seemed extremely unsafe; although, as a realist, she may have felt no other decision possible, and it had certainly become very difficult for her and her daughters to remain at Westminster. However, Vergil claims that she also wrote encouraging her son the

Middleham Castle, childhood home of Richard III, where he lived with the Earl of Warwick's family. Richard's son, Edward of Middleham, was born in the castle and also died here on 9 April 1484 (Wikimedia Commons/CC-BY-SA 3.0).

Marquess of Dorset to return to court, telling him to expect good treatment from Richard. Dorset was subsequently prevented from leaving France by adherents of Henry Tudor, but his mother's earnest letter entreating him to return may have been indicative of some sort of arrangement between Richard and his sister-in-law, whereby her son would have a role in the king's new regime.[11]

Gatehouse of Middleham Castle (Wikimedia Commons/CC-BY-SA 3.0).

Barely a year later, at the end of March 1485, Richard was still beset by problems from all sides. His only son, Edward of Middleham, had died on 9 April 1484, and in December of that year, he dispatched Sir John Kendall to Rome with a view, it has been suggested, to asking for papal dispensation to lift the Titulus Regius and reinstate one of his nephews.[12] Kendall was later a supporter of the "feigned boy," Perkin Warbeck, so this is not impossible, although no evidence exists to support the view that either Edward or Richard were alive at that time. Richard received what many saw as final divine vengeance on 16 March 1485, when his wife and constant companion, Anne Neville, finally expired after a prolonged illness, probably consumption. In the aftermath of this sad event, he also found himself forced to deny rumors that were circulating about his intention to marry his niece, Elizabeth of York, fueled by another story about his alleged poisoning of his wife to make way for the younger woman. Richard does seem to have entertained the idea of this marriage, despite their over-close relationship, in an attempt to buy back Woodville support and destroy Henry Tudor's validity as heir to the throne; but his closest associates told him bluntly that any such action would forfeit the support of the northern gentry upon which he placed so much reliance. It seems that it was not the incestuous relationship that worried Catesby, Ratcliffe and the others but rather the possibility of being dispossessed of lands Richard had granted them and that he had taken from the very Wydeville adherents he was now proposing to allow back into favor.[13]

By the summer of 1485, Richard must have been growing desperate. The southern counties were still not fully settled under their new, northern overlords, and he continued to be seen by many in country as an illegal usurper—and worse, a child murderer.[14] More importantly, his treasury was empty, and he could no longer expect support from much of the nobility, particularly the minor southern officials and placemen who had previously been an important part of his brother's regime. Bereft of this support and able to rely only upon his northern sympathizers, Richard reluctantly took up the only option left to him and prepared to fight. If he could destroy Henry Tudor and his southern allies in one final battle, his problems would be resolved, at least temporarily, since no other acceptable candidate for the throne would then remain at large and he would no longer need the expensive coastal defenses that were destroying his solvency. More importantly, if he could make a clean sweep of the southerners who had sided with Tudor, their former tenants would have no option but to accept their new northern overlords, since there would be no members of the old families left to replace them.

Henry Tudor

After his abortive invasion attempt in November 1483, Henry Tudor had returned to Brittany, and almost immediately, Richard began a campaign to induce the vacillating ruler of the Bretons, Duke Francis, to hand the Tudor pretender over to his custody. Breton politics were in a state of violent flux, one section of the nobility demanding closer cooperation with France while

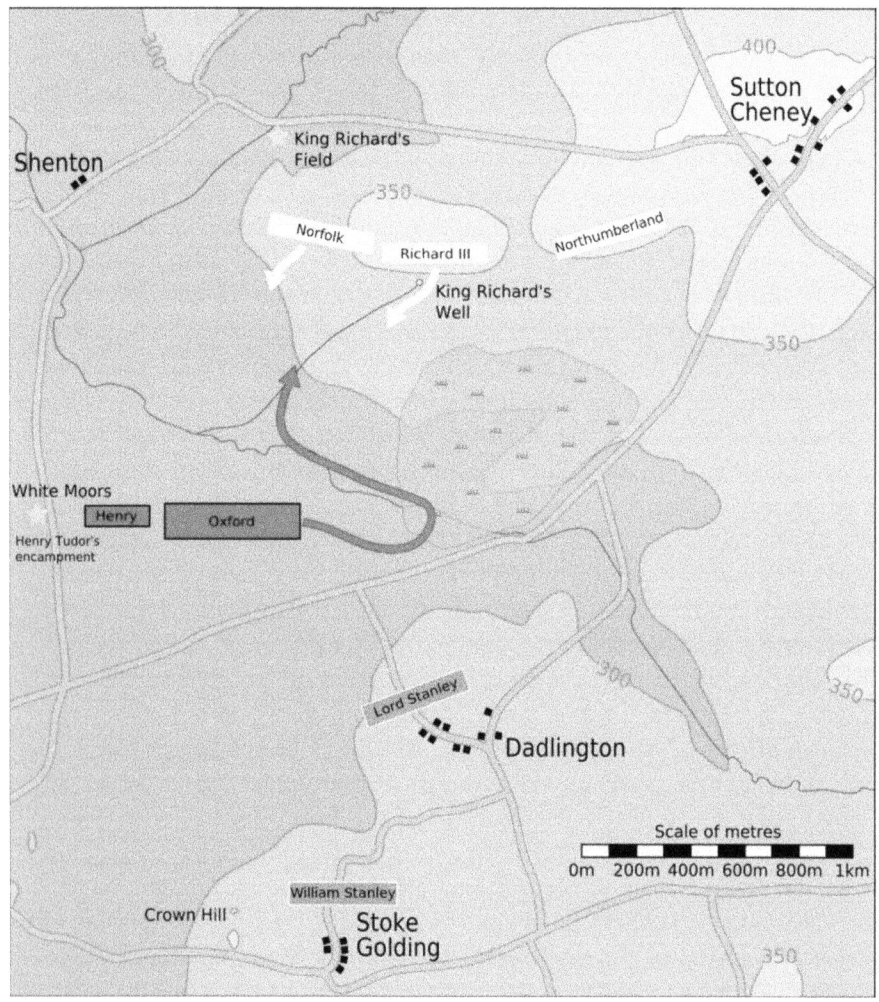

Map of the battlefield at Bosworth, showing the dispositions of Richard and Henry Tudor's armies and the Stanleys to the south, waiting to pounce (Wikimedia Commons/CC-BY-SA 3.0).

an opposing faction advocated an English alliance against the French. Intent upon forcing their overlord's hand, Richard increased his naval operations against the Bretons early in 1484 and by June of that year had concluded a treaty with Francis, whereby the English agreed to supply a company of longbowmen to assist the duke against France, in return for the delivery of Henry Tudor. Tudor, unfortunately, was warned about the plot and decamped to France, where feeling was running high against England. By the summer of 1485, the French regent, Anne of Beaujeu, had been persuaded to place a fleet of ships and part of the French army at Henry's disposal, and with this substantial force he embarked for England.[15] In contrast to his position during the abortive revolt in October 1483, with this sort of military backing, Tudor was no longer in the position of consort; his aim now could realistically be the throne in his own right, with marriage to the daughter of Edward IV as much-needed reinforcement.

Bosworth Field

The Tudor forces sailed from Harfleur on 1 August 1485 and landed at Milford Haven on 7 August. Henry's army consisted of roughly 4,500 men, later increased by the addition of 500 Welshmen recruited by Richard's lieutenant in West Wales, Rhys ap Thomas. By 15 or 16 August, the united army, now around 5,000 strong, had reached Shrewsbury. Leaving Shrewsbury without too much delay, Henry moved slowly eastward, picking up men as he proceeded, including Sir Gilbert Talbot and a number of other supporters. As well as collecting men, Tudor reestablished contact with the Stanleys, with whom he had been in communication before arriving in England. The Stanleys were deployed as scouts ahead of the Tudor forces as they approached the Bosworth battlefield, and on 21 August, they made camp on a hill north of Dadlington, with Tudor's army a little way off to the northwest.

Richard had received the news of Tudor's landing on 11 August and by 16 August his army was gathering, Norfolk and Northumberland bringing their men to Leicester to join their king. Richard joined his allies on 20 August at Leicester, having taken Thomas Stanley's son, Lord Strange, as a hostage to ensure his father's cooperation, and the army moved westward, camping on Ambion Hill on the evening of the 21 August.

On the morning of 22 August, Richard deployed his men along the ridge of Ambion Hill, with Norfolk's group or "battle," consisting of about 3,000 men, on the right protecting both the cannons and a company of about 1,200 archers. Richard's group of 3,000 dismounted infantry formed the center, with Northumberland's battle of 4,000 infantry, some of them mounted, on the left. The Stanleys, fielding approximately 6,000 men, were waiting on the Tudor right and some way behind those forces, on Dadlington Hill. Seeing his enemy mustering, Richard sent a message to Thomas Stanley, threatening to execute his son, Lord Strange, if Stanley did not immediately attack the Tudor ranks, to which Thomas Stanley replied that "he had other sons." Richard gave orders for his captive's immediate execution but his officers temporized, suggesting that, as battle was imminent, the execution could be delayed until the fighting was over. At about the same time, Tudor also sent a messenger to Stanley, asking him to declare his allegiance, but Stanley continued being evasive and Tudor was forced to confront Richard's forces alone and outnumbered about two to one.

Lacking any experience of battle, Henry Tudor had given command of his army to the vastly more knowledgeable Earl of Oxford, who now organized his men in a tight formation, protected by horsemen. These forces began to advance upon Richard's lines but were forced to turn left and maneuver around an area of marsh, which allowed Richard's forces to direct their cannon fire against the Tudor army's tightly packed ranks. Having bypassed the area of marsh, the Tudor forces were met by the advancing lines of Norfolk's men and part of Richard's force. In the ensuing combat Oxford's men began to gain a slight advantage, and Richard signaled for Northumberland's group to come to his aid. Northumberland's battle, however, showed no sign of movement, either from a failure in communications or because the earl refused to order any movement forward.

With the battle reaching a critical point, Henry Tudor was seen moving towards the Stanleys, and Richard impetuously decided to finish the battle with a single stroke, by killing the enemy commander. He charged into the group surrounding Henry Tudor with an unknown number of his own men (some sources insisting it was as many as 800–1,000 knights), initially killing Henry's standard-bearer, Sir William Brandon. Stanley now chose his side, attacking Richard's men and eventually driving them into the marsh, where Richard was killed. Examination of Richard's skull after the discovery of his body in 2013 showed eight wounds, including one that had hacked away part of the rear of the skull.

It has always been claimed that after the battle was over, Thomas Stanley found Richard's crown on a hawthorn bush and carried the circlet to Henry, who was subsequently crowned on Crown Hill, near the village of Stoke Golding. This event may be reflected in the hawthorn bush incorporated into Henry's coat-of-arms.[16]

Three. The Road to Bosworth Field

Lord Stanley delivering the crown to Henry VII at the Battle of Bosworth Field (Wikipedia).

Aftermath to the Battle

Rumors about his nephews' death had died down, although they had by no means disappeared altogether, when Richard was killed at Bosworth on 22 August 1485. Conveniently, they could now be once more resurrected in the autumn of 1485, turning Henry's triumph into that of a God-appointed savior dealing his just deserts to Richard, a disloyal, unnatural regicide and "spiller of infant's blood," an accusation included in the Act of Attainder that was passed against Richard in Henry's first Parliament.

After Bosworth, Richard's friends and followers scattered. Brackenbury, John Howard, Duke of Norfolk and Sir Richard Ratcliffe were killed in the battle alongside their friend and king. William Catesby was captured alive but was executed three days later at Leicester. Lovell fled to Colchester, where he was to remain for six months while negotiating with Henry over the arrangements made for Elizabeth Wydeville and her daughter, before heading for Ireland and involvement in Lambert Simnel's abortive attempt on the throne.[17] The purge of Richard's adherents subsequently occupied the first

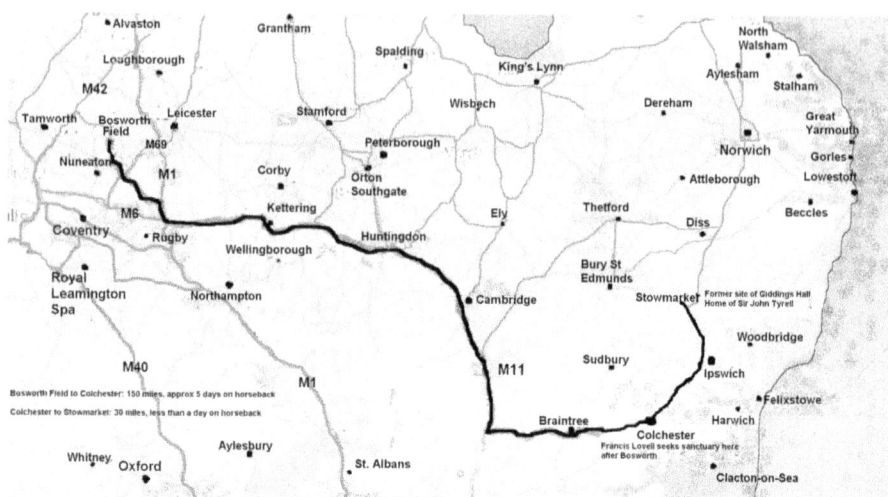

Map showing the route from Bosworth to Stowmarket, via Colchester, which may have been taken by Lovell and the Stanley brothers, including distances and estimated times to complete the journey on horseback.

two years of the new king's reign, although after that period, Henry proved ready to accept those prepared to submit to him, whatever their former allegiances, including Sir James Tyrell. Richard was gone, if not forgotten, and in future it was the myth propagated by Tudor's historians and propagandists that would predominate, masking the man himself.

Politics, Propaganda and the Paradoxes

Whatever view is taken of the character of Richard III, his ascent to the throne had all the appearances of a masterpiece of ingenuity, manipulation and misdirection. His arrest of Grey, Rivers, Vaughan and Haute, which allowed him to exert his own influence upon Edward, and the entry into London with wagonloads of weapons claimed to have been captured from Woodville adherents intent upon his murder, combined to show his opponents in the worst possible light and ensured that his protectorship would be confirmed.[18] Once made protector, he then extended his campaign of misdirection and negative propaganda, implicating the Woodvilles in the theft of the royal treasury, executing Hastings for treason and then forcing Elizabeth Woodville to relinquish her youngest son into his charge. Hasting's execution and the dissolution of the Woodville faction removed his main political opponents, whereupon his nephews and nieces were almost immediately disinherited because of their illegitimacy, leaving him the only candidate for the throne.[19]

Whether his response was the result of careful planning or was the action of a desperate man forced into taking extreme measures to protect himself has been (and still is) the subject of acrimonious debate, although deliberate, planned usurpation seems the most likely motivation for his actions.[20] Certainly, if he had not made plans to usurp the monarchy before or soon after his brother's death, it is remarkable how circumstances aided his decisions; and the speed and efficiency with which he neutralized the Woodville faction, in particular, suggests at the very least some careful consideration on his part.

Until his coronation in July 1483, Richard's conduct, especially towards his nephews, had clearly been circumspect and devious enough to allay any suspicion about his motives among the vast majority of his subjects. He had observed the required forms in his dealings with Edward, according him all the rights and privileges of a future king and never deviating outwardly from his posture as a loyal subject, convinced of his nephew's right to rule. It was not until the revelations by a collection of ostensibly "disinterested" third parties, first Stillington and then Shaa in the course of his sermon, that Richard appeared to allow himself to be convinced both of his nephew's illegitimacy and that his own duty lay in accepting the crown. He had eschewed violence as a solution, except in the case of Lord Hastings, where Richard's accusations against his brother's friend could be claimed to justify firm action, and his ascent to the throne continued to be a model of subtle dissimulation and manipulation of public opinion.[21]

Memorial to King Richard III in Leicester Cathedral. The inscription reads: "Richard III / King of England / Killed at Bosworth Field in this county / 22nd August 1485 / Buried in the Church of the Grey Friars in this Parish (Wikimedia Commons/CC-BY-SA 3.0).

Even the executions of Rivers, Grey and Vaughan had been given a superficial air of legality; they were also conducted away from London and in the heart of Richard's northern support network, so the executions hardly stirred public opinion until later, when rumor accused him of murdering his nephews and his execution of these gentlemen could be used to add weight to the charge. Besides, the men were Wydeville adherents and stood condemned in the eyes of most of the populace by the contaminating propaganda Richard had so carefully spread.

Consequently, in late July 1483, his position looked reasonably strong, although he still had a considerable amount of work to do before his role as king was completely accepted by nobles and commons alike.[22] The throne that was now his had been offered to him by the Lords Spiritual and Temporal and his claim subsequently ratified by an act of Parliament, although popular acclamation seems to have been sadly lacking. More importantly, the only alternative claimants, his royal nephews and nieces, were discredited by their father's immorality and safely imprisoned, guarded by men like Brackenbury, whose loyalty to Richard was guaranteed by both their own integrity and informed self-interest. It seemed probable that he only need be circumspect in his dealings with the remaining members of Elizabeth Woodville's family and friends to establish a quiescent, if not entirely loyal group, mainly confined to the southern counties of England, where they could be contained and gradually deprived of power and any remaining influence, in the same way his handsome, energetic elder brother had dealt with his own political opponents. It was certainly true that his nephews might still form a focus for rebellion and Henry Tudor would have to be dealt with, but while the boys were locked away from their mother and her friends, it would be difficult for them to implement any form of organized resistance. Who was going to support two young boys or an obscure great-great-grandson of John of Gaunt, whose patronage in terms of land and positions at court remained very much an unknown quantity? More importantly, few if any in the country considered Henry Tudor a likely candidate for kingship: his elevation to the role of contender for the crown would only come at Buckingham's instigation and after the beginning of the October revolt.

Now, however, instead of building on the foundations that he had so carefully constructed, Richard apparently completely discarded his previous subtlety, and in an act of pointless savagery—it is claimed—he ordered the immediate murder of his nephews. More importantly, he made no attempt to either deny his involvement or portray the deaths as having happened by accident, natural causes or murder by someone else. Instead, he allows the rumor that he killed them to spread and gain credence throughout the whole country, with its inevitable effects on the conduct of his reign and subsequent defeat at Bosworth.

Richard's conduct during the period from July to December 1483 seems difficult to reconcile with his previous subtlety. In particular:

- Why, if he murdered the boys, did he not invent some innocuous explanation for their disappearance? It was certainly not impossible for him to arrange for the two corpses to appear to have expired of natural causes, especially if the two deaths were separated by a reasonable period and he delayed any examination until decomposition was fairly well advanced.
- Why, if another person was responsible for their deaths or they died of natural causes, did he not put the bodies on public display, as Henry IV had done with Richard II, and his brother Edward had done with Henry VI? Then he could have simply played the part of the grief-stricken uncle, tearfully admitting his culpability in not having been able to protect the two boys committed to his sacred charge.
- Why not display the bodies and play the grief-stricken uncle anyway, whatever the cause of the boys' deaths? It would certainly seem to be the simplest, perhaps even the best way out for a murderous relative.
- If they were not dead, why did he offer *no sort of explanation of any kind* for the boys' disappearance, when the suspicion that he had murdered them has always been claimed to be one of the main reasons for the October Rebellion and Henry Tudor used the murder of his wife's brothers as a rallying point before Bosworth? Why did he not do something to stop the rot that unsupported rumor was spreading throughout the land?
- And finally, if he planned to usurp the throne and dispose of the boys from the time of his brother's death, why did he wait so long? Why not arrange an accident for Edward before he reached London, or even before he met the boy at Stony Stratford when the blame could be passed to Earl Rivers, and for Richard soon after he entered the Tower? Then there would have been no question of usurpation, simply a natural process of inheritance, because Edward's daughters would not have counted in that scheme of things. Certainly, he did not lack opportunity to dispose of the boys.

Whatever his detractors have claimed for him, no author has ever considered Richard to be unintelligent or incapable of judging properly the political climate in which he lived and operated. Why then did he allow the rumor that his nephews were murdered to become accepted as fact and, more significantly, make the monumental political error of leaving himself to be seen by the majority of his subjects as the only reasonable culprit?

The October Rebellion: A Second Paradox?

Fifteenth century life among the nobility was concerned with wealth and position, almost to the exclusion of everything else, and wealth was measured by possessions, particularly land. A family's place in the hierarchy was dependent upon its land holdings, which was why so much time was expended by the Wydeville clan, Richard (then Duke of Gloucester) and George, Duke of Clarence, in presenting innumerable petitions to the king over land they might have title to, by marriage, inheritance or just plain avarice. Nor were these activities confined to just the king's family. Manipulation of the courts, giving daughters in marriage and even the occasional clandestine murder were all reasonably common practices among landed families intent upon increasing their holdings and thus their influence locally in the county and nationally with the king.[23] Consequently, it is difficult to understand what motivated so many of these frankly avaricious, land-hungry county magnates to organize a rebellion in October 1483, from which they could hope to gain so very little and, in failing, would lose everything.

Why should such a group of former Yorkist court officials, administrators and servants of the late king risk everything to depose another Yorkist king, when there seemed to be so very little to be gained from either the accession of a Wydeville-dominated minor or a Lancastrian monarch in the person of Henry Tudor and, more importantly, so much more to be gained from Richard's continued patronage? Richard, frankly, was intent upon buying friends in this unsettled period after his coronation, and loyalty was being lavishly rewarded, perhaps even too lavishly. An altruistic concern for the dead heir of Edward IV, although usually offered as the reason, seems too flimsy. After all, whatever his royal and governmental responsibilities, advancement was the sole prerogative of the king; and advancement and the acquisition of land and thus, power, that accompanied it was the overriding concern of most of these gentry. If it had not been, they would not have reached the positions in the court of Edward IV that they all had held. Moreover, many of their northern, eastern and Welsh contemporaries choose the easy option, offered their loyalty to Richard and found themselves adequately, if not handsomely, rewarded.[24]

More than that, why did so many flee overseas, rather than accept Richard's clemency, which he seems to have been ready to extend to the vast majority who took part in the rebellion? Avoiding an Act of Attainder would not have prevented them from continuing to plot with Henry Tudor, and if they fled because of uncertainty over what form Richard's wrath would take, why not return when it was clear he was inclined to be merciful, following the example of Elizabeth Wydeville's son, the Marquess of Dorset?

One explanation of this apparently anomalous behavior is that the rebellion originated and continued after the princes' disappearance not as an attempt to crown Henry Tudor (an explanation that may have been the result of hindsight by Tudor historians intent upon justifying the dynasty's frankly wobbly claim)[25] but was instead intended to place Edward IV's eldest daughter, Elizabeth of York, on the throne, complete with Tudor as a convenient but ineffectual consort. To the southern Yorkists this would probably have seemed to be a much more satisfactory scenario than being forced to accept the usurper Gloucester and his avaricious northern rabble at the center of affairs. Manipulation of Elizabeth and a pusillanimous husband would probably have been seen as significantly easier for her father's old friends and supporters than extracting favors from an experienced courtier like Richard, especially when surrounded by ruthless opportunists such as Robert Ratcliffe and his ilk.

Buckingham

If the southern rebels had little to gain and much to lose from the untimely rebellion they orchestrated, the involvement of Henry Stafford, Duke of Buckingham, with the rebellion to put another contender on the throne is even more difficult to understand. By July 1483, he had been given more land than any supporter of Richard in the kingdom, and it would be no exaggeration to say that he was the most powerful and influential man in the land, after the king himself.[26] He was also considerably more secure, because the king was dependent upon his support, while Buckingham's acquisitions had made him dependent upon nobody, not even Richard. What more could he have hoped to gain if Henry Tudor or Elizabeth of York came to power?

Clearly, he could expect very little improvement under either regime, but if his plan was not to allow the reestablishment of the old Yorkist dynasty, but rather to place himself upon the throne, his defection begins to make considerably more sense. He had better qualifications than either Henry, who was only a descendent of the Plantagenet line through a very distant, nebulous relationship to John o' Gaunt, and Elizabeth of York, who was a woman and so useful only for the sort of husband she could attract, especially considering her youth. Certainly, Elizabeth of York would have been too inexperienced to be able to exert the same influence at court or among the noble families that her mother had wielded or her redoubtable future mother-in-law, Margaret Beaufort, would exert during her son's reign. Consequently, Stafford may have calculated that, with Richard gone, his chances of outfighting and then replacing both of the more obvious contenders for the throne would have been excellent.

Whether he would have had better luck than Richard in usurping the throne is debatable. Not being particularly likeable, he had not attracted the sort of support network Richard had established among the northern magnates, but he seems to have been a man indifferent to those around him and may have felt that the sheer force of his personality would carry him to the crown. Of course, he would not have been the first to think that the strength of political feeling in England could be hacked through with the sword.

Elizabeth Woodville

Elizabeth Woodville's behavior during this period also requires some explanation. She began what amounted to a campaign of attrition against Richard in the autumn of 1483, when Vergil claims that negotiations were opened between her and Henry's mother, Margaret Beaufort, which led to Henry promising on Christmas Day, 1483, that he would marry Elizabeth of York as soon as he became king. This has frequently been interpreted as evidence that she knew her sons Edward and Richard were dead and so had decided to ally herself to the regime most likely to replace their murderer. In view of past events, that seems eminently reasonable, but if she was intent upon siding with Henry and his mother, why did she give her daughters so wholly into Richard's care when it is claimed he forced her to leave the sanctuary of Westminster? Moreover, why compound what could have been a fatal error by writing to Dorset, her last remaining son, telling him to return to England, thus placing him in the hands of the very man who, it is claimed, she thought murdered his half-brothers? Most interesting of all, why did Henry turn on her after Warbeck's appearance, deprive her of her dower lands and give them to her daughter, Elizabeth of York, as part of her dowry? Did she know or had she recently discovered something about her two sons' whereabouts that he dare not let her reveal?

Section II
Life for Edward and Richard

CHAPTER FOUR

Life in Fifteenth Century England

Although the daily life of the general population surrounding the king and his court is an aspect of the problems associated with Richard III and his nephews that is rarely discussed, it is of considerable importance to have an understanding of the general living conditions in England during that period. Life for the boys and their uncle was not as hard as it was for those in the lower social classes, but the prevalence of infectious disease and commonplace violence surrounding the throne and those who occupied it gives their lives and, more especially, their disappearance a perspective that does repay closer examination. The boys were also undergoing a rigorous training implemented by their father; and this period, including details of contemporary accounts of the time they spent in the Tower, is described in this section.

England's Social Organization in the Middle Ages

England's medieval population was divided into a number of groups: the king and his nobles; the gentry, which included the richer merchants, yeoman farmers and craftsmen; the tenant farmers, who rented their land from the gentry; and at the bottom of the pile, the wage laborers. These groups were not as firmly fixed by social constraints as is often supposed, however, and upward and downward movement seems to have been a reasonably common phenomenon in modifying the social hierarchy of the period, especially between the laboring class and the group of less-well-to-do merchants.

At Court

A medieval English king such as Edward IV was not an arbitrary, authoritarian ruler. He was certainly perceived as king by divine right, anointed

Late fifteenth century artistic portrayal of the Battle of Barnet: Edward IV (left), wearing a circlet and mounted on a horse, leads the Yorkist charge and pierces Richard Neville, Earl of Warwick, "the Kingmaker," with his lance. In reality, Warwick was not killed by Edward (Wikipedia).

with holy oil and considered by the church as God's lieutenant upon earth, but his freedom to act was constrained by the laws and precedents, and he was expected to rule according to Christian standards, in the public interest for the common good. Government was created for the benefit of the governed, not the divine ruler. Consequently, the king could only operate for just as long as he made the majority of the nobility and a significant proportion of the common people content with what he was doing. This necessity ensured the development of the system of favors, land deals and arranged marriages that characterized much of the political life of medieval courts in Britain and Europe.[1]

Life for an ambitious nobleman or noblewoman during this period centered on the court. Advancement was solely the prerogative of the king, who

Depiction of the battle of Tewkesbury from a fifteenth century Ghent (Flemish) manuscript. This battle secured the throne for Edward IV and resulted in the death of Edward, Prince of Wales, the only son of Henry VI (Wikipedia).

was also responsible for the distribution of lands (and their associated revenues) and lucrative court appointments such as chancellor, royal chamberlain and constable of the Tower. Land was wealth during this period, and the more land a noble or member of the gentry had, the more highly he or she was regarded, although female heiresses were usually only esteemed for their matrimonial potential and were bestowed upon a loyal subject in the same way that the king might pass on any of his other possessions. Hence, land was also the currency with which the king bought and sold the loyalty of his subordinates. From this it follows that a king without independent power to grant land to his supporters, as Edward became after entering London with his uncle, was a king in name only, without any real means of ensuring the functioning of his administration or that his supporters would remain loyal. Edward was further handicapped by his association with the Wydevilles. His mother's family had a reputation for greed that set them apart, even from the majority of courtiers who had surrounded Edward IV, and this may have resulted in a reluctance on the part of the big landowners, such as the Stanleys, to transfer their loyalty to Edward's son—if they thought their rewards, doled out by a Wydeville-dominated Royal Council, would be niggardly.

Whatever the limitations imposed on Edward by his age and relative inexperience, the same was not true of his father.[2] Edward IV had been particularly adept at imparting favors where they would do him most good and subsequently manipulating those he had advantaged. He began his rise to the throne when, together with Richard Neville, Earl of Warwick, he captured Henry VI, after the battle of Northampton, on 10 July 1460. Edward ruled England in Henry's name until the end of the year; and after the death of his father and brother at the battle of Wakefield in December 1460 and his victory over the Lancastrians at Mortimer's Cross in February 1461, Edward joined forces with Richard Neville and entered London, where he was crowned king on 4 March 1461. Although the years between 1461 and Henry's readeption (his restoration to the throne) in 1470 saw much fighting, Edward also attempted to win over his father's former Lancastrian opponents by the bestowal of royal favors, although he was not always successful, as in the case of Sir Ralph Percy and the Duke of Somerset, who both entered his service, only to subsequently change sides again.

His marriage in 1461, although unfortunate for a number of reasons, did give him the opportunity for allying himself more strongly with some of the most powerful figures in the English nobility.[3] By 1463, Edward had arranged marriages for five of the queen's six sisters to Henry Stafford, Duke of Buckingham, Lord Herbert and the heirs of the Earls of Kent, Essex and Arundel, in a series of associations probably welcomed by both sides. Of course, one individual whom these arrangements did not suit was Richard Neville, Earl of Warwick. Edward's unwelcoming response to Neville's proposal of marriage between his daughter and George, Duke of Clarence signaled the beginning of an estrangement that erupted into rebellion in 1469. The deaths of Warwick, Henry VI and Henry's son, Edmund, strengthened Edward's regime significantly when he returned to the throne, although he still used favors in the form of land to strengthen his hold on his supporters. Most significant of these was the appointment of his brother Richard as "Lord of the North," replacing Neville authority in the region, while William Herbert, later Earl of Pembroke, controlled South Wales on Edward's behalf (although with the birth of his sons, Edward then began to rearrange the hierarchy in the west and east of the country in favor of the boys).

The Nobility

This term is applied loosely to those who bore some form of title, conferred upon them by the king or inherited through the ownership of ancestral lands. The Crown, senior churchmen (abbots and bishops were also barons with noble status) and other members of what may be loosely termed the noble class represented less than 0.01 percent of the population (200 men out of a population of between two and three million), although they owned over 75 percent of the land, which made them correspondingly wealthy. Incidentally, it is worth mentioning here that lands and titles could only be inherited by legitimate offspring, that is; children that were the result of a liaison between a legally married couple. Property could be passed on to illegitimate offspring under a parent's will, but title could still be uncertain.[4]

Life for the Rest

Most of the population, including the nobility, were dependent upon the rural economy for their livelihood, although 10 percent of peasant boys are thought to have entered the priesthood, for which they were required to be able to read Latin. Although land, effectively, was wealth, a family's management of its property could cause a considerable variation in the money that became available from it.

Towns were small, having approximately 200–300 houses, often less, and were occupied almost exclusively by merchants and craftsmen and the families they employed. The necessary internal organization of the town was overseen by the town council, which included members of both the merchant and craftsmen's guilds. Towns also had intimate commercial links with the surrounding countryside.

Outside the towns, those who worked the land lived either in small villages or adjacent to the land they worked. Lowest in rank was the villain, a serf or semi-slave who was obliged to pay for his right to work the land by laboring on the adjoining lands of the lord of the manor and who could not leave his land without his landlord's permission. By 1480, however, the decrease in population brought about by the Black Death ensured that this system was being largely replaced by paid service or tenure by rent; such people were increasingly referred to as smallholders, cottagers or cottars. Free craftsmen also lived in the rural villages, particularly those such as blacksmiths or wheelwrights who needed to be near their customers.

Both urban and rural populations appear to have lived in substantial houses, a household usually consisting of a husband and wife, together with their children, and presumably those family members who found it convenient to live in such a group. Lives were passed in quite reasonable comfort, some houses having upper rooms to ensure at least a modicum of privacy as well as wooden floors and locks for both doors and chests. They were well fed, having a diet that included meat (pork, lamb, beef and game such as rabbit), as well as fish, cheese (from goat or sheep), fruit, vegetables and homemade bread. Ale and wine was usually drunk in preference to water, which was frequently unsanitary and a source of water-borne diseases. Everyone worked hard, usually from dawn to dusk, but there was sufficient time for leisure, books being not uncommon possessions and many homes also possessed games such as chess. And, of course, training with the longbow had been compulsory for every man and boy from an early age since the decree of Edward III in 1363, so most Sunday mornings after church would be spent upon the butts. It is also significant that coins are often found in these peasant villages, indicating that the people who lived there were not part of a subsistence economy but used money as well as barter to obtain both necessities and possibly luxury items. Specialist occupations were also becoming common, such as baker, brewer, butcher, cobbler as well as silver-, gold- and bronzesmiths. More importantly, instead of being subject to the arbitrary decisions of their landlords or overlord, people were now able to seek justice in the local assize court, with a specially appointed judge sitting regularly in most counties.[5]

Health

Average life expectancy at birth during the fifteenth century was only 30 years. However, a significant proportion of the population did live into their fifties, the figure of 30 being statistically biased because approximately 30–50 percent of the population died before reaching 16. Subsequently, an individual might survive to 50 or even 60, with a significant proportion reaching 70 or more, although this included a much lower proportion of women, due to the lack of contraception and the consequent dangers of repeated childbirth.[6]

Medical knowledge was scanty, and doctors relied on information for their diagnoses that they learned by rote from books written centuries before, rather than observation and experience. These failings in the medical profession meant that common diseases such as measles, mumps, scarlet fever and smallpox resulted in a mortality of over 50 percent of those contracting the disease, and ailments such as syphilis and typhus were widespread. Bubonic plague was also a significant mortality factor during the fifteenth century, an outbreak in 1471 causing the deaths of 10–15 percent of the population, with a later outbreak in 1479–1480 claimed to have been responsible for the deaths of approximately 20 percent of the remainder. Malaria was also common, particularly in residents of the riverside London boroughs, because of their proximity to low-lying, marshy areas of the Thames.[7]

Table 4: Infectious Diseases in Fifteenth Century England

Disease (common name)	Cause and prevalence	Symptoms and external signs	Mortality in the 15th century (%)
Dysentery or bloody flux	Caused by bacterial contamination of water or food by fecal material. Common in cities among both nobility and common people.	Diarrhea, arthritis, meningitis. Externally: Few signs except weight loss.	High in infants, less dangerous in older individuals
Influenza ('flu)	Extremely contagious viral infection of the upper respiratory tract, spread by inhalation. Common in cities among both nobility and common people. Possibly the cause of London's "sweating sickness" in 1485.	Fever, high temperature, headache, muscular aches, and may develop into bronchitis and pneumonia. Externally: Few signs.	Significant mortality. Particularly prevalent in England during the fifteenth century.

Four. Life in Fifteenth Century England

Disease (common name)	Cause and prevalence	Symptoms and external signs	Mortality in the 15th century (%)
Malaria (the ague)	Protozoan disease spread by mosquitoes. Widespread in marshy areas of southern and eastern England. Found commonly in the London boroughs of Lambeth, Southwark and Westminster because of their proximity to marshy areas of the Thames.	Shaking, severe headache, very high temperature. Symptoms appear 12–18 days after being bitten. Externally: Few signs.	~1% of population annually. Children most at risk.
Measles	Extremely contagious viral disease transmitted by inhalation. Widespread.	High temperature and cold-like symptoms. Externally: Red spots inside mouth, then characteristic red rash.	Mortality: ~1% of cases.
Plague	Bacterial infection transmitted by fleas or inhalation. Outbreaks usually widespread, although sometimes confined to discrete areas.	Headache, high temperature, delirium, which in 20% of cases is followed by lung infection. Externally: Characteristic swelling of lymph nodes in neck, armpit and groin.	Mortality: 50–100%
Smallpox (the Red Plague)	Extremely contagious viral disease transmitted by inhalation. Widespread.	Symptoms: High temperature, headache and backache. Externally: Itchy red rash	Mortality: 1–30% of those infected.
Typhoid	Bacterial infection, transmitted by faecal contamination, often of water supply. May be widespread, depending upon sanitary measures.	Diarrhea, high temperature, headache and cough. Externally: Patches of red on abdomen, and wasting.	Mortality 10–20% of those infected.

Disease (common name)	Cause and prevalence	Symptoms and external signs	Mortality in the 15th century (%)
Tuberculosis (consumption)	Bacterial infection, transmitted by inhalation.	Symptomless in most cases, because immune system in a healthy person will deal with the bacterium. Bacteria may lie dormant, however, and then become active. When active, symptoms include high temperature, loss of appetite and weight. Externally: Little change except weight loss.	Mortality: 100% once disease becomes active.
Typhus	Highly contagious bacterial disease spread by fleas or lice. Widespread in dirty conditions.	High temperature and delirium. Externally: gangrenous sores.	Mortality: 30–70%, although may be much higher in children.

Literacy and the Dissemination of Information and Propaganda

William Caxton established his first printing press in London, at Westminster, in 1476. By 1500, it is estimated that 40 percent of male householders in London could read Latin, with an even higher percentage also able to read English, although in rural areas literacy rates were very significantly lower.[8] Printed matter was certainly available for the dissemination of information and many of the nobility and merchant classes possessed quite respectable libraries, but it is unlikely that Richard's enemies were able to use it to much effect, because the broadsheet, which was the most common medium for political information before the general availability of books or newspapers, was not widely used until the end of the reign of Henry VIII.[9] Unfortunately for Richard and his cause, information was definitely being shared, Croyland specifically describing an instance where "it was spread abroad that King Edward's sons were dead."

There was a widespread conviction that the princes were dead, and many apparently believed Richard was responsible, although it is hard to determine how such information can have been disseminated. Presumably, simple word of mouth was the main channel, since few other means existed. It is not inconceivable that Buckingham or one of his subordinates also made a public proclamation to the rebel troops under his command, although there is no record of this happening.

Writing seems to have been a less common achievement than reading, probably not more than 10–25 percent of the population being able to do more than "make their mark"; and this may be one of the reasons little information has been retained about the fate of the boys.[10] Until recently, Polydore Vergil, Henry VII's paid historian, has also been blamed for the destruction of many historical sources by Ricardian revisionists, although this has been shown to be an invention of certain sixteenth century rivals who had been made unhappy over his comments about the legend of King Arthur. However, although Vergil has been cleared of blame, it is not impossible that Henry himself destroyed documents that described the fate of the boys after he came to power in 1485.

CHAPTER FIVE

Edward and Richard: The Princes in the Tower

Most of the research into Richard's treatment of the boys has centered upon events after the death of Edward IV in April 1483, but it is possible that their upbringing and early education may have influenced their uncle's behavior during the usurpation in a way not exhaustively considered previously. In particular:

- How did Edward's regime for his childrens' education fit them for a governing role?
- Would that educational regimen also have made them fit to be highly placed administrators, rather than monarchs?
- Perhaps most importantly, were they necessarily so intransigent as to feel nothing less than the crown was acceptable, especially after their illegitimacy was an established fact?

Edward (1470–83[?]): Birth and Early Childhood

Edward V, eldest son of Edward IV and Elizabeth Wydeville, was born in sanctuary at Westminster on 2 November 1470 (making him 12 years and 8 months in July 1483), during his father's enforced sojourn in Burgundy as a result of the Neville rebellion. He was the fourth child born to Edward and his queen, being preceded by 3 sisters whose use to the dynasty was limited to obedient components in possibly advantageous political marriages. Edward's role was far more important. As his father's first surviving son, he was heir to the Yorkist throne, and it soon became clear that Edward intended him to be fully trained for that role, both intellectually and physically.

The process began as soon as his father was reestablished in England. Within a month of his father's defeat of the Lancastrians at Tewksbury and the death of Edward of Lancaster, Edward was created Prince of Wales and

Earl of Chester. On 3 July 1471 the Lords Spiritual and Temporal took the oath of allegiance to him as heir to the throne, a group that included his uncle Richard of Gloucester.[1] The rule of his household and lands was also organized during this period, a council being appointed to administer them until he was fourteen. The council was headed by his mother, Elizabeth Wydeville, his paternal uncles, the dukes of Clarence and Gloucester, and his maternal uncle, Anthony Woodville, Earl Rivers. Along with these members of the royal family itself, membership also included many of the leading servants of the royal household, as well as a collection of experienced administrators. This group included Thomas Vaughan, who had been appointed to the post of Edward's chamberlain as early as 8 July 1471, only seven months after Edward's birth. Two years later this council was enlarged and on 10 November 1473, John Alcock, Bishop of Rochester, was given responsibility for Edward's education, also being made president of his household council, with Anthony Woodville ordered to act as his governor. From 1476, Edward's council was based at Ludlow, near Shrewsbury in Shropshire, and during this period it developed into the main agent of royal authority in Wales, while the prince's territorial interests expanded to encompass lands attached to the earldoms of March and Pembroke.[2] He also made several trips away from Ludlow, on one occasion in 1481 reviewing the fleet with his father, such duties being considered essential to the process of grooming the boy for kingship. After the death of Edward IV, Edward's council was disbanded and his Welsh possessions were transferred to Henry Stafford, Duke of Buckingham, together with the revenues accruing to those lands, on 15 May 1483, four days before his transfer to the Tower and over three weeks before that most significant council meeting on 9 or 10 June.[3]

Richard (1473–83[?]): Birth and Early Childhood

Richard, second son of Edward IV and Elizabeth Woodville, was born at Shrewsbury on 17 August 1473 (this would make him 9 years and 11 months old in July 1483). He was created Duke of York on 28 May 1474, knighted on 18 April 1475, and made a Knight of the Garter, along with his elder brother, on 15 May 1475, all three titles being conferred before his second birthday. Land that had previously belonged to the Welles and Willoughby families was settled on him in March 1475, just before his knighthood, and he acquired more land upon his marriage to Anne Mowbray, the sole heir of John Mowbray, Duke of Norfolk, which took place on 15 January 1478, in St. Stephen's Chapel, Westminster.

Gatehouse of Ludlow Castle, home to Prince Edward during much of his childhood (Wikimedia Commons/CC-BY-SA 3.0).

He had previously received all the former Mowbray titles in an agreement ratified before this marriage, being initially made Earl of Nottingham on 12 June 1476, and then Duke of Norfolk and Earl Warenne on 7 February 1477. He also became earl marshal, and lord of Seagrave, Mowbray, and Gower. In addition, an act of Parliament of 1478 gave him a life interest in the Mowbray lands even if his wife died childless (as she did). More land was ceded to him in his father's will, drawn up in 1475 prior to Edward's French expedition, which stipulated that when Richard came of age at 16, he was to inherit a group of estates wholly confined to the northeast of England, specifically in East Anglia, Norfolk, Northamptonshire, Rutland and Lincolnshire, much of it repossessed from Edward's Lancastrian opponents. These lands were in addition to his Mowbray acquisitions in Norfolk and those of the Welles and Willoughby estates in Lincolnshire. In May 1479 Richard was also appointed Lord Lieutenant of Ireland, an appointment renewed for a further twelve years in the following year. By 1480 he also had his own officers, which included his chamberlain, the East Anglian gentleman Sir Thomas Grey. It seems probable that these were not Richard's appointees but rather men seconded from his father's household, which was certainly the case with Grey, who was also a Knight of the Body (an honorary post as bodyguard to the king).[4]

Daily Life for the Boys

In common with most noble ladies of the period, Elizabeth Woodville did not nurse her children from birth, responsibility for this being delegated to a wet-nurse. In Edward's case this is thought to have been Mrs. Avice Welles, although by November 1472, her services were no longer required and he may have been transferred then to the care of the royal nursemaid, Elizabeth, Lady Darcey. In general, royal and noble children of this period did not live with their parents, and Edward's childhood seems to have followed this pattern. Certainly, by 28 September 1473, when he would have been less than three, he had a separate establishment of his own, which was probably what necessitated the expansion of his council.[5] By 1476, Edward's council was firmly established at Ludlow, where it controlled Wales and the Welsh border country, and Edward seems also to have been in residence there, although he was aged only five. Richard's early life was slightly different, since it is known that he lived with his mother for most of the period before his father's death. It is unfortunate that fewer specific records exist describing the sort of regime he experienced during his childhood.

Although by modern standards the daily life of the two boys was circumscribed to an incredible degree, Edward's education, at least, was unusual in that he was brought up and educated in an establishment of his own rather than in an established household with his father, mother or some noble of high rank. His father may not have been close at hand to oversee his eldest son, but Edward IV certainly intended his heir to be fully trained for kingship. With this end in view, the king was careful to fully delineate his son's activities and education, with a series of written ordinances drawn up governing every aspect of the boy's life until he was fourteen. Responsibility for the implementation of these ordinances fell the prince's uncle, Anthony, Earl Rivers, who as Edward's "governor and ruler" was responsible for "the guiding of our said son's person."[6]

The following account is based on Edward's regime, as decreed by his father, and his younger brother, Richard, probably followed a similar timetable[7]:

> Edward rose early, probably before dawn in winter, and immediately celebrated Matins with his personal chaplain. With Matins over, he then went to his own personal chapel, where he celebrated early morning Mass. Mass was followed by breakfast. After finishing his meal, he would receive instruction in "such virtuous learning as his age shall suffer to receive." Presumably reading and writing were on the curriculum, and it is recorded that Edward IV granted a Master John Giles £20 a year for life on 1 May 1476 for teaching his sons Latin grammar. Giles was also paid to teach the princes French, then the language of international diplomacy and a necessary accomplishment for an English king intent on being involved in European politics.[8] In addition, the boys certainly would have received considerable religious instruction, whatever their other studies might have included, and much of their day was centered around religious observances.

Arrangements for the midday meal were more elaborate than those for breakfast in that Edward's dishes were to be "borne by worshipful folks and squires, having on our livery; and that all other officers and servants give their due attendance, according to their offices." During the midday meal, Edward was read the sort of stories considered suitable for a royal prince and chosen by his guardian, Earl Rivers, consisting of: "nothing that should move or stir him to vice." After lunch, Edward went back to his books, although towards the middle of the afternoon, he took part in training and other activities that would fit him for participation in a military role, should that be called for. Presumably this included exercises with the bow and other weapons; and lessons in jousting and horsemanship; and more social pursuits such as hunting and hawking. Rui de Soussa, the Portuguese ambassador, also claimed to have seen Richard "singing with his mother and one of his sisters and that he sang very well and that he was very pretty and the most beautiful creature he had ever seen, and he also saw him playing very well at sticks and with a two-handed sword."[9]

So the education of the brothers undoubtedly included some knowledge of music, singing and probably dancing, as well as instruction in the more robust arts necessary for a medieval king and his younger brother. After this afternoon exercise period, Edward celebrated Evensong, then went to his supper, again elaborately served by servants and squires. After supper, he was allowed a period of recreation before going to bed at about eight o'clock, several attendants being assigned to remain with him throughout the night. Incidentally, Edward's literary knowledge and attainments seem to have been considerably more extensive than many of his contemporaries in this late medieval period, Mancini himself complimenting the boy on his accomplishments and breadth of learning, claiming that "in word and deed he gave so many proofs of a liberal education, of polite, nay, rather scholarly attainments far beyond his age..[and] his special knowledge of literature, which enabled him to discourse elegantly, understand fully, and declaim (i.e., make a speech) most excellently from any work whether in verse or prose which came into his hands, unless it were from amongst the most abstruse authors."[10]

Richard's itinerary may have been more relaxed, since he was only the youngest son and not heir to the throne, although doubtless it would have followed the same general form, especially where the religious observances were concerned. Moreover, he was living with his mother, who may have allowed a less rigid atmosphere, although Elizabeth Wydeville's reputation suggests she would have been unlikely to encourage idleness.

The boys' education was clearly intended to turn them into dutiful children, both properly disciplined and well educated, who could be expected to develop into self-disciplined, conscientious adults. It seems likely that their father had purposely implemented such a regime so as to mold his sons into the useful functionaries and administrators he needed, both to meet his own requirements within his established power-base and to ensure a stable government after his death. Edward had made his eldest son's future clear when he said, "[We] purpose by God's grace to purvey that he shall be so virtuously, cunningly [knowledgeably] and knightly brought up to serve Almighty God, christianly and devoutly, as accords to his duty and to live and proceed in the world honourably after his estate and dignity."[11]

Family, if its members remained loyal, was a much more reliable source for court officials, administrators and landholders than the noble classes whose sympathies could be bought and sold by the next rebel who felt the crown was within his grasp. Moreover, if Edward wanted an example of family loyalty when things got rough, he need only look to his younger brother, who had supported him through all the difficulties of the first part of his reign.

Household Servants and Functionaries

Edward was anything but isolated. His chamberlain, Thomas Vaughan, was in constant attendance almost from birth, and as he grew older, his retinue grew to include chaplains, tutors, servants and mentors such as Earl Rivers. Most importantly, Edward also had carefully selected companions of his own age and social standing, who were intended to set him an example in "virtue, honour, cunning [knowledge], wisdom and deeds of worship and nothing that should stir him to vices."[12] These positions around the prince, the prince's "henxmen," were coveted, being seen as the first step in a subsequent career in royal service, so the young lordlings appointed to be Edward's companions were carefully screened and their behavior continually scrutinized. It was also ordered, possibly by Rivers, that Edward should be accompanied everywhere by "two discreet and convenient persons"—not noble companions, but more in the way of bodyguards and personal servants. In additions to these close companions, servants, cooks, grooms and hangers-on finally constituted a household that grew from around fifty in 1472, when it was first established, probably to several hundred by the time of his father's death. The names of some of these retainers are known:

Sir Richard Croft: Treasurer, assuming his duties before 1480.
Richard Minors: Usher of Edward's chamber, assuming his duties before 1474.
Nicholas Here: Yeoman porter in 1477.
John Argentine: Edward's doctor from 1478 until 1483.[13]

Intended Political and Military Roles

The role that Edward intended his sons to play in a future England dominated by a Yorkist monarchy is made fairly clear from the lands he bestowed upon them in their earliest years, as well as the prescribed, well-regulated life he ordered for them during their childhood.

Edward, with lands in much of Wales and Pembroke, and appointments as both Earl of Chester and Duke of Cornwall, seems to have been intended to oversee the west and southwest, while Richard's place lay in the east, controlling East Anglia and the Midlands, both areas previously dominated by Lancastrian nobles. The boys' uncle, Richard, Duke of Gloucester, was presumably intended to continue his governing role in the north, where he would also act as a buttress against any Scottish incursion. This would leave Edward free to strengthen his grip in the south and southeast, playing politics with his allies and those less friendly to his administration in Kent, Wiltshire and Somerset, while also advancing his cause in France. Whatever the outcome of this perhaps oversimplified interpretation of Edward's machinations, what is clear is that their father intended his sons to play a major part in helping him to govern his possessions, and they were being groomed to both accept and expect responsibility when they came of age.

Marriage

Marriage for the heir apparent to the English throne was seen as an essentially political arrangement. Alliances between royal children were intended to strengthen already-established political ties or establish new, advantageous relationships. A royal father's overriding concern was that his offspring be contracted in marriage as soon as reasonably (or even unreasonably) possible. Marriages were contracted early. Edward was a typical example, being immersed in this maelstrom in 1476, at the age of six, when a match was suggested for him with the Spanish infanta, Isabella, the daughter of Ferdinand and Isabella. Other suggestions for a future alliance included the daughter of Galeazzo Sforza, Duke of Milan, as well as the sister of Maximilian, Archduke of Austria and Duke of Burgundy. These earlier arrangements appear to have been rejected by 1480, however, when negotiations began for his marriage to the three-year-old Anne, Duchess of Brittany (1477–1514), a treaty ratifying this marriage being signed in 1481 between Edward IV and her father, François II, Duke of Brittany.[14]

Richard suffered a similar fate, married to the Mowbray heiress, Anne Mortimer, on 15 January 1478 at St. Stephen's Chapel, Westminster, when he was four and she was five. Anne Mortimer died on 19 November 1481, at Greenwich, and Richard's father had not managed to arrange another, suitably lucrative match before his own death in 1483.[15]

The Monarchy Under Edward V, and the Woodville Influence

Edward's period as a prospective king of England lasted only about three months, from his father's death on 9 April until Shaa's declaration of his illegitimate status on 25 June. Although Richard and Buckingham had removed Edward's former attendants at Stony Stratford on 30 April and made it clear to him that it was their wishes that counted, not his, there is some circumstantial evidence that both men tried to win his confidence and trust. All three appear to have signed their name to a slip of parchment—Gloucester and Buckingham also appending their mottoes after their respective signatures—and they may have succeeded in impressing the boy enough to ensure his cooperation.[16] After all, both were young men, and Edward may well have appreciated the less constrained atmosphere he experienced while journeying with them to London.

When news of the coup reached the capital on 1 May, the queen and Dorset tried to raise an army to rescue the prince, but they met opposition from an unexpected quarter, as Crowland explains: "When they had exhorted certain nobles who had come to them and others to take up arms, they perceived that mens minds were not only irresolute, but altogether hostile to themselves. Some even said openly that it was more just and profitable that the youthful sovereign should be with his paternal uncle than with his maternal uncles and uterine brothers."[17]

On 2 May, Richard wrote to the City Corporation and Royal Council, with a copy of the letter also dispatched for public proclamation, declaring his loyalty to the new king and explaining that the actions he had taken were only intended to remove the Woodvilles from power and remove any influence his family might have exercised over the new king. These letters served to convince the London councilors of his good intentions, and he was admitted to the city unopposed, accompanied by Buckingham and Edward. Still acting the part of a loyal subject, Richard obliged all the lords and city council to swear allegiance to the new king, himself accompanying them in the oath-taking. He was now well established because, with the queen and Dorset in sanctuary, Sir Edward Wydeville gone to sea but deprived of his command of the fleet, and Rivers, Grey and Vaughan incarcerated, the Woodville faction of the king's council no longer existed. Despite the solidity of his position, he then further strengthened it by successfully implicating the queen, Dorset and Sir Edward in the theft of the late king's treasure, although it was pretty well known in court circles that Edward had left an empty treasury.[18] With the demise of the Wydevilles, the household of Edward IV was now transferred wholesale to his son, with Hastings retaining his post as chamberlain, while Lord Stanley remained as steward. Richard was now firmly and solely in charge, with seven weeks to mature any plans he might have, the new king's coronation having been rearranged for 22 June, at which point his uncle's protectorate would end.

Despite Richard's machinations prior to his appointment as protector, he was still observing the niceties towards his royal nephew. Edward was accorded all the honors of a prospective king after his arrival on 4 May, apparently at the command of his uncle Richard, who achieved his desired protectorship about a week later, on 10 May. Administration in the period before his coronation was carried on in the same way as it had progressed under his father, although international relations were in a much more unstable condition.[19]

Minor administrative business included:

- 21 April: Mayor of the Staple of Calais admitted, Royal Judges reappointed, sheriffs and escheators appointed (escheators are persons responsible for administration of escheats, i.e., property of persons who had died intestate and whose property was transferred to the Crown or a feudal overlord).
- 23 April: Coroners appointed.
- 26–27 April: Commissions appointed against piracy (French vessels were raiding Channel shipping); commissioners also appointed to look into the taxation of aliens.

After 9 May, Edward began issuing instructions under his own signet (i.e., using his own seal ring for ratification of documents) and using his own name. Only seven warrants under the Great Seal are known that bear the future king's signature, his "sign manual," and this includes one authorizing the summons of Parliament.[20] Although these documents show Edward beginning to play a major part in government and that his signature was regarded as significant by those in authority, his was still only a minor role. In reality, as the "Crowland Continuator" wrote, Gloucester "exercised this authority with the consent and goodwill of all the Lords, commanding and forbidding everything like another king, as occasion demanded."[21]

Some time between 9 and 16 May, Edward was moved to the Tower in preparation for his coronation, and there is no evidence to suggest that his life there did not proceed in its normal, well-regulated fashion, with the requisite number of servants and attendants. The Tower during that period was simply another royal palace, more secure and better appointed than most, and Edward probably still had his familiar adherents about him, including John Argentine, his physician. He is claimed to have spent much of his time shooting and playing in the gardens, probably with his brother Richard, after the Duke of York was sent to join him on 16 June. One disadvantage of the Tower, however, was that it was some distance from Westminster. This may have been seen by Richard as an advantageous change, brought about to distance Edward from governmental decision-making.

Decision-making in Edward's name appears to have lasted only from 14 May, when the justices of assize were appointed to four home counties, until

9 June, the day the precontract between Edward IV and Lady Eleanor Butler was first revealed, the last document bearing his signature being dated 10 June 1483. There may be significance in this, in that the transition period between Edward's prospective monarchy and Richard's assumption of power is thus shown to be far more abrupt than was previously supposed. Edward appears to have been deprived of his governmental prerogatives and therefore his right to the monarchy from the time of the first council meeting (9 June) rather than with the presentation of the Titulus Regius (26 June), as is more usually supposed, and this could indicate planning, either by Richard or someone else.

Edward's position changed irrevocably after that council meeting of 9 June, and by 26 June he found himself illegitimate and confined to the Tower with his brother, who had been removed from his mother's custody ostensibly to make preparations for his attendance at his older brother Edward's coronation. The day after Richard joined his brother, the coronation was canceled for the indefinite future and on Sunday 22 June, the Shaa sermon had laid bare his father's indiscretions to the view of the whole country. Edward's monarchy had ended in degradation before it had properly begun.

Table 5. Children of Edward IV
Legitimate Children (by Elizabeth Woodville)

Name and Title	Born–Died	Notes
Elizabeth of York, queen to Henry VII	11 February 1466–11 February 1503	
Mary of York	11 August 1467–23 May 1482	
Cecily of York	20 March 1469–24 August 1507	Married first John Welles, 1st Viscount Welles and 2nd Thomas Kyme or Keme
Edward V of England	2 November 1470–1483?	
Margaret of York	10 April 1472–11 December 1472	
Richard of Shrewsbury, 1st Duke of York	17 August 1473–1483?	
Anne of York, Lady Howard	2 November 1475–23 November 1511	Married Thomas Howard (later 3rd Duke of Norfolk)
George Plantagenet, 1st Duke of Bedford	March 1477–March 1479	
Catherine of York	14 August 1479–15 November 1527	Married William Courtenay, 1st Earl of Devon
Bridget of York	10 November 1480–1517	Became a nun

Note: Of Edward and Elizabeth's ten children, seven were still living by 1483, Mary (died age 15), Margaret (died age 9 months) and George (died age 2 years), all predeceasing their father.

Illegitimate Children (by Elizabeth Lucy)

Name and Title	Born–Died	Notes
Elizabeth Plantagenet	1464–?	
Arthur Plantagenet, 1st Viscount Lisle	1470–3 March 1542	

Mother Unknown

Name and Title	Born–Died	Notes
Grace Plantagenet		
Mary Plantagenet		

Table 6. The Members of Edward's Councils[22]

Members of Edward's First Council, 1471

Member	Relation to Edward	Role in Edward's Council	Role After 1483
Elizabeth Woodville	Mother	Councilor	In sanctuary at Westminster until March 1483, then involved in schemes to marry Elizabeth of York to Henry Tudor
Cardinal Thomas Bourchier, Archbishop of Canterbury	Great uncle	Councilor and administrator	Possibly involved in the various conspiracies against Richard III. Crowned Henry VII in 1485 and Elizabeth of York in 1486.
George, Duke of Clarence	Elder paternal uncle		Executed 1478
Richard, Duke of Gloucester	Youngest paternal uncle	Advisory	King Richard III
Robert Stillington, Bishop of Bath and Chancellor of England	No relation	Advisory	Advisor to Richard III. Responsible for evidence

Member	Relation to Edward	Role in Edward's Council	Role After 1483 upon which the "Titulus Regius" was based
Thomas Millyng, Abbot of Westminster, Bishop of Hereford, king's councilor	Godfather	Chancellor, 1471–1483	Survived into reign of Henry VII
Laurence Bothe, Bishop of Durham	No relation	Advisor on religious questions	Died 1480
Anthony, Earl Rivers	Eldest maternal uncle	Tutor and governor from 1473	Executed 1483
William, Lord Hastings, chamberlain of the king's household	No relation	Chamberlain	Executed 1483
Richard Fiennes, Lord Dacre, steward of the king's household	No relation	Steward	Died 1483
Sir John Fogge, treasurer of the king's household	No relation	Chamberlain and tutor	Participant in 1483 rebellion (Kent)
Sir John Scott, controller of the king's Household, Administrator of the Devon properties	No relation	Chamberlain and tutor	Died 1485, after coronation of Henry VII
Sir Thomas Vaughn, treasurer of the king's chamber	No relation	Chamberlain, appointed 1474	Executed 1483
John Alcock, dean of St. Stephen's Chapel, Westminster, later Bishop of Rochester and Winchester	No relation	Teacher and president of the council from 1473	Served under Richard III. Temporarily appointed chancellor under Henry VII, until Morton's return.
Richard Fowler, esquire, chancellor of the Duchy of Lancaster	No relation	Advisory	

Members Added to Edward's Council in 1473[23]

Member	Relation to Edward	Role in Edward's Council	Role after death of Edward IV
Edward Storey, Bishop of Chicester, queen's chancellor	No relation	Possibly religious advisor	Removed himself from public life.
John, Earl of Shrewsbury	Distant cousin	Advisory	Not known
Walter Devereux, Lord Ferrers of Chartley	Distant in-law	Tutor and councilor	Possibly associated with Buckingham's rebellion. Killed at Bosworth.
Sir John Needham, justice of the King's Bench	No relation	Legal advisor	Died in 1480
Sir Richard Chok, Justice of the Common Pleas	No relation	Legal advisor	Died 1483
Dr. Richard Martin, chancellor of the Earldom of March	No relation	Tutor and councilor	Died 25 March 1483
William Allington, esquire, royal councilor, possibly chancellor of the Duchy of Cornwall	No relation	Tutor and councilor	Died 16 May 1479
Richard Haute, esquire	Maternal cousin	Controller	Participant in 1483 rebellion and attainted. Property returned in 1485, died in 1487.
John Sulyard, sergeant-at-law	No relation	Legal advisor	
Geoffrey Cottesmore, lawyer	No relation	Legal advisor	

Chapter Six

Sojourn in the Tower

After 16 June 1483 when Richard joined his brother, several contemporary accounts have the boys still in the Tower, possibly until the early autumn, although subsequently, they were not reliably reported to have been seen again there or anywhere else. It is usually claimed that the boys were lodged in a tower facing the river and erected as part of the south curtain wall, which surrounded the inner ward. During the reign of Edward IV, this structure was referred to as the Garden Tower because its upper story opened on to the Constable's Garden, and it did not become known as the Bloody Tower until 1585, when it was given this label after Henry Percy, 8th Earl of Northumberland, committed suicide within its walls. Fabyan's account of the boys being seen "shotyng and playyng in the Gardyn of the Tower by sundry tymys" was probably the basis for the legend about the boys' prison ("Garden of the Tower" being misread as "Garden Tower"). The Garden Tower itself does not seem to have been a particularly secure place to incarcerate two valuable prisoners such as Edward and Richard. It is on the perimeter wall of the inner ward facing Tower Wharf and has a number of windows overlooking the river, which would have made it a relatively easy matter to slip over the outer wall one moonless night, get the boys out through a window and put them on a ship anchored in mid-river. Moreover, there is only a single apartment on the first floor that would have been even barely suitable as royal accommodation, and housing the brothers here would have been fraught with security problems, the Garden Tower being the main entrance to the inner ward. Thus the entrance, which is immediately adjacent to those apartments, was certain to have seen a lot of foot and horse traffic, making the boys more readily accessible than perhaps would have been advisable, in view of their extreme political value.

It seems much more probable that Edward and Richard were housed initially in what was usually referred to as the Royal Palace, which comprised secure apartments located in St. Thomas's Tower and the two adjacent towers of Wakefield and Lanthorn. Henry VI is thought to have been imprisoned there on 11 April 1471, and he died or was murdered in the chapel of the Wakefield Tower after the death of his son at the battle of Tewksbury in 1471. So it is not unreasonable to suggest that Richard may have housed his nephews in these palatial rooms, especially as Edward was moved to the Tower in the expectation that his coronation was imminent. He was not a prisoner at that point, and so would have expected appropriate accommodation and treatment in accord with his status. Wakefield Tower is also next door to the Garden Tower, making the Constable's Garden convenient for the boys and perhaps explaining why they were seen playing there, if Fabyan's informant was correct about what he or she had observed. None of the contemporary accounts mention precisely where the boys were imprisoned, and the Palace apartments are perhaps a more probable location.

The Contemporary Accounts

DOMONIC MANCINI

The most comprehensive of these accounts was written by Domonic Mancini, an Italian scholar who had been employed to report on conditions in England by Angelo Cato, one of the counselors of Louis XI of France. Mancini appears to have left England on or just before Richard's coronation on 6 July, and he delivered his written report to Cato sometime in December 1483. He is thought to owe much of his information to John Argentine, an English-born doctor who was serving as Edward's physician at the time, and although he states that the princes disappeared, he is also clear that their fate was uncertain. He wrote:

> After Hastings was removed, all the attendants who had waited upon the king were debarred access to him. He and his brother were withdrawn into the inner apartments of the Tower proper, and day by day began to be seen more rarely behind the bars at the windows, till at length they ceased to appear altogether. A Strasbourg doctor (thought to be Argentine, although he actually trained in Italy), the last of his attendants whose services the king enjoyed, reported that the young king, like a victim prepared for sacrifice, sought remission of his sins by daily confession and penance, because he believed that death was facing him.... I have seen many men burst forth into tears and lamentations when mention was made of him after his removal from men's sight; and already there was a suspicion that he had been done away with. Whether, however, he has been done away with, and by what manner of death, so far I have not at all discovered.

The last document signed by Edward was dated 10 June; Hastings was executed on 13 June; and Edward's brother, Richard, joined him in the Tower on 16 June. This may not have been the last sighting of Edward, since the wardrobe account suggests that he may have been present at his uncle's coronation on 6 July. Mancini claims, however, that no one saw the boys after Richard entered the Tower in the middle of June, except perhaps through the barred window of their apartments, although Mancini left London himself soon after 6 July, so his statement referring to a suspicion that Edward had been done away with seems a little premature, especially since there was an attempt to remove the boys from the Tower a month later, at the end of July, which resulted in the execution of four of the men involved.

Mancini's description of the boys being "withdrawn into the inner apartments of the Tower proper, and day by day … seen more rarely behind the bars at the windows, till at length they ceased to appear altogether" is also interesting, implying that the boys were moved from their original lodging, whether in the Royal Palace or Garden Tower, to a more secure location. The "Tower proper" usually refers to the White Tower; and this suggests that the boys may have been moved to that building some time in July, perhaps for their own safety, rather than remaining where they had been originally housed.[1]

Robert Fabyan

More contemporary evidence is included in the text of "The Great Chronicle of London," composed by the London cloth merchant and city alderman Robert Fabyan, writing in the reign of Henry VII, although the record refers to a period before 29 September 1483, which was the end of Sir Edmund Shaa's mayoral year.

Fabyan records simply that "King Edward V, with his brother the Duke of York, were put under sure keeping within the Tower in which wise they never came abroad after." Later in the manuscript, he also claims, "During this mayre's year, the childyr of Kyng Edward were seen shotyng and playyng in the Gardyn of the Tower by sundry tymys."

Although this observation is usually thought to refer to a period when Sir Edmund Shaa was lord mayor, from October 1482 to October 1483, it has been suggested, because of an incorrectly written date, that it may have referred to the following year when Robert Billesden was the incumbent, although this is now considered to be unlikely.

Fabyan's wording also suggests that he was reporting something he was told, not a direct observation he made himself, and that the boys were seen not once but "sundry" or several times. Moreover, whoever told Fabyan about the boys must have been a regular visitor to the Tower and most probably employed there, because the garden where it is claimed the boys were seen playing and shooting is not visible from beyond either the inner or the outer curtain wall, so they could not have been seen by anyone passing by chance.

Finally, Fabyan concludes, "The common fame went that King Richard put unto secret death the two sons of his brother."[2]

The Croyland Chronicler

Another, almost contemporary account of the boys' fate is included in the Croyland Chronicles, a description of events in England kept intermittently from 655 to 1486. The relevant part concerning Richard's reign was written in the Benedictine abbey at Crowland, Lincolnshire, in April 1486, and the writer is even more vague than either Mancini or Fabian, simply stating that about the time of the Buckingham rebellion, which could have been as early as August or as late as October 1483, "when the peoples about London … made a rising on their behalf, publicly proclaiming that Henry, Duke of Buckingham, repenting the course of conduct he had adopted, would be their leader, it was spread abroad that King Edward's sons were dead, but by what kind of violent death is unknown." In this passage the writer is clearly implying that the rumor was "spread abroad" after the duke had decided to lead the rebellion, the rumor arising as a result of Buckingham's decision and not as the cause of it.

Moreover, earlier in the Chronicle, the same writer records: "While these things were passing in the North, King Edward's two sons remained under certain deputed custody for whose release from captivity the people of the southern and western parts began very much to murmur."[3]

The "things passing in the North" mentioned in this passage refers to the tour made by Richard to York from July to September 1483, *after* the coronation, so someone was sufficiently well informed to reassure the general population that the late king's sons were still alive at that time. In this passage, the Chronicler appears to be implying that the condition of the boys was generally well known; if that is so, how was such information being spread and by whom? It also suggests that no concern was felt by the general population of London for the safety of Edward's sons just after their incarceration in the Tower in June and early July, specifically because they had been consigned to the safekeeping of a person of appropriate rank, possibly Brackenbury. This certainly seems to disagree with Mancini's account, who claims to have seen men lamenting their fate because they were thought to have been "done away with" before he left the country some time after 6 July. According to Croyland, uncertainty only set in after Buckingham's rumor became general knowledge from August to October 1483, the implication being that the possibility of Richard's murdering the boys was not an idea that had been generally considered likely. Consequently, when the rumor of their death became prevalent, it was greeted with a horror greatly increased by the surprise that many must have felt when faced with an event so unexpected and wholly unthinkable as a royal uncle's murder of his nephews. In that context, it would be interesting to know what might have been said in earlier bulletins or letters originating from Richard that would have reassured people that he had some specific role planned for his nephews and so increased the general surprise and horror at the report, however unsubstantiated, of the boys' death.

The reticence of the Chronicler about their eventual fate is surprising as well, since he was thought to be a highly placed courtier who had served in the courts of Edward IV, his son and his brother, Richard, so he might have been expected to be able to supply significantly more detail about what really happened to the boys.[4] Despite what he might have known, in his later passages the Chronicler only confirmed his earlier statement, while writing from memory in 1486, that "the rumor arose in September, 1483, that … the princes, by some unknown manner of destruction had met their fate."

THE CELY LETTER

George Cely, a London merchant, claimed in a letter that he was concerned for the life of the king, although he gives no reason for the fear he expressed, and he also appears to have harbored similar concerns for the safety of Richard, Duke of Gloucester, the Duke of Northumberland and John Howard. He gives no reason why he supposed these three to have been in any danger either, although the letter is thought to have been written some time between the death of Hastings at the council meeting on 13 June and the creation of John Howard as Duke of Norfolk on 28 June; so Cely may have heard the rumors of a plot against Richard.

The relevant text is as follows:

> Her ys grett romber in the reme, the scottes has done grett yn Ynglond, schamberlayne [the chamberlain Hastings], ys dessesset in trobell the chaunseler [the ex-Chancellor, Thomas Rotherham] ys dysprowett and nott content the boshop of Ely [John Morton] nny ys ded yff the kyng [Edward V] God saffe his lyfe wher desset, the Dewk of Glosetter wher in any parell, geffe my lorde prynsse [my lord prince, referring to Richard, Duke of York] wher God defend wher trobellett, yf my lord of Northehombyrlond wher ded or grettly trobellyt, yf my lorde Haward wher slayne.

The rest of the letter is missing. It may be significant that this source describes only an uncertainty about what had happened to Edward, although the writer also expresses some concern as to the fate of Richard.[5]

The Colchester Oath Book

This is an extract from the Borough Records of Colchester, which was found in a collection of documents referred to as the Oath Book. The pages referring to the fifteenth century take the form of a year-by-year listing of both bailiffs and burgesses, together with a summary of other documents registered as received in the borough during the year. The records themselves were probably brought up to date at the end of the civic year, Michaelmas Day (29 September), which means that the record for 1483 was made just before the October Rebellion and only three months after Richard was crowned.

The record for this period (30 September 1482 until 29 September 1483) is remarkable in that it includes the reigns of three kings, and the compiler, John Hervey, a local lawyer who also served as town clerk, found that sufficiently unusual to make careful note of it. Analysis of his entry has also shown that the account for 1483 was probably written on or shortly after 29 September 1483. The original text is in Latin and the English translation reads:

> In the time of John Bisshop and Thomas Cristemesse, Baliffs of the town of Colchester from the feast of St Michael the Archangel in the 22nd year of the reign of Lord Edward IV, late king of England, now deceased, up until the 8th day of April first following; and in the first year of the reign of King Edward V, late son of the lord Edward IV after the Conquest, up to the 20th day of June then first following; [and] in the first year of the reign of Richard III after the Conquest, from the beginning, and thence until the first feast of St Michael the Archangel there after as for one complete year.

This account thus suggests a date for Edward's death of 20 June 1483, a short while before Mancini left England, when he made reference to Edward, claiming, "There was already a suspicion that he had been done away with." It may also be significant that this is another account in which no reference is made to the whereabouts of Richard of York, nor is any authoritative source given for the information. In view of the distance from Colchester to London and the relative obscurity of that city as a commercial center, this lack of corroboration might suggest that information would have arrived there belatedly and possibly in a garbled form.[6]

Robert Ricart, Recorder of Bristol

Robert Ricart was town clerk or recorder of Bristol, probably from 1478 until 1506, and was responsible for the production of a book, *The Maire of Bristowe Is Kalendar (Ricart's Calendar)*, a history of Britain and particularly Bristol, in six parts. The Kalendar begins with a history of Britain and includes an entry under the year ending September 1483, probably Michaelmas Day, like the Colchester Oath Book, saying, "In this year the sons of King Edward were put to silence in the Tower of London." No source is recorded for the information.

Anlaby Family Cartulary

This book is a history of the Anlaby family of Etton, begun by one of the family's scribes in 1450. The entry concerning the princes was written some time in 1509 and it simply and confidently states that Edward V died on 22 June 1483. Doubt has been cast on the veracity of this source because the writer incorrectly recorded the date of Edward IV's death. However, all his other dates are correct, including the date for the birth and accession to the throne of Edward V himself, although the writer does not include details of any source for the information he recorded.[7] This is another source that records only the death of Edward and does not mention Richard of York in any context.

Middleton Collection, University of Nottingham: King List

This is a list included in the Middleton Collection Deeds in the University of Nottingham Library, which notes that Edward was murdered on the day after his uncle took possession of the throne, i.e., 27 June 1483. This entry, however, raises at least one significant problem, in that it describes Edward's body as "submersum fuit" ("was drowned"). Nor does it mention anything about what happened to Richard.[8]

Guillaume de Rochfort

Guillaume de Rochfort, chancellor of France, made a speech to the Estates General at Tours in January 1484, in which he stated that, as they knew, after the death of Edward IV his sons were murdered and the crown was given to the murderer.

It is difficult to know how much credence to give this account, since by this time the French were supporting Henry Tudor against the established Yorkist monarchy, Henry having proclaimed himself king and promised to marry Elizabeth of York at Rheims Cathedral on 25 December 1483. Consequently, any adverse propaganda directed against Richard would certainly have been to the advantage of the French and most especially to the benefit of their Tudor protégé; so the report of the princes' death may have been wishful thinking on the part of the esteemed chancellor.[9]

Later Accounts

THE ROUS ROLLE

John Rous, the Warwickshire cleric, writing approximately six years after the event, some time in 1489, recorded, "He received his lord king Edward V blandly [at Stony Strattford on 29 April] with embraces and kisses and within about three months or a little more he killed him together with his brother." Rous may be unreliable, having written at least three versions of his Rolle, the first pre–Tudor, extolling the virtues of Richard and his son, while the second and subsequent work first omitted him completely, then in a later version castigated him as a monster. He even implies in one version of the Rolle that the boys were murdered before Richard was crowned, so his accuracy on other questions is dubious, at the very least.[10]

PHILLIPE DE COMMYNES

Phillipe Commynes (1447–1511) was a Flemish historian and former advisor to Louis XI, and so was probably predominantly pro–Tudor and anti–Richardian in his views. In his *Mémoires de Phillipe de Commynes,* completed around 1500, he gives three different accounts of the princes' fate. Initially, he states that Richard had his nephews murdered, then assumed the throne. In a later passage, he reverses the order of events, having Richard crowned before murdering his nephews, before finally confirming that it was really Buckingham who was responsible.[11]

JEAN MOLINET

Jean Molinet (1435–1507) was a French poet and historian who worked for Charles the Bold, Duke of Burgundy, from 1463 until his death in 1477 and then seems to have been employed about the Burgundian and Austrian courts in a number of scholarly capacities. He wrote his book *Chroniques de Jean Molinet (1474–1506)* during this period, although it is not quite clear when it was finished. Molinet's *Chronicles* also contains an account in which he claims that the princes were smothered about five weeks after being imprisoned (around 22 July) and subsequently buried in the grounds of the Tower, a story suspiciously similar to the account given in Sir Thomas More's *History*.[12]

The other contemporary accounts from a number of foreign sources, such as Casper Weinreich of Danzig and Jan Allertz, recorder (town clerk) of Rotterdam, are equally vague and seem to be the result of collected rumor or, as in the case of the French chancellor Guillaume de Rochefort, possibly wishful thinking.[13]

Uncertainty and Later Writers

Polydore Vergil

Polydore Vergil (1470–1555) was Henry VII's official historian. He wrote his commissioned history *Anglica Historia* or *History of England* between 1505 and 1513, finishing the text under Henry VIII. It was first published in Basle, now northern Switzerland, in 1534 and covered events up to 1509, with a subsequent second edition published in Basle in 1546. A completed third edition of the book with an amended text describing events up to 1537 was subsequently published, once again in Basle, some time during 1555. As might be expected, it has a very pro-Tudor bias, which is understandable considering that Henry Tudor was paying Vergil for his work, and Vergil has been accused of destroying documents that did not agree with his views, although this has now been shown to be one thing he was not guilty of. Significantly, it is the first work in print to accuse Richard of killing his nephews, over twenty years after the event, basing the account of the boys' death on the confession of Sir John Tyrell, which is also the basis for Sir Thomas More's famous story. Virgil, who was age 15 in 1483, was not certain about exactly what happened to the boys, however, and even admitted that "a report prevailed among the common people that the sons of Edward the king had migrated to some part of the earth in secret, and there were still surviving."[14]

Sir Thomas More

Written during 1512–1519 and published some time after More's death, *The History of King Richard the Thirde (unfinished)* was accepted for several hundred years as the definitive account, both of Richard's reign and his murder of the princes in the Tower. More (1478–1535; age 5 in 1483) goes into great detail about Richards' plot to kill the princes, accusing Sir James Tyrell of arranging the murders and claiming the bodies were buried "at a stayre foot" before being moved, on Richard's orders, to a "more fit place the pair bein kings' sonyes." There was much confusion over this passage, after it was claimed that the bodies of two children were found in chest during demolition of an exterior staircase abutting the White Tower, and who were subsequently said to be Edward and Richard.

More's main source was thought to be Richard's long-time enemy, John Morton, so he could hardly have been treated to a balanced tale. Further more, his contemporary sources were all likely to have been pro–Tudor since most of Richards' friends and supporters, few enough to begin with, would probably have been dead or keeping their mouths shut. Sir Thomas was executed in 1535 and the book was published after his death.

Even Sir Thomas appears not to be absolutely sure about the princes' fate. More wrote, "[The princes'] death and final infortune hath nathless so far comen in question that some remain yet in doubt whether they were in his [King Richard's] days destroyed or no."[15]

Although Caroline Halstead claimed that this quote indicated that Sir Thomas was not sure about the fate of the boys, reading the whole passage in context shows that what More actually meant was that, although some may have doubted that the boys were killed by Richard, his account is the true story. He continued after the passage quoted above and wrote: "But in the meane time for this present matter [i.e., the death of the princes], I shall rehearse you the dolorous end of those babes, not after euery way that I haue heard, but after that way thay I haue so hard by such men & by such meanes, as me thinketh it wer hard but it should be true."[16]

Francis Bacon

Francis Bacon (1561–1626), who had served as both attorney general and lord chancellor of England, published his *History of the Reign of King Henry VII* in 1621. The text revealed him to be convinced of Richard's guilt, and he certainly contributed to the former king's "Black Legend," but even Bacon was forced to concede: "Neither wanted there even at that time [the reign of Henry VII], secret rumors and whisperings, which afterwards gathered strength, and turned to great troubles, that the two young sons of King Edward IV, or one of them, which were said to be destroyed in the Tower, were not indeed murdered, but conveyed secretly away and were yet living." Later, he added, "And all this time it was still whispered everywhere that at least one of the children of Edward IV was still living."[17]

Putting aside all the conjecture and based on just the contemporary accounts and later versions by More, Bacon and Vergil, the only certainty is that the boys were alive on 16 June 1483 and the *general opinion* was that they were dead by the autumn of 1483. It may also be of significance that of the twelve contemporary sources included here, four of them, specifically the Cely Letter, the Colchester Oath Book, the Anlaby Family Cartulary and the Middleton Collection Deeds King List, claim that it was only Edward who was known to have died or whose life was despaired of, and they make no mention of the fate of Richard of York.

It is not clear, however, whether the consensus found among these various accounts is the result of information becoming available from a number of authentic, independent sources or was part of a well-planned conspiracy, giving rise to several coherent rumors that had their origin in a single source. That the origin of the story of the boys' death has been claimed to be both Buckingham and Richard himself only serves to add to the confusion, although further examination of the sources listed here shows that only one, the Cely Letter, actually originates from a period before the Rebellion. More importantly, Cely only states that he is fearful for the life of the young king and makes no claim that either of the boys were killed during this period. Nor does he say who he thinks may have been threatening the children at this point. No contemporary writer could offer absolute, incontrovertible proof of what happened to them nor produce a story with sufficient detail to be convincing. Apart from Sir Thomas, even those writing in the Tudor period did not include details of the murder or the subsequent treatment of the bodies and, with the exception of More's *History*, this sort of information is entirely missing.

Perspectives

Although documents referring to Edward and his little brother are less common than is desirable, a reasonably clear picture still emerges of the character of the boys and the future their father intended for them. Their early education and the lands settled upon them indicate that they were intended for significant roles within the royal hierarchy, as both administrators within the court and major landowners. Their father may have intended them also to have some European involvement, since both boys were taught to read and write English and French as well as the more usual Latin. It is also perhaps indicative of this feature of the king's future plans that Prince Edward had been betrothed to Anne, Duchess of Brittany, which gave the king an ally by marriage on the French mainland and a good chance that his son would inherit her father's title, Francis II having no male heir. Edward was undoubtedly intent upon turning the monarchy into a family business as far as possible, and he probably adopted this course because of the fickle nature of the men who surrounded him at court, in particular the various members of the Stanley family, Buckingham and the rest of his wife's acquisitive relations. Unfortunately, his brother George, Duke of Clarence, had proven unreliable and disloyal, forcing Edward to order his execution in 1478, but with his trusted brother Richard holding the north and his two sons controlling the west and east, once they were of age, he might have been forgiven for thinking that his own future and that of his family were both in the process of being properly and firmly secured.

Edward had also been careful to ensure that his sons were instilled with a strong sense of responsibility and a clear knowledge of their place in the established hierarchy. However, this type of training would also have made them well aware of not just their own positions but also the responsibilities that devolved upon them as both Yorkists and inheritors of the Plantaganet monarchy. With that sort of conditioning, begun in their earliest years, it does not seem impossible that, with their illegitimacy an accomplished and—perhaps more importantly—a generally acknowledged fact, Richard may have felt he could convince them that their best and safest course, perhaps even the most honorable one, lay as administrators in his monarchy, albeit highly placed, serving him and later his son, as the Mortimers served Henry V after his father's death.[18] Effectively, it was the same role their father had intended for them while he was alive and with a good chance of inheriting the monarchy itself, if Richard's own son, Edward of Middleham, did not survive to become adult. With their courtly education, particularly in the European diplomatic languages, as well as their other skills and Yorkist background, they were a considerable asset and not one to be lightly discarded. Richard may have foreseen this possibility early in the period after his brother's death, and this could have been the reason for his cultivation of Edward's friendship after the events at Stony Stratford. Certainly, with the youthful king in his power, Richard had no real need to humble himself in the way he did to obtain Edward's acquiescence, especially if he intended to murder one or both of the boys at the earliest opportunity.[19] Unfortunately, no letter or other document has ever been located giving details of the future Richard had planned for his nephews, although it must have been occupying his thoughts, especially after his coronation in July 1483.

Whatever Richard's real intentions towards the boys, it is certain that, before the publication of Vergil's book, nobody had claimed in writing that they really knew Richard had murdered them, although, according to Croyland, many in the country were sure that Richard had intended to displace his nephew Edward and occupy the throne from the time of his elder brother's death. More importantly, and despite some later writers suggesting that one or both of the boys might have survived their uncle's enmity and escaped the Tower, it is clear from most sources that, despite the complete lack of evidence, by December 1483 a very large proportion of Richard's subjects had either been convinced or persuaded themselves that he had murdered the boys or, at the very least, had given the orders for their deaths. This fixed belief in Richard's guilt, combined with what many apparently saw as the blatant usurpation of his brother's throne, was certainly a major contribution to the unrest that erupted into the October Rebellion and his subsequent continued failure to obtain support from many Yorkist nobles. This, in turn, was instrumental in ensuring his eventual defeat and death at Bosworth; and despite Richard's talent for self-promotion, he appears to have been unable to counter or even discourage this flow of negative publicity. Consequently, it may be of interest to consider who in Henry Tudor's regime was sufficiently talented to circumvent Richard so adroitly. Moreover, if they could deal with Richard so easily, how successfully might that person, whoever he or she was, have conducted a search for information leading them to the princes? Bray, Morton, even Margaret Beaufort are all suitable candidates, and it may have been fear of Tudor's embryonic intelligence organization that obliged Richard to keep the boys hidden, even when the worst effects of the October Rebellion had subsided, without being entirely dissipated.

Timeline 1.
Evidence for the Location and Fate of the Princes After July 1483, from Contemporary Sources

June, 1483

9: Edward's own servants paid off.

10: Last document bearing Edward's signature.

13: George Cely: "Not long after 13th June ... feared that Edward V was in peril of his life."

Hasting was executed on this day, and Richard was not sent to the Tower until 16 June 1483. Cely's letter was written between 13 June 1483 and 28 September 1483.

16: Richard of York sent to the Tower to join his elder brother.

20: Colchester Council Oath Book, written September 1483, gives 20 June as the date for Edward's death.

22: Anlaby Family Cartulary, written some time before 1509, gives 22 June as the precise date of Edward's death. This is only six days after Richard joined his brother in the Tower, and the account specifies only Edward's death.

July, 1483

6: Mancini leaves England, considering that Edward and Richard are already dead. His account was written late in 1483.

The attempt to remove the boys and their sisters took place some time before 29 July and Fabyan describes the boys in the Tower "shootng and playng" possibly as late as October.

20: Richard left for his northern progress some time from 18 to 20 July; Croyland claimed that the boys were under "certain deputed custody" while Richard was in the north. This statement could have covered the period from 18 July until as late as 11 October, when the king reached Lincoln, so Mancini's contention that the boys had disappeared or "been done away with" before he left the country, seems, at the very least, dubious.

20–25: Jean Molinet stated, "The Princes were smothered about 5 weeks after being imprisoned." Molinet wrote his account some time after the events he described, but certainly before 1509.

Richard was imprisoned on 16 June 1483, so Molinet's date would be 5 weeks later, on 22 July, four days before Richard departed for the north.

30: John Rous, writing during the reign of Henry VII: "He received his lord king Edward V blandly [at Stony Strattford on 29 April] with embraces and kisses and within about three months or a little more he killed him together with his brother."

That makes the date Rous claims the boys were killed approximately 30 July.

August, 1483

8–10: Sir Thomas More's account claims that the king was at Warwick when he ordered Tyrell to murder them, making the date of their death some time soon after he arrived in that city and within the same time period as that claimed by John Rous.

September

The Croyland Chronicle stated, "The rumour arose in September, 1483, that … the princes, by some unknown manner of destruction had met their fate." The "rumour arising" does not mean that the boys could not have died before this date and it is not suggested here that Richard killed them. The Croyland account is usually claimed to have been written sometime in 1486.

15: Robert Ricart in his Bristol "Kalender" also claims Edward and Richard were killed sometime before this date. Ricart's account was written before 1506 and possibly much earlier.

29: In the "Great Chronicle," written in the reign of Henry Tudor, Fabyan claims that, in the period before 29 September 1483, which marked the end of Sir Edmund Shaa's year as mayor, "The childyr of kyng Edward were seen shotyng and playyng in the Garden of the Tower by sundry tymys."

October

Fabyan claims, "The common fame went that King Richard put unto secret death the two sons of his brother."

Collectively, these accounts suggest that the boys must have disappeared some time from 13 July 1483 (*Cely*) up to the end of October 1483 (*Fabyan and Croyland*).

Section III
Which Road from the Tower?
What Might Have Happened to Edward and Richard?

Introduction

There are certainly good circumstantial reasons to believe Richard was responsible for the boys' deaths, sometime from July 1483 to the autumn of that year; significantly, this is the period suggested in all the contemporary accounts.[1] Undoubtedly he had means, a strong political motive, opportunity and what seems to many historians to be a clear historical precedent for disposing of rival claimants to the throne, a precedent reestablished as recently as his brother's probable assassination of the elderly Henry VI. More important than these theoretical considerations is that, at least according to Croyland, most of the country was convinced he was responsible. The behavior of the boys' mother, Elizabeth Woodville, is certainly very suggestive of secret knowledge relating to their disappearance.[2] Circumstantial evidence and an undeniable popular certainty are not proof of Richard's involvement in their disappearance, however; and suggestions with regard to possible alternative murderers have also included Henry Stafford, Duke of Buckingham, and even Henry VII and his mother, Margaret Beaufort. Despite these theories, which are only those most usually presented, in reality, there is no evidence of any sort to show that either of the boys died from any cause during this period nor, in fact, what had eventually happened to them.

However, rather than reiterate all the old arguments favored by Richard's detractors and supporters, it may be more instructive to look at what might have happened in that summer and autumn of 1483 and then examine how the available evidence supports these possibilities.

The main questions concerning the boys and their disappearance may be briefly summarized:

- Were the boys murdered or is it possible that they died of natural causes?
- If they died or were killed in the Tower, what really happened to the bodies?
- If they did not die in the Tower in 1483, as the whole country supposed, what *did* happen to them?

On the basis of these questions three possible fates are indicated:

- Death by natural causes
- Murder by a person or persons unknown
- Escape or rescue by a person or persons unknown

And, at least as important as any conjecture about their fates: Who might have *known or guessed* what had really happened to them?

CHAPTER SEVEN

The First Solution: Did They Simply Die?

Death from natural causes is certainly a possibility that has to be considered. In Tudor England, 30–50 percent of all children died before their sixteenth birthday from accident, murder or diseases such as smallpox, measles, malaria, typhus or influenza.[1] Noble children were probably more isolated from disease than their low-born contemporaries, but there may have been other factors that balanced out the overall death rate, such as a failure to develop natural immunity because they were not exposed to the sort of rigorous environment experienced by the poorer children. It may also be significant in this context that Edward was being attended regularly by a doctor, John Argentine, who was effectively the Court physician. He was recorded by Mancini as the last man to see both the boys alive. He may simply have been attending them as a precautionary measure, but if Edward was seriously ill during this period and he eventually died from whatever was wrong with him, it could explain Argentine's contention that the boy believed death was facing him and so sought comfort in "daily confession and penance." Moreover, it does seem unlikely that a doctor like Argentine would be visiting so regularly if both the boys were healthy. That may add weight to the supposition that one or both were suffering from a serious illness. Incidentally, Edward and Richard's religious observances may not be as significant as previously thought, because the boys' normal timetable shows that they usually celebrated Matins, Mass and Evensong every day, and would probably have made a daily confession simply as part of that process. Consequently, what may have been normal religious observances for them might have been considered an excess of religious zeal by a man like Argentine, although if Edward was dangerously ill, and seeking relief in prayer, it would explain the boy's disappearance soon afterward. There are, however, no records to show that his younger brother, Richard, was anything but perfectly healthy when he joined his brother in the Tower, so even if Edward died naturally, what happened to his brother? One simple, obvious answer is that Edward was suffering from some infectious disease, which his brother caught and subsequently died from, although neither Mancini nor Argentine left a record of this. More significantly, if this is what happened, why were the boys not buried with the pomp and ceremony becoming nephews of the king, whereupon they could be abruptly and conveniently forgotten?

The Health of the Princes

Edward and Richard were young, 12 and 10 respectively, and so well below the age of 16 years that may be considered arbitrarily the "safe" point.[2] Edward had been living previously in relative isolation at Ludlow castle, while Richard was with his mother at Westminster. Consequently, the new king's arrival in London would have exposed him to a huge array of potentially dangerous microorganisms that his immune system might not have been robust enough to cope with. Moreover, the Tower was just across the Thames from Southwark marshes, which, along with the adjacent Westminster and Lambeth marshes, are now known to have been a breeding place for malaria-carrying mosquitoes of the genus Anopheles. The boys were incarcerated there in the early summer and remained in residence until the autumn, the period when mosquitoes are most active. Symptoms of malaria appear 12 to 18 days after initial infection and are known to frequently cause death in children as young as 10 (Richard's age when he entered the Tower). Death sometimes occurs within days or even hours of the initial infection, and mortality rates from malaria in the fifteenth century were approximately 1 percent of the population annually, with children considered most at risk.[3]

Influenza was another common fifteenth century disease that was very infectious and could be fatal in a short period of time, especially in young children. The outbreak of 1918 caused between 50 and 100 million deaths worldwide. A particularly virulent strain has been suggested as the cause of an outbreak of "sweating sickness" in London that also resulted in several thousand deaths, including two lord mayors in rapid succession, between August and October 1485. Although this seems too late for the disease to have been responsible for the boys' deaths, the Croyland Chronicle did record that Thomas Stanley, first Earl of Derby, claimed the sweating sickness as an excuse for not joining Richard at Bosworth, so it may have been prevalent before any official notice was taken of its incidence. Dysentery, measles, smallpox, typhoid, tuberculosis and typhus were also common ailments among the poorer sections of the population, and the nobility themselves were certainly not immune to such diseases. This would have been especially true of any malady, such as typhus, which was borne by a parasitic insect or other invertebrate, and diseases caused by macroscopic helminths, such as tapeworms and nematodes. Such helminth infections must have been more common in the nobility than the poorer classes, because the diets of rich people contained more meats, such as pork and beef, that contain the infective stage of those parasites, although, unless the infection is uncharacteristically heavy, tapeworm and nematode infections do not usually kill the host. Bubonic plague, although more dangerous, tends to have an epidemic nature so that its incidence in the population was sporadic, unlike the more common diseases, although when it did appear the mortality rate was from 50 to 100 percent of those infected.[4]

Evidence

Apart from that passing reference in Mancini's text, there is no evidence to show that either of the boys were ill at the time they were moved to the Tower, Edward during 16–19 May and Richard a month later, on 16 June. Even circumstantial evidence is missing, except for the inference possible from the description of daily confession and penance.

The Bodies in the Tower

In 1674, during the reign of Charles II, the remains of two children were found by workmen while they were digging in the foundations of the White Tower. The bones were said to have been enclosed in a wooden box, buried 10 ft (over 3 meters) below the existing ground level, under the staircase leading to the chapel of the White Tower (which is the oldest part of the Tower of London, built by William I and finished around 1100, possibly earlier). John Knight, principal surgeon to Charles II, was an eye witness and reported the find:

> Upon Friday the ... day of July, An. 1674 ... in order to the rebuilding of the several Offices in the Tower, and to clear the White Tower of all contiguous buildings, digging down the stairs which led from the King's Lodgings, to the chapel in the said Tower, about ten foot in the ground were found the bones of two striplings in (as it seemed) a wooden chest, which upon the survey were found proportionable to ages of those two brothers viz. about thirteen and eleven years. The skull of one bring entire, the other broken, as were indeed many of the other bones, also the chest, by the violence of the laborers, who ... cast the rubbish and them away together, wherefore they were

caused to sift the rubbish and by that means preserved all the bones. The circumstances of the story being considered and the same often discoursed with Sir Thomas Chichley, Master of the Ordinance, by whose industry the new buildings were then in carrying on, and by whom the matter was reported to the King.[5]

These remains, categorically stated to be the bones of Edward and Richard on the basis of Sir Thomas More's writings, were placed in an urn designed by Sir Christopher Wren and interred in Westminster Abbey, in the wall of the Henry VII Lady Chapel. A monument, also designed by Wren, marks the resting place of the putative princes. Wren also had something to say about the location of the bones, describing them as "about ten feet deep in the ground ... as the workmen were taking away the stairs which led from the royal lodgings into the Chapel of the White Tower,"[6] which corroborates Knight's account.

The bones were removed and examined in 1933, by Lawrence Tanner, at that time the archivist of Westminster Abbey, Professor William Wright, a leading anatomist, and George Northcroft, then president of the British Dental Association. Measurements of certain bones and teeth led them to conclude that the skeletons were those of two children who had been aged five to fourteen years when they died, which is broadly within the correct age range to include the princes, although the two skeletons were incomplete and chicken and other animal remains had also been included in the urn, along with three rusty nails. One skeleton was larger than the other (four feet, nine and a half inches, and four feet, six and a half inches, respectively), but many of the bones were missing, including part of the jawbone of the smaller skeleton and all of the teeth from the larger one, and many of the bones that did remain had been broken by the original workmen. The skeletons were thought to be related, with evidence of consanguinity including congenitally missing teeth and similarities in structure of Wormian bones found in both skulls. No attempt was made to determine whether the skeletons were from male or female children, the three men admitting in their final report that they had assumed that the bones were those of the princes and consequently concentrated their efforts on looking for pathological signs of suffocation upon the surface of the bones, particularly the two skulls.[7]

Other skeletons found in the Tower that have been identified as the princes included two children found in a walled-up room when Sir Walter Raleigh and Lord Grey of Wilton were imprisoned there, which gives a date for their discovery of some time between 1604 and 1614. The remains, which were not preserved, were claimed at the time to be the bones of Edward's sons, even though they seemed to the men who found them to be more characteristic of children aged six to eight, rather than ten to twelve and half, the ages of Richard and Edward in 1483. The remains were not preserved and the only record of their existence and subsequent examination is a statement by a Mr. Johnson made in 1647, about a report he heard from a John or Jonathan Webb some thirty years before.[8]

Another discovery that may have a bearing on the remains found previously in the Tower concerns a body excavated in 1977. This skeleton was found buried in a shallow grave just northwest of the Lanthorn Tower, which was subsequently shown to be that of a boy originally aged thirteen to sixteen years. Carbon-14 dating showed him to have been placed there sometime AD 1 to AD 140 (early Roman or late Iron Age), roughly 1,300 years before the alleged burial of the princes. This particular burial is of interest because details from the original excavation describe the find as being only about 5 feet (1.45 meters) below the level of the surrounding earth. The alleged burial of the princes was described as being 10 feet below ground level and in a place where there must have been little surface deposition, since construction of the White Tower was begun in 1078. From the depth at which they were buried by comparison with the early Roman boy, this seems to suggest that the two bodies found in 1674 are much older than the 1977 find and had been buried on that site long before the foundations of the White Tower were laid.[9] Queen Elizabeth II has consistently refused to allow further examination of the bones in Westminster Abbey, including any attempt at C-14 dating, for both personal and constitutional reasons. Until such permission is granted, the age and family relations of these two individuals remains to be elucidated.

CHAPTER EIGHT

The Second Solution: Was It Murder?

Richard III

Richard, of course, must be the favorite candidate for their murderer, since he had means, an ostensibly sound political motive, and no lack of opportunity.[1] Even if he did not murder them, undoubtedly he knew what had happened to them and was keeping quiet about it. There is, however, a significant flaw in what is generally accepted as the neat picture of a wicked uncle conveniently disposing of his two main rivals to the throne and thus profiting by their deaths.

All the events recorded before July 1483 show Richard to be an adept politician with a clear, well-planned agenda designed to put him on the throne with the least difficulty. He even arranged for the throne to be offered to him by Parliament, a body that had previously been a Woodville instrument. After his nephew's incarceration, however, it is suggested that all his subtlety deserted him and, throwing away all this hard-won political advantage in an act of monumental stupidity, he simply murdered Edward and Richard and allowed their deaths to become a rallying point for his enemies. Now, far from aiding his cause, the boys' deaths were held against him by the overwhelming majority of his subjects and became a major contributing factor to the lack of support that resulted in his defeat at Bosworth. All his benign legislation, his attempts at fair dealing (even towards those who conspired against him), and the death of his wife and son elicited no support nor even sympathy, because he was seen as having murdered his nephews, an act for which, in the minds of his subjects, there could be no forgiveness in heaven or on earth. As one of the *London Chronicles* records:

> In this year many knights and gentlemen of Kent and other places gathered them together to have gone toward the duke of Buckingham ... which intended to subdue King Richard; for anon as the said King Richard had put to death the lord chamberlain

and other gentlemen ... he also put to death the two children of King Edward, for which cause he lost the hearts of the people. And thereon many gentlemen intended his destruction.[2]

Richard, known not just for his considerable political acumen but also for his ability to employ propaganda, must have acknowledged at least the possibility of such a reaction on the part of his subjects and would surely have planned to circumvent it if possible.[3] Even his worst enemies acknowledged his subtlety and intelligence. Croyland says of Richard, "He never acted sleepily, but incisively and with the utmost vigilance,"[4] while Polydore Virgil wrote of him, in 1513, "Truly, he had a sharp wit, provident and subtle."[5]

Moreover, even if he was indifferent to the effects his actions would have on public opinion, his councilors certainly were not. Later in his reign, when he suggested a marriage between himself and his niece, Elizabeth of York, two of his most intimate friends and advisers, Catesby and Ratcliffe, told him it would not be possible, unless he wished to lose the support of the whole country by entering into an incestuous union. The king seems to have listened to them and acted upon their advice.[6] If Richard and his councilors were astute enough to foresee trouble in such a marriage, they must surely have also realized previously how inadvisable it would be for Richard even to be suspected of murdering his nephews, who were seen by his subjects as a sacred trust, given into his care by his dead brother. The worst possible outcome for Richard was what happened, their disappearance becoming a mystery and more importantly, a mystery that many solved by declaring him the murderer of his nephews. Even two dead children would have been easier to explain away, especially if it *looked* as though they had died naturally. A number of diseases that quite commonly affected children at that period, such as dysentery, influenza, malaria and tuberculosis, would have left no external postmortem signs discernable by a fifteenth century physician.[7] Consequently, if Richard had murdered the boys in a way that left no obvious traces, displaying the bodies, together with producing evidence from an unscrupulous physician who was ready to state that the boys had died of one of these ailments, would have been an effective way of disposing of them without inconvenient questions being asked. Even a pair of convenient "accidents" would probably have created less furor, especially if the two boys died some months apart and there was, once again, a convenient barber-surgeon to certify an innocuous cause of death.

Richard certainly had ample precedent for murdering rival claimants to the throne. His older brother, Edward IV, had adopted just this approach when he wished to rid himself of the embarrassing presence of Henry VI, claiming that Henry died the day after his son's death at Tewksbury of depression and melancholy. Two other famous royal murders that are also often cited as giving Richard a pointer as to his attitude to his nephews are Edward II, probably murdered by his wife's lover, Roger Mortimer, after some months in captivity, and Richard II, who is claimed to have died of starvation, either self-inflicted or encouraged by Henry IV.

However, it is significant in the context of Richard's supposed secret murder and concealment of his nephews' bodies that, although the alleged murders of all three kings took place in secret, their subsequent treatment and interment could not have been more public. Moreover, the cause of death in each case was ascribed to natural causes by the men who were most likely to have ordered the murders. Edward II was buried by the high altar of Gloucester Abbey in 1327, three months after his death, the cause of which was not described at the time, although Edward III executed Roger Mortimer for his father's murder, among other things. The body of Richard II was displayed in the old St. Paul's Cathedral in London, before being interred in King's Langley Church in March 1400; and Henry VI was buried in Chertsey Abbey in 1471, before being moved to St. George's Chapel at Windsor Castle, on the orders of Richard III himself. No royal successor ever tried to get away with concealing the evidence after their secret murder of a royal predecessor, and both Henry IV and Edward IV at least offered some sort of natural explanation of their defeated rival's death that could be accepted by the nobility and the general population. So, if Richard was ultimately responsible for the murder of the boys, why did he not adopt the same policy? After all, he had no lack of opportunity to incriminate some innocent victim, and there were at least two beautifully convenient suspects on whom he could pin the murder: Henry Stafford, who was dead by 2 November 1483, and Henry Tudor, trapped in the French court and unable to offer a word in his own defense.

Henry Stafford, Duke of Buckingham

Henry Stafford, Duke of Buckingham, has also been seen as a reasonable culprit by some authors, although realistically he lacked opportunity, having left London before the last sighting of the boys in the Tower. He certainly had a more than adequate motive, however, being related closely enough to the royal family to be considered a candidate for the throne himself—and, as Croyland's entry has shown, the rumor about the boy's deaths only became current after he had decided to lead the rebellion, so he could have been responsible for the propagation of the story himself. Some authors have suggested that he may have done this in order to reduce Richard's standing in the eyes of his subjects, thus ensuring the success of the revolt. He is, however, also accused of the murders by at least one historical source, where the author writes that Edward and his brother were "put to deyth in the Towur of London be the vise of the duke of Buckingham."[8] "Be the vise" in this context means either "on the advice of" or "by the device of." Another account suggests that Richard consulted him before ordering the murders.[9] Whatever view one takes of Duke Henry's culpability, however, it is not plausible to suggest that he could have carried out the murders without Richard's knowledge and connivance. If Buckingham did orchestrate the murders, Richard was at best criminally negligent and at worst a willing accessory.[10]

Henry Tudor

The last popular suspect, Henry VII, is even less realistic than Buckingham. In 1483, he was a distant cousin to the royal line, without money, influence or supporters. It was only after his mother supposedly contracted his marriage to Elizabeth of York and rumors of the boys' deaths had become sufficiently widespread to undermine Richard's standing in the eyes of his subjects that he gained enough support to make his successful attempt at the throne. If the boys died some time in 1483, he could not have killed them himself; and at that time, he probably would not have been able to persuade anyone else with sufficient influence to enter the Tower and perform the deed for him, since his qualification for kingship was only ratified in December 1483, upon his betrothal. Murder after he became king was certainly a possibility, as he was even better qualified in terms of means, opportunity and particularly motive than Richard had been, since in declaring his prospective wife a legitimate child of Edward IV, he also helped the boys regain their status as the rightful heirs of Edward IV; they thus became potentially better qualified candidates for the throne he was occupying by right of conquest and marriage. By then, however, they had disappeared completely not only from the Tower but also from all public notice. Moreover, if he did find them somewhere else and subsequently quietly murdered them, why all the fuss about the Lambert Simnel and Perkin Warbeck insurrections? If he knew the boys were dead and could prove it by showing the bodies, regardless of who killed them, why not just do so, while blaming Richard or Buckingham for their deaths, rather than expose himself to all the trouble he had from those two imposters, especially Warbeck? In the popular mind, Richard had already been condemned as the culprit, so if he had the bodies, Henry had the perfect opportunity to exonerate himself if he had conspired to murder his wife's brothers. In support of this suggestion that Henry murdered the boys after ascending the throne, there are two pieces of evidence available that might suggest that the boys were alive after December 1483. There is, first, an ordinance regulating the king's household in the north at Sheriff Hutton, dated 24 July 1484, stating that arrangements were specifically made for some unspecified children at a breakfast. Consequently, it has been suggested that the children referred to were the princes, although there were probably other children living in that household, and two of Edward's daughters and the Earl of Warwick, Clarence's son, were also living at Sheriff Hutton during this period. The second piece of evidence is a warrant that was issued on 9 March 1485 for clothing to be given to the "Lord Bastard," although this probably refers to Richard's own illegitimate son, John.[11] Neither of these vague allusions are convincing, however, and they really prove nothing about Henry's potential involvement in the boys' disappearance.

Although Henry probably did not murder them, it would be naïve to suppose that he did not know what happened to them, or rather, what had not happened to them. He had access to all the servants, guards and officials who had been working in the Tower at the time the boys disappeared, and either he or his intelligence agents must have questioned them thoroughly. It was, after all, even more to his advantage than to his predecessor's to have two dead heirs to the throne to display, mourn over and then conveniently forget about in the natural course of events, because of the implications involving his wife's legitimacy and right to the crown. If Henry had known where his young brothers-in-law were hidden, their corpses would undoubtedly have been brought to light, victims of their uncle's brutal regime, even if Henry had been required to arrange their murders in secret himself.[12]

Margaret Beaufort

His mother is an even more unlikely candidate than Henry Tudor himself. She would not have been able to commit the act herself, and it would not be plausible to suggest that between June 1483 and August 1485 she could have influenced anyone capable of gaining access to the boys to commit the murder for her. In effect, she was the mother of an aspirant to the hand of presumptive queen and few, if any, would have given anything for Henry Tudor's chance at the throne much before March 1484, when Richard's son died and the succession was once again an open question. Her chances after Bosworth were certainly much improved if she knew the boys were alive and where they were living, but the same objections apply to her as to Henry. If she killed them, why allow her son to experience all the trouble with Simnel and Warbeck?

John Morton

John Morton was an unlikely candidate by himself, but if Henry was involved, then, almost certainly, so was Morton. Murder before Bosworth would have been difficult, although in the eighteen months between the October Rebellion and the battle that ended his reign, Richard and his cronies were certainly aware of propaganda being spread, which undermined the king's position and credibility. There is no evidence to connect Morton with this whispering campaign, although his undoubted subtlety and hatred of Richard certainly qualified him for the role, and if his agents were spreading propaganda there is no reason to suppose they could not have been searching for the boys at the same time, if Morton knew, or had reason to suspect, they were alive. However, once again, the same old objections arise. If he had them murdered, why not conveniently "find" the bodies in a location that clearly implicated Richard and deal summarily with those now proven imposters, Simnel and Warbeck?

CHAPTER NINE

The Third Solution: Did They Escape?

Escape by Richard's Connivance

Although there is no significant documentary evidence to indicate Richard's intentions towards his nephews, he may have felt he had a sound political motive for keeping the boys alive. His wife was ill, possibly dying of tuberculosis and, depending upon circumstances, his son may also have been unwell, having contracted the disease from his mother. If Richard knew that his wife was unlikely to live for much longer and that his son was "delicate" and so was also not certain to survive, he may have felt that Edward's sons would have been a plausible alternative that would keep the House of York in power, if they could be persuaded to accept their illegitimacy unreservedly. Richard's son, Edward of Middleham, Prince of Wales, did pass away in March 1484, from an unknown cause, although the fact that both he and his wife were "almost out of their minds for a long time when faced with sudden grief"[1] suggests that the death was unexpected and not the result of long-standing illness.

Richard also had good reasons for moving the boys from London in September or October 1483, if he was intent upon preserving their lives. Buckingham's rebellion began in the autumn of 1483, and his supporters from Kent and the southeast were only stopped by John Howard at Gravesend, 25 miles from where the boys were living in the Tower. Croyland claims Richard had information about the rebellion from his spies even before Howard learned of it, and he may have felt it expedient to move the boys for their own safety because of a very real danger to their lives at Buckingham's hands.[2] Having broadcast the rumor of the boys' death after his public proclamation as leader of the rebellion, Buckingham had narrowed his options so effectively that the boys could not be allowed to survive if the rebellion was intended to depose Richard and put Henry Tudor or Buckingham himself on the throne, with or without Elizabeth of York as queen. Consequently, Richard may have moved them safely out of harm's way, having his own ideas about their political usefulness if they could be persuaded to actively support his regime.

The Boys' Destination and the Possible Role of Sir John Tyrell

Where the boys might have gone after their escape or release is impossible to say, but their mother, Elizabeth Woodville, left sanctuary for an unknown manor in March 1484, having been granted a yearly stipend of 700 marks (approximately £500).[3] Her destination cannot be established either, although there have been a number of suggestions. It is possible that she may have been been taken by the man who was her guardian at Westminster, John Nesfield, to be lodged in his manor of Haytesbury in Wiltshire, where she was conveniently out of the way and where one or both of her sons may have joined her. However, that still leaves open the question of where the boys lived from July 1483 to March 1484.[4] There was also a rumor in the Tyrell family that the former queen and some of her children lived at Gipping Hall, Sir James's Tyrell's house, near Stowmarket, Suffolk. This tradition was apparently of long standing, specifically worded, and it went back well before the eighteenth century, being handed down from generation to generation "that the princes and their mother Elizabeth Woodville lived in the hall by permission of the uncle."[5] This uncle can only have been Richard because their other uncle, George, had died before their father, who would have been the one to issue such permission during his reign. An extended stay at Tyrell's house and subsequent escape from there to Flanders may also account for his suggested involvement in the boys' disappearance. Sir Thomas More's *Historie* implicated Tyrell unequivocally in the murder of the Edward and Richard and was said to have been based on Tyrell's own confession, obtained before his execution in 1502. This signed confession of his, admitting to the murder, would have been a good counter to any story that they were alive and had been living at Stowmarket before Bosworth, since such a story could be dismissed simply as a belated attempt to establish Tyrell's innocence in the face of his confessed crime, by either his family or supporters of the princes. More evidence with a possible bearing upon Tyrell's involvement is contained in the Harleian Manuscript 433, the docket book of Richard's Privy Seal, which has an entry referring to Sir James Tyrell and concerning a journey he undertook in late 1484 "over the See into the parties of Flaundres for diverse maters concernyng gretely oure wele." This may have been a trip either to check on one or both of the boys, if they were already with their aunt, or to arrange for their reception at her court in the event of things going wrong for Richard in England, the latter being more plausible if one or both of the boys were still at Gipping Hall. Of course, it is also perfectly possible that Tyrell was upon some other errand entirely, such as seeking military support from prospective Continental allies or making arrangements connected with his appointment as commander of the castle at Guînes. Tyrell also received payment of the enormous sum of 4,500 marks upon his appointment to Guînes in January 1485. The reason for giving him such an enormous amount of money, equivalent to Richard's total revenue for that year, has never been clarified with any degree of satisfaction.

There is a further incident that is suggestive of the involvement of Tyrell and his home as the boys' hiding place. After Bosworth, in August 1485, Francis Lovell and Humphrey and Thomas Stafford escaped from the battlefield. Instead of riding north, where they had lands and friends to protect them, they turned roughly southeast and a week later arrived at Colchester. It could be argued that they took this route intending to escape overseas, perhaps to Richard's sister, Margaret, in Burgundy; but if that was their plan, they abandoned it fairly quickly. After approximately six months in sanctuary at St. John's Abbey in Colchester, during which time Henry opened discussions with them about the fate of Elizabeth Woodville and her daughter, all three abruptly left Colchester and went north, clearly intent on continuing the fight.[6] So why Colchester, and how does it reflect on the story of the princes? Colchester is only thirty miles, four hours or less on a fast horse, from Stowmarket, where Tyrell had his family home and where the princes might have been living. Richard may have ordered Lovell to leave Bosworth and make this detour to warn Elizabeth Woodville and one or both of her sons, while Lovell and the Stafford brothers remained in Colchester to draw Henry's attention away from the boys' departure.

Although Tyrell's involvement in the boys' removal from the Tower and subsequent concealment is by no means proven, it is at least curious that an individual around whom this number of rumors and possibilities seem to have developed should be the one whose confession, unseen by any but Henry and Sir Thomas, implicated him so unequivocally in the murder. Moreover, the question naturally arises, what did Tyrell actually confess to?

- Was it to the murder of the boys, or did he actually admit only to moving the boys, first from the Tower and then overseas out of Henry's reach?
- Did he also give Henry the names of his accomplices, so that Henry

could be sure that anyone else involved in the disappearance and likely to be believed was dead?

- If all the other courtiers and nobles involved in the plot were dead, did Henry use the opportunity presented by the execution of Tyrell—who may have been the last survivor who really knew and perhaps could *prove* what had happened to the king's brothers-in-law—to concoct a story that could not be challenged by anyone living, since he had just executed the last witness?

Escape or Rescue by Their Own Supporters

An escape managed by supporters of the late king, Edward IV, seems less likely, although it has been suggested.[7] If the boys escaped or were rescued, their obvious course would surely have been to contact the rebels then mobilizing in the south to depose Richard, whose original intention appears to have been to place a son of Edward IV on the throne. However, since the course of the rebellion had been changed fairly quickly after it began, possibly by Buckingham, and the duke had also made his own intentions towards Henry Tudor known, it is must have been clear to their rescuers that neither of the boys would have survived their first meeting with him. They may also have eschewed the rebels' cause as hopeless, even dangerous, and gone into hiding, which brings us to another dead end: where did they hide, and why did Richard not find them and bring them back into circulation after the rebellion was over? One explanation of this disappearance is that they may have left England, taken out of the reach of Richard, Buckingham and Henry Tudor, possibly to their aunt Margaret in Burgundy or hidden with Yorkist sympathizers in Ireland.[8]

Life Abroad

If one or both of the boys did escape abroad, the question naturally arises, where did they finish up? Traveling in a foreign country in late medieval times was not simple, and it was not an adventure two young boys could have undertaken without some expert help and plenty of ready money, which implies considerable preparation by someone. Where might be their best refuge?

Certainly not France. Henry Tudor was under the protection of Frances II, Duke of Brittany, from 1471 to 1483, and the French were clearly sympathetic to his cause because they supplied him with troops and equipment for his second successful invasion in 1485.[9]

Ireland might have seemed like a good option for a son of the House of York. The most important Irish nobles had all been enthusiastic supporters of their father, and the suggestion has been made that Edward, Earl of Warwick, may have been hiding in Ireland prior to the beginning of the rebellion of 1487.[10] It has also been claimed that the boy later displayed as Lambert Simnel and the individual imprisoned in the Tower as the Earl of Warwick were both imposters, substituted by Henry Tudor to conceal his murder of the real son of George, Duke of Clarence.

Their aunt, Margaret of York, would probably have been their best destination, whether they were sent to her by their uncle Richard or by former adherents of their father. Margaret had been another of those royal girls whose political role seemed destined to be limited to their ability to attract a potentially useful husband. In Margaret's case, this was Charles the Bold of Burgundy. The match had been slightly unusual in that it was arranged by her brother, not her father. Margaret, however, was far from being simply another ducal ornament and by 1475, she had begun to take a significant and very active role in the administration of Burgundy. She had also previously sheltered her two brothers, Edward and Richard, during the time when England had become too hot for them and they were driven out by the Earl of Warwick, in September 1470. Richard was on good terms with her and even visited her and her step-daughter Mary in February 1471, before his return to England with Edward a month later, on 3 March 1471.[11]

Consequently, it is not inconceivable that Richard made arrangements with his elder sister to shelter one or both of his nephews until conditions in England were more settled.

Sir George Buck was certainly convinced that Richard at least had escaped overseas. He wrote that there had been "English noblemen and gentlemen which were privy to the conveyance of the Prince Richard ... and who knew where he lurked or lay close." Later in the same text he concluded:

> Some write that they were both secretly taken out of the Tower and both set afloat in a ship and conveyed together over the seas. But because I find no mention of the being of the elder brother in Flanders, but very frequent mention of the younger brother's being there and of his other adventures and travails, I will let the elder brother, Edward, rest, and speak of his brother's transportation and the rest of his actions and life.[12]

In referring to the "very frequent mention of the younger brother being there" (i.e., in Flanders), Buck seems to be referring to the stories that were circulated about Warbeck, his escape from the Tower and subsequent sojourn on the Continent. Clearly, he also thought that the boys had been sent overseas at around the time of the October Rebellion, unless he had evidence, which he did not include, that they remained in the Tower for a period after the rest of the country assumed they were dead.

The "Pretenders"

Henry Tudor had trouble with two pretenders to his throne, Lambert Simnel and Perkin Warbeck, difficulties that he could have easily avoided if he had been able to reveal the burial place of his two brothers-in-law. Simnel was said to have been born in Oxford, although it has been suggested that he may have been a substitute for the real pretender, who had been living in Ireland since before Bosworth, while Warbeck was claimed to be a Flemish merchant's son.[13] Hence, both originally appear to have had vaguely overseas origins, which agrees with Buck's contention that Edward's sons were sent abroad. Simnel was initially said to be Richard of York, before his asserted identity was changed to Edward, Earl of Warwick; while Warbeck also claimed to be Richard, at least until he was captured. This could be the basis for Buck's claims about the stories he had discovered concerning the boys. Their foreign origins after Bosworth may also implicate Margaret of Burgundy in their original rescue and shelter either in July 1483 or after August 1485, especially since she had a significant role in aiding the second candidate for Henry's throne, Perkin Warbeck.

Lambert Simnel

Born some time in 1476 or 1477, Simnel's real name is not known, contemporary records referring to him as John. It was even suggested that his surname may have been assumed, taken from the name given to a variety of grain. He was certainly not from the nobility, and current research suggests that he was most probably the son of Thomas Simnel, a carpenter and organ builder.[14] However, Simnel's real identity cannot be established with any certainty, and almost all that is known about him is derived from Tudor sources, with their usual bias. There is even some confusion about whether he originally claimed to be Clarence's son, Edward, Earl of Warwick, or Richard, Duke of York, the younger of Edward IV's sons. This confusion may have arisen, as Vergil claims, because the conspiracy began life as a movement to reestablish Prince Richard on the throne but then quickly shifted its focus to his cousin, the Earl of Warwick.

The plot had its origins in Oxford during 1486—if not earlier—that city's continually changing population of clerks and scholars making it a convenient location for a conspiracy based on impersonation. While it may have originated in the mind of a single priest, named variously as Richard Simon, Richard Symonds, Richard Simons or William Symonds, who is claimed to have educated Simnel and refined his manners during the boy's stay in Oxford, it may be significant that two of the leaders of the subsequent revolt had their principal seats near the town: the Earl of Lincoln at Ewelme and Francis Lovell, Viscount Lovell, at Minster Lovell. Another conspirator was also resident in Oxford during this period: Robert Stillington, bishop of Bath and Wells, who had retired to his former college at Oxford after the battle of Bosworth. Henry must have felt himself to have good reason to suspect the old bishop's involvement in a plot on behalf of Clarence's son because he summoned Stillington in February 1487 to answer charges regarding certain unspecified conspiracies.

During much of the autumn of 1486 there were conflicting rumors about a Yorkist pretender overseas, and although it is clear that Simnel was not the only candidate, by the end of 1486 he was established in Ireland, backed in turn by Thomas Fitzgerald, chancellor of Ireland, and then by his brother Gerald Fitzgerald, eighth earl of Kildare and the king's deputy, together with Walter Fitzsimons, the archbishop of Dublin.

This seems to have had all the characteristics of a serious conspiracy, at least to Henry Tudor, because the king is said to have gone to the trouble of sending a herald to question Simnel about his background. This is corroborated by a payment that was made to Falcon Pursuivant of the Herald's College for a mission to Ireland in the king's service in March 1487. Simnel must also have had some former courtiers in his entourage; and Lovell, who had escaped after Bosworth, may already have been active in the conspiracy, because Symonds confessed that after he took Simnel to Ireland, he and Lovell had investigated a potential landing site in the Furness Fells in north Lancashire. Margaret of York, dowager duchess of Burgundy and Clarence's sister, also began to lend support to the enterprise, providing a base for defectors and some financial assistance as well as sheltering the Earl of Lincoln from some time early in 1487.

Henry must have been getting worried by now because on 2 February 1487, the real Earl of Warwick was paraded through London from the Tower to St. Paul's Cathedral, on orders originating directly from the king's council. If Henry hoped that this display would dispel interest in the pretender, he was to be disappointed. Support continued to grow. Even John de la Pole, Earl of Lincoln, nephew to Edward and Richard and consequently another legitimate claimant to the throne, supported Simnel—and even declared him to be the real Warwick. By the end of April 1487, Lincoln and Lovell, together with a number of other Yorkist exiles and a company of German mercenaries under the Swiss captain Martin Schwartz, had sailed to Ireland. Upon the arrival of these supporters in Dublin, Simnel was crowned in Christ Church Cathedral on 24 May 1487 as Edward VI, confirming his claim as Edward, Earl of Warwick. All due observances were made to the new pretender, with a parliament held in Dublin in the new king's name. Coins were struck and proclamations issued. Henry later used these events to make fun of the gullibility of the Irish, claiming, "They would crown apes at last."

However comic events in Ireland may have seemed to the king, the new pretender's invasion of England was a serious affair. Simnel, Lincoln, and a mixed force of around 6,000 men, consisting of Yorkist nobles, 1,500 German mercenaries, and about 4,000 poorly armed Irish infantry, landed in Furness on 4 June 1487. They moved quickly from the invasion site, traveling eastwards across northern Lancashire and over the Pennines into Wensleydale, where they found fresh recruits among the local gentry. On 8 June 1487, a letter in the name of "Edward VI" was dispatched from Masham to York, advertising his cause and seeking "relief and ease of lodgings and victuals."[15] Subsequently, John Scrope, fifth Baron Scrope of Bolton, and Thomas Scrope, sixth Baron Scrope of Masham, also led a company of horsemen to York, proclaiming the new king at Bootham Bar, although despite these importunings the city remained loyal to Henry. Meanwhile the main rebel army had begun to move south, desperately hoping to embarrass and eventually destroy Tudor's army by a quick advance.

Henry had anticipated the insurrectionist's movements, however, and having raised significant support was able to make a well-organized advance from his original base at Leicester. He rested at Nottingham to consolidate his forces, and upon leaving that city on 15 June 1487, he had managed to gather an army that outnumbered his opponent's significantly. On the morning of 16 June the rebels crossed the Trent upstream from Newark and positioned themselves on the hillside overlooking the road from Nottingham where a short, brutal encounter took place, later to be known as the battle of Stoke. The Earl of Lincoln, usually regarded as the real leader of the rebellion, was killed during the battle, but Lovell escaped and fled to Scotland, Simnel apparently being captured by Robert Bellingham.[16]

According to Vergil, Henry spared Simnel and put him to service, first in the scullery and later as a falconer. It is also claimed that Henry had his new scullion formally presented to a group of Irish lords in 1487, in order to emphasize the folly of their actions. Vergil reports that Simnel was still alive when he completed his *Anglica Historie*, in 1534.

Perkin Warbeck

Pastel drawing of Perkin Warbeck, the "feigned boy." Some contemporary observers claimed to see a likeness between this portrait and the former king, Edward IV (Wikipedia).

According to Warbeck's final confession, made in 1497, he was born at Tournai, France, the son of John Osbek, comptroller of the town of Tournai, and Kataryn de Faro. In reality, his parents are thought to have been Jehan de Werbecque and Nicaise Farou, members of Tournai's prosperous class of leading artisans, small merchants, and civic officials, and his real name is thought to have been Pierrechon de Werbecque, born in 1474. The boy who would become pretender to the throne of England began his travels early with a series of journeys between 1484 and 1487 to Antwerp, Bergen op Zoom, and Middelburg, where he completed his education by learning Flemish, probably while working in the cloth trade. In April or May 1487 he moved on to the Portuguese court in Lisbon, together with Lady Margaret Beaumont, who was the wife of the Anglo-Portuguese Jewish convert, courtier and international trader Sir Edward Brampton. He appears to have taken service in Lisbon with the explorer and royal councilor Pero Vaz de Cunha, transferring his services in 1488 to the Breton merchant Pregent Meno, with whom he sailed to Cork in December 1491 to sell silks. There he was persuaded by Yorkist elements in the city, led by the former mayor John Atwater and the English exile John Taylor, to begin his masquerade as Richard, Duke of York.

Warbeck's supporters, in a desperate search for patrons, first gained the support of the Earl of Desmond; but it was Charles VIII, king of France, whose fleet brought Warbeck from Cork to Harfleur in March 1492 and consequently established the pretender on the European political stage. Warbeck and his adherents escaped to Mechelen in November 1492, when a treaty between Henry Tudor and Charles meant the French king had no more use for Warbeck, and he was fêted in that city by Margaret of York, dowager duchess of Burgundy, as her miraculously preserved nephew. Early in 1493 and within months of his arrival at Margaret's court, senior figures at the English court began to be drawn into plotting on Warbeck's behalf: John, Lord Fitzwalter, Sir Robert Clifford, William Worsley, dean of St. Paul's, and even the chamberlain of the king's household, Sir William Stanley. The recruitment of these men ensured that there now began in the summer of 1493 a protracted political struggle involving both sides in the use of espionage, propaganda, murder and intrigue. Unfortunately for Warbeck's supporters, their various plots failed, an invasion from the Netherlands had to be canceled, and in what must have been almost a last resort, Warbeck was sent on to Vienna to meet Maximilian, king of the Romans (reign: 1493–1519), and secure his support.

Maximilian was convinced by the pretender's credentials, and Warbeck accompanied him when he returned to the Low Countries in August 1494 for the ceremonial reception of his son Philip the Fair as ruler of a number of Dutch principalities. Unfortunately, the plans of Warbeck and his highly placed adherents were considerably damaged when Sir Robert Clifford fled from Mechelen, taking Henry clear evidence of the treason of Stanley, Fitzwalter, and the others, and this information led to the arrest and subsequent execution of many important figures in the conspiracy. Despite this setback, there was renewed rebellion in Ireland, and an invasion of England, given financial backing by Maximilian, was attempted in the summer of 1495. A small advance party landed at Deal on 3 July but, while Warbeck and the remainder of his army were still on their ships, this vanguard was overwhelmed by the local levies, with 163 men captured and perhaps as many as 150 killed. Apparently undeterred, Warbeck's flotilla sailed on to Youghall and Waterford, where they joined the Earl of Desmond in his unsuccessful siege. Despite this string of failures Warbeck soon found another patron in James IV of Scots, and on 20 November he was being welcomed at Stirling Castle.

Although not all James' adherents were convinced by Warbeck's claims, James himself demonstrated his apparent belief in Warbeck by marrying him, on or about 13 January 1496, to Lady Katherine Gordon, daughter of George, Earl of Huntly, and a distant royal relative by marriage. Soon afterward he made Falkland Palace available as a base for Warbeck's adherents and from there began to plan an invasion of England. James and Warbeck crossed the border on 21 November, although Warbeck almost immediately withdrew, discouraged by his failure to elicit any visible English support for his cause, which he had expected to materialize after issuing a proclamation denouncing

Henry's misgovernment. James soon followed, his support for Warbeck now starting to have far too big a price, as Henry prepared a huge army to invade Scotland.

However, it appeared that all was not quite lost. In May 1497 Henry's heavy taxation sparked rebellion in Cornwall, with trouble spreading into Somerset. As the rebels prepared to march on London they apparently called on Warbeck to lead them. Henry's army stopped the rebels at Blackheath on 17 June 1497, driving them back to Cornwall, where they welcomed Warbeck when he landed at Whitesand Bay on 7 September. Although his Irish sojourn had gained him little support, chiefly because of the pacification of the country by the Earl of Kildare, in Cornwall his small original force of approximately 300 multiplied rapidly, and his army numbered over 8,000 by the time they laid siege to Exeter on 17 September. The siege was again unsuccessful, the Earl of Devon and his garrison repelling their attacks, and Warbeck's army withdrew to Taunton, arriving there on 19 September. Henry's army was in close proximity, however, and Warbeck's supporters began to disappear, the pretender himself and his closest followers making their own escape on 21 September. John Taylor, who had been one of Warbeck's first promoters, escaped to France, while others took sanctuary in London. Warbeck and three companions took sanctuary at Beaulieu Abbey, Hampshire, but were captured and brought before Henry and his nobles at Taunton Castle on 5 October 1497, where Warbeck is said to have confessed his imposture.

Upon the king's return to London, Warbeck was repeatedly paraded through the city, before accompanying Tudor on his progresses until 9 June 1498, when he escaped, perhaps with the king's connivance. He was quickly found and subsequently twice displayed in the stocks before being secured in shackles in the Tower of London for life on 18 June. There, in the summer of 1499, he became inveigled into one final misadventure, an attempt to free his fellow prisoner Edward, Earl of Warwick, and himself, with a view to placing one of them on the throne. Exactly what part he played in the conspiracy, and in its betrayal to the king on 3 August, is hard to establish, but Henry and his council resolved to punish all the principal participants. Warbeck was tried on 16 November in the White Hall of the Palace of Westminster together with Taylor and Atwater, who had been recovered from France and Ireland, and all three men were condemned to death. On 23 November 1499, after one final confession that he was no Plantagenet, Warbeck (alias Richard Plantagenet, duke of York) was hung, drawn and quartered at Tyburn.[17]

Perspectives

The deaths of the boys from disease or some other natural cause is not a possibility that can be simply discarded, although evidence from any contemporary source to suggest either of the boys was ill is lacking. Despite little consideration having been given to the possibility that Edward and Richard died from disease or other natural causes, life in the fifteenth century was no sinecure, even for well-provided sprigs of the nobility. Although they were more carefully protected than other children, this may have been to their detriment rather than otherwise, since it would have meant that their immunity to common diseases would have been considerably less than the children of commoners enjoyed. It may have also been less even than the immunity of noble children who had lived all their lives in London and who the princes probably mixed with on a daily basis. Certainly, Edward and Richard were not as safe from the normal hazards of fifteenth century life as a cursory examination of their lifestyle may have suggested. Perhaps most significantly, they were also confined in a riverside prison during the summer months, where malaria-carrying mosquitoes would have been commonplace. Consequently, death by natural causes such as malaria, smallpox, influenza or even a fatal accident is not impossible, but this leaves two questions:

- If his nephews died of something other than murder, why did Richard keep quiet about it?
- More importantly, what possible advantage could such an action have held for him?

Murder by any of the three most likely candidates is no more convincing as a solution than a simple death by disease or accident. Richard was the only good candidate for the role of murderer, and there were circumstances surrounding the early part of his reign that suggest that he would have been reluctant and rather more than unwise to allow the deaths of his two nephews to become linked to him in the way they finally did. More significantly, such a disadvantageous connection could have been prevented quite easily. Buckingham, Henry Tudor and the rest are simply not serious contenders because they had absolutely no reason to conceal the deaths, which could have been convincingly blamed on Richard, and Henry had several good reasons for bringing the bodies to light after Bosworth, before then allowing the rumor that Richard killed them to become accepted fact.

Escape and subsequent concealment by either Richard or the former friends and associates of Edward IV seems on balance a marginally more likely scenario, but even this solution is fraught with difficulties. If they were hidden:

- Where were they hidden?
- Who hid them?
- If it was Richard, why did they not return to London when the October Rebellion was over?
- If their mother knew they were alive, why did she not withdraw from the Tudor match and convince Tudor's supporters, most of them formerly adherents of Edward IV, to change sides and support her and her sons against Richard, rather than focus the rebellion on Tudor's frankly nebulous claim?

Nor are the two collections of bones found during the excavation of the staircase in the reign of Charles II either convincing as the remains of the two princes or helpful in determining the date or cause of their deaths. The depth of the burial suggests that the two unfortunate children were interred some considerable period of time before 1483, and postmortem examination by several eminent experts could not or did not determine either the gender or period of time the skeletal remains had been in the ground, although the estimated ages at death, somewhere between 5 and 14 years, did correspond very broadly to that of Edward and Richard. Skeletons are not uncommon finds in the ground upon which the Tower stands, however. The remains of two children were found in a locked room in the Tower some time between 1603 and 1614, as was the skeleton of a youth of around 13 years of age in 1977, which turned out to have been there since the Roman invasion and was located at only half the depth below ground level that the 1674 remains were found.

Simnel and Warbeck, the two pretenders, are not easily disposed of either and are still arousing controversy among historians even up to the present. Put simply, the question that needed to be answered was this: imposters or not imposters? Certainly, Simnel does not seem a good candidate for the surviving son of Edward IV. Although he was originally paraded as Richard, Duke of York, his cronies quickly changed direction and lauded him as Edward, Earl of Warwick, whom Henry Tudor had safely locked in the Tower. Nor does Warbeck seem to have any more authentic credentials, although he certainly managed his imposture, if that is what it was, with more success than Simnel.

Section IV
Witnesses

CHAPTER TEN

Who Might Have Known?

The fate of Edward and Richard must have been known to a considerable number of people who survived Richard's reign, and consequently, it is perhaps surprising that this is a feature of the boys' disappearance that has been so little considered by many who have written about Richard and his nephews.[1] Although Mancini claimed that their own retainers were withdrawn and it is recorded that eighteen were to be paid soon after 9 June 1483,[2] boys of the age and social status of the princes would still have needed a significant number of servants, including clerics—either their own or new people appointed by Richard—and these individuals would certainly have known where the boys were and what they were doing for a significant part of every day. Even if they were imprisoned alone and without servants, Sir Robert Brackenbury, as constable of the Tower, cannot have been ignorant of the whereabouts of such important prisoners; neither would their uncle Richard, his successor Henry VII or their mother Elizabeth Woodville. A huge staff would have been required to run an establishment like the Tower of London, and gossip must have circulated with a rapidity that would have rivaled or even exceeded the present, as anyone who has been the subject of office rumor, particularly if its nature was malicious, would probably agree.

A lot of people knew what happened to Edward and Richard; so why is there not some more precise record?

The Fate of Possible Records

Literacy Among the Witnesses

One significant factor that must be considered when trying to explain this absence of records is the literacy of any possible witnesses. As has been seen, fairly reliable estimates give a figure for literacy of over 40 percent for male London householders at the beginning of the sixteenth century, although it is not possible to be absolutely sure that such individuals could write as well as read.³ Even among the nobility, reading and writing was not universal accomplishments. It is probable that such skills were more prevalent among the clergy and middle class merchants, whose business transactions would have necessitated considerable correspondence, than among the titled landowners, whose orders would perhaps have been conveyed more conveniently to their mostly illiterate servants by word of mouth. Literate nobles and merchants included members of the Stonor, Paxton and Cely families, and these men and women have all left significant collections of correspondence dating from that period. Unfortunately, it is mostly concerned with family matters and business affairs, not court politics, although occasional mention of Richard's actions are found in these letters, most notably those from the Stonor and Cely families. Unfortunately, the Stonor correspondence finishes on 11 October 1483, in a letter written on the eve of the October Rebellion, and the Cely letters contain only one very short passage from the period 13 to 28 June, professing concern for the life of king Edward V but giving no clear indication of his fate.

However educated these representatives of the noble and merchant classes may have been, it is unfortunately almost certain that most of those who knew exactly what had happened to the boys would not have belonged to either of these groups. Rather, the most knowledgeable would have been found within the partially literate group responsible for doing the menial work about the Tower or Palace of Westminster, and the likelihood of anyone of this status leaving a written record is remote.

Destruction of Relevant Documents

It has also been suggested that this puzzle, which should never have become such a mystery, is the fault of Polydore Vergil, historian to Henry VII. Some authors have claimed he destroyed many of the documents that could have enlightened later historians about Richard's reign and revealed the answers to some of the mysteries surrounding it, which are not confined to the fate of the princes. This claim, however, was based on evidence from later historians in the seventeenth century, and it now seems probable that it is unfounded.

However, Henry himself may also have destroyed or hidden certain documents that indicated the fate of his wife's brothers. He is known to have been responsible for calling in and destroying every copy of the Titulus Regius, with the exception of one that was retained secretly and later included in full in the Croyland Chronicles. In addition to the Rolle there are also a number of significant documents missing from Richard's reign and the later part of Henry's monarchy that might have served to elucidate the fate of the boys. These include records of the following:

- The council meeting on 9 or 10 June 1483
- The council meeting on 13 June 1483
- The Shaa sermon
- The July rescue attempt
- The October Rebellion and Buckingham's role
- Sir John Tyrell's confession
- Perkin Warbeck's original confession, made at Taunton

The Council Meeting on 9 or 10 June 1483

This is the meeting at which Stillington is said to have presented "instruments, authentic doctors, proctors, and notaries of law with depositions of divers witnesses" proving that Edward IV had entered into a pre-contract with a noblewoman called Eleanor Butler and consequently was legally married to her before his marriage to Elizabeth Wydeville. None of the depositions from "diverse witnesses" have been preserved nor has any record of the meeting, which, unlike the meeting of 13 June, is not included in Sir Thomas More's account and is only inferred from a passage in one of the Stonor letters. The destruction of any document describing the course of this meeting would have been of significant benefit to Henry Tudor, since, in its absence, no proof is available concerning the alleged pre-contract between Edward IV and Eleanor Butler, and consequently, his wife's illegitimacy.

The Council Meeting on 13 June 1483

This was the meeting at which Lord Hastings was arrested and summarily executed and Stanley, Morton and Rotherham were arrested. The only record of this meeting, which is claimed to originate from a member of the council who was there, is Sir Thomas More's account, said to have been given to him, like much else in his *Historie*, by Chancellor John Morton. No documents referring to the imprisonment of any of the others are known to exist, nor is any written instruction to Buckingham about Morton's incarceration at his castle in Brecon.

The Shaa Sermon

There is no record of the complete text of the Shaa sermon, describing the precontract between Edward IV and the unknown noblewoman (usually claimed to be Eleanor Butler), in existence, the only record of what Shaa said being in contemporary reports. From the viewpoint of Henry VII, any record of the text of this sermon would have been a very damaging document indeed, specifying as it did the reasons behind the Titulus Regius and the evidence confirming the illegitimacy of his new wife.

The July Rescue Attempt

The names and even the occupations of the four men most closely involved in what is usually referred to as an attempted rescue are recorded in the relevant documents of the period as well as one of the contemporary histories.[4] No information is included, however, about the more important figures behind the plot.

The October Rebellion

The almost complete absence of documentation arising from the rebellion is suspicious in itself, suggesting that documents describing the motivation of the rebels may have been suppressed by someone interested in concealing the original cause of the revolt. There are no contemporary statements by the rebels of their intentions, no letters, proclamations, notes, or other documentation at all suggesting how a coherent organization was developed to control and direct the rebellion, nor any manifestos or placards, although it is known that they existed.[5] This lack of evidence contrasts markedly with the level of information available about the much earlier Peasant's Revolt of 1381, for example, which took place during the reign of Richard II, and where the causes of the revolt, the names and motivations of the rebels and even the records of their trials and subsequent punishments are well documented.

Nor are there any documents, letters or other written evidence describing Buckingham's motivation during this period. Vergil states that he wrote to Henry, telling him to come and marry Elizabeth of York and share the throne with her, but that letter is missing, as is all the other correspondence that must have passed between these people:

- Elizabeth Woodville and Margaret Beaufort about the proposed marriage
- Henry Tudor, or perhaps more probably Margaret Beaufort, and John Morton with regard to how Buckingham might be suborned
- John Morton and Henry Tudor, regarding Morton's role in the new Tudor regime

Sir John Tyrell's Confession

Henry VII claimed that Tyrell stated that he murdered the boys, in a final confession made in 1502 just before he was executed. This document is exhaustively quoted in Sir Thomas Moore's *History*, but no copy of the actual text has ever been found. Whatever its validity, dissemination of the "facts" contained in Tyrell's confession was undoubtedly instrumental in finally dispelling the rumors that Edward and Richard were still alive. Whether Tyrell was actually responsible for a single word of the document he is claimed to have signed is debatable, and it may have been his close association with the late king that prompted Henry to implicate him in the murders. He was certainly considered by many to be a plausible culprit, and his confession was extremely convenient from the viewpoint of the new Tudor dynasty, which was still shaky, despite the efforts of Henry and his chancellor, John Morton.

Perkin Warbeck's Confession

Warbeck is claimed to have made his initial confession before Henry VII and his nobles at Taunton Castle on 5 October 1497. He is said to have explained that in reality his name was Perkin Warbeck (Pierrechon de Werbeque) and that he was the son of John Osbek, comptroller of the town of Tourai, in northern France. The original document recording his confession in his own words is missing, although he later repeated the contents of this confession before he was tortured and finally executed at Tyburn. The text of this confession was recorded and is included in full in the Great Chronicle of London.[6]

Perspectives

All the documents described above are missing from the official records, and their absence helped no one but Henry VII. Clearly, much else is also missing, probably because a substantial number of witnesses to Richard's activities either died with him at Bosworth or were executed immediately afterward, leaving no record. However, there are still parts of the accepted story and alternative theories suggested here that can be tested. The possible involvement of Richard, Buckingham and Henry VII has already been touched upon, but who else might conceivably have known?

These are some of the groups who might be expected to have shared knowledge about the fate of the boys:

- The family of Edward and Richard
- Members of Edward's council and the servants, priests and tutors who attended the princes

- Richard's associates
- Henry Tudor's associates
- Those involved in the July rescue attempt and the October rebels

The possible involvement of these persons and the location of any records associated with them are described in the following chapters.[7]

CHAPTER ELEVEN

The Family of Edward and Richard

Richard III (1452–1485; age in 1483: 31)

Whether or not he was responsible for their disappearance, it is difficult to imagine that Richard did not know what had happened to his nephews. Croyland implies that his intelligence system was efficient prior to the beginning of the October Rebellion, so he must have had good information about the disappearance of his nephews, even if he was not responsible for organizing it, which seems unlikely.

Anne Neville (1456–1485; age in 1483: 27)

Anne Neville, younger daughter of Richard Neville (Warwick the Kingmaker), married Richard, Duke of Gloucester, in March 1472, after her first husband, Edward, Prince of Wales, was executed after the Battle of Tewkesbury. She became Richard's queen in 1483, although she does not appear to have played much part in court politics, possibly because of her ill health and retiring personality. She died on 16 March 1485, aged 29, and subsequently, Richard was obliged to offer a formal denial of any plans to marry his niece Elizabeth of York in an attempt to counter the rumors that were circulating that he had poisoned his wife to make way for his brother's daughter.[1]

Elizabeth Woodville (1437–1492; age in 1483: 46)

Wife of Edward IV and mother of Edward and Richard, Elizabeth Woodville was certainly a political schemer, although she proved no match for

Richard after her husband's demise. She married Edward IV after the death of her first husband, Sir John Grey, by whom she had two children: Thomas Grey, later Marquess of Dorset, and Richard Grey. Sir John was killed at the second battle of St. Albans fighting on the Lancastrian side, so when Edward assumed the throne after the battle of Towton, she found herself in some difficulties with her late husband's estate. Desperate for money, she appealed to a distant relative, William, Lord Hastings. Hastings agreed to help but only after certain conditions had been agreed; most importantly the marriage of her son, Thomas Grey, to an unborn daughter of Lord Hastings, with a further provision that her younger son, Richard, should marry the girl if his elder brother died. With these conditions agreed on 13 April 1464, Hastings ensured that Elizabeth's suit was successful. It is claimed that her evidence was presented to the king in person, and she must have been very effective because three weeks later she and Edward were secretly married, on 1 May 1464.

After her husband's death and her brother-in-law's capture of Grey, Dorset, Vaughn and Haute, she entered sanctuary at Westminster on 1 May 1483 and did not leave the abbey until 1 March 1484, and then only after extracting promises from Richard guaranteeing the safety and future marital prospects of her daughters. When Henry Tudor defeated Richard at Bosworth, she was restored to her dower lands for a short period, until the Great Council deprived her of those lands in February 1487 and she withdrew from the world to live in Bermonsey Abbey, where she died on 8 June 1492, aged 55.[2]

Edward and Elizabeth's Children

Edward IV and Elizabeth Woodville had ten children, three boys and seven girls. Three of them did not survive their father: George Plantagenet (1477–1479), Mary of York (1467–1482) and Margaret of York (April 1472–December 1472). The rest are listed here by age, eldest first.[3]

ELIZABETH OF YORK (1466–1503; age in 1483: 17)

Elizabeth of York was the first child of Edward IV and his queen, Elizabeth Woodville. She was initially betrothed by her father to the Dauphin Charles, son of the king of France, although the marriage did not take place. Her father died in 1483 before contracting another match and in April 1483, Elizabeth, together with her mother, sisters and brother, Richard, Duke of York, entered sanctuary in Westminster Abbey. Henry Tudor took an oath in Rennes Cathedral on Christmas day, promising to marry Elizabeth if he became king, and driven by the need to resolve the situation at Westminster, Elizabeth Wydeville and Richard reached an accommodation in March 1484. The dowager queen would leave sanctuary, trusting her children to Richard's care, on the proviso that he found husbands for them. This would have been unfortunate from Tudor's viewpoint, since Elizabeth of York was included in the arrangement, although fortunately for him, Richard kept his niece unwed until Bosworth deprived him of any interest in the matter. It is not known where Elizabeth of York lived between March 1484 and August 1485, but she is known to have spent Christmas 1484 at court because Croyland criticizes the extent of the celebrations and claims that the queen and her niece-by-marriage even exchanged clothes. This sent a significant message to all and sundry: Edward's illegitimate children were now accepted back into the royal family. This represented a sharp change in the direction of official governmental thinking, because as late as March 1484, Elizabeth Woodville was still being routinely referred to simply as "Elizabeth, late wife of Sir John Grey." Richard's wife, Anne Neville, died on 16 March 1485, and Elizabeth of York appears to have been considered her successor, although political considerations ensured that Richard was forced to deny that he had ever thought about the match. About this time, Sir George Buck claims that Elizabeth wrote a letter to Richard professing her love for him, although that letter is now lost, if it ever existed.

After Bosworth, Elizabeth lived with Tudor's mother, Margaret Beaufort, and when some pressure had been exerted on Henry by both Lords and Commons, the pair were married on 18 January 1486, the new queen receiving her mother's dower lands as part of her marriage settlement. Elizabeth appears to have been quietly influential in court circles, rather than provocative, in direct contrast to her mother-in-law, the redoubtable Margaret Beaufort. Five of her seven children survived infancy, but complications during her last pregnancy caused her death on 11 February 1503, aged 37.[4]

Cecily of York (1469–1507; age in 1483: 14)

Cecily was the subject of two abortive marriage alliances before 1483 when she entered sanctuary with the rest of her family. After the conclusion of negotiations between her mother and uncle, she married Ralph Scrope, the brother of Baron Scrope of Masham. The marriage was annulled in 1486 to allow Cecily's marriage to Henry VII's half-uncle John, Viscount Welles. After his death on 9 February 1499 Cecily married an obscure Lincolnshire landowner, Thomas Keme, sometime from May 1502 to January 1504. Records indicate that she had two children from this marriage, and having incurred the king's displeasure because she failed to consult him before marrying Keme, she lived in relative poverty until her death in 1507, aged 38.[5]

ANNE OF YORK (1475–1511; age in 1483: 8)

Initially her father arranged her marriage to Philip, the future Duke of Burgundy, but the marriage agreement was repudiated after Edward's death. In 1484, in an attempt to establish closer links with the Howards, Anne was betrothed to Thomas Howard, later third Duke of Norfolk. Bosworth interrupted the match, but Howard persisted and on 4 February 1495, the pair were married. They had children, although the only one whose history is known, albeit scantily, is Thomas Howard (1496–1508) and there may have been at least three others who died either stillborn or very young. Anne died in 1511, aged 36.[6]

CATHERINE OF YORK (1479–1527; age in 1483: 4)

Catherine was initially promised in marriage by her father to John, Prince of Asturias, eldest son of Ferdinand and Isabella, although the marriage arrangements were never concluded. Henry attempted to negotiate a marriage for Catherine to James Stewart, Duke of Ross and son of James III of Scotland, but the marriage settlement was not pursued after the death of James III in 1488. By 1495, Catherine was married to William Courtenay, Earl of Devon, by whom she had three children: Henry, Edward and Margaret. Courtenay died in 1511 and Catherine refused to remarry, taking a vow of chastity to confirm her wishes in this matter. She died on 15 November 1527, aged 48.[7]

BRIDGET OF YORK (1480–1517; age in 1483: 3)

Her parents seem to have decided soon after her birth that Bridget should be intended for a religious life, and she was sent to Dartford Priory, in Dartford, Kent, some time from 1486 to 1492. She was ordained and lived most of her life in the priory, only leaving for her mother's funeral in 1492. She is thought to have had one illegitimate daughter, Agnes of Eltham, who was made a ward of the priory, presumably to conceal her parentage. Bridget died in 1517, aged 37.[8]

THOMAS GREY, MARQUESS OF DORSET (1455–1501; age in 1483: 28)

Thomas Grey was the eldest son of Sir John Grey, first husband of Elizabeth Woodville, who was killed fighting on the Lancastrian side during the second battle of St. Albans on 17 February 1461. His mother, being left a widow and almost penniless, married him in 1466 to Anne Holland, daughter of the exiled Duke of Exeter. He fought with the Yorkists at Tewksbury in 1471 and was created Earl of Huntingdon in 1471, although he resigned this position when he became Marquess of Dorset. After the death of his first wife, he married the Bonville heiress, Cicely Bonville, which brought him lands in Devon and Cornwall as well as northern England, which resulted in Grey being created a knight of the Bath and Marquess of Dorset. The betrothal of his son to Anne St. Leger also brought him a portion of the estates of the Duchy of Exeter.

The death of Edward IV marked a turning point in Dorset's fortunes, the hostility between Dorset and Hastings being one factor that contributed to the relative ease with which Richard, Duke of Gloucester, managed to occupy the throne. Dorset must have been politically quite naïve, because, according to Mancini, he is said to have boasted at a council meeting in April 1483, "We are so important that even without the king's uncle, we can make and enforce these decisions."

After Gloucester arrested Rivers and Grey at Stony Stratford, Buckinghamshire, on 30 April, and took charge of his nephew, Dorset abandoned the Tower of London, where he was in control, and followed his mother, Queen Elizabeth, into sanctuary at Westminster Abbey. Having escaped from the abbey, Dorset joined the October Rebellion; but the collapse of this ill-planned revolt compelled him to take refuge in Brittany, where he was obliged to remain for over two years, having been attainted by the parliament of 1484 and having forfeited his estates. He joined Henry Tudor at Rennes, but shortly before Henry's successful invasion of England in August 1485, Dorset received a letter from his mother, who had come to terms with Richard III, and he decided to abandon the Tudor cause. He had no more success in this than in his earlier ventures, being intercepted at Compiègne, en route for Flanders and then England, and was subsequently left in Paris with John Bourchier, Lord Berners (d. 1533), as security for a loan made to Henry Tudor by the French government. He was not allowed to return to England until Henry VII was safely installed as king.

Dorset's attainder was reversed in November 1485 and his land and titles restored, although Henry never really trusted him; during Simnel's rising in 1487, he was even imprisoned in the Tower until after the battle of Stoke. He is known to have been an early patron of the young Thomas Wolsey and is believed to have been responsible for the building of Bradgate Hall in Leicester, which became his family's principal residence. He died in 1501 and was buried in Astley, Warwickshire, aged 46.[9]

Margaret of York and Burgundy (1446–1503; age in 1483: 37)

Margaret of York, third daughter of Richard of York and Cecily Neville, was born on 3 May 1446, probably at Fotheringhay Castle in Northamptonshire, and after her brother Edward's seizure of the crown in 1461, she divided her time between Bayard's Castle, the Yorks' London home, and Greenwich. As the sister of the king of England she was considered a very eligible match, and in June 1468, she married Charles, Count of Charolais. The happy couple seem to have spent little time in each other's company but relations seem to have remained amicable, although by 1475 Charles's military commitments forced Margaret to assume a much larger administrative role than might have been expected of her. She mediated between Charles and her brother Edward on several occasions and even presented Charles's demands for men and money to his estates general in 1476, shortly before his death at Nancy on 5 January 1477. In the relative chaos following her husband's death and Louis XI's invasion of Burgundian lands, Margaret organized support for the new duchess, Marie, who responded by confirming Margaret's claim on the extensive dower lands that Charles had conferred on her. This included the city of Mechelen (Fr.: Maline; Eng: Mechelin), which was to become the dowager's principal place of residence. She was involved in the negotiations that brought about the marriage of her stepdaughter Marie to the Hapsburg duke Maximiliam, which took place in August 1477, and she visited England in 1480 to persuade her brother Edward to return to his old alliance with the Burgundians.

Her stepdaughter Marie died in March 1482, and following her brother Richard's death in 1485, she refused to accept Henry's accession as valid, and her court became a refuge for Yorkists exiles and pretenders of all kinds. She promised finance for an abortive expedition to England in 1486 and also paid for a group of Maximilian's mercenaries, recruited in the Netherlands, to support the Lambert Simnel conspirators. After 1488, European complications occupied her attention, but she continued her intrigues against Henry, as witnessed by the activities of her envoys at a number of European royal courts, including that of James IV of Scotland.

She appears to have been involved in the Perkin Warbeck conspiracy from about February 1492, despite Henry's envoys presenting her with evidence that the "feigned boy" was almost certainly an imposter who was being used to implement French policy against England. Despite Henry's assertions, Margaret publicly recognized him as her nephew, Richard of Shrewsbury, Duke of York, providing him with funds and writing to the pope on his behalf in May 1495. Unfortunately, Warbeck's landing in England in that summer was a failure, forcing him to escape to the Scottish court, where he eventually found refuge and a bride. Despite his obvious incompetence and the increasingly unlikely chance of his ever ascending the throne, Margaret's support for him continued in a surreptitious way until his death in October 1497. She eventually made peace with Henry in 1498, five years before her death in 1503, aged 57.[10]

Evidence from Edward's Family

From July 1483 to August 1485, Richard's main residences were London, Canterbury and York, although he seems to have been fairly mobile and there may be other locations where he might have left written evidence. He has been confirmed as the owner of several books and was able to both read and write, being known to have affixed a postscript in his own handwriting to the letter to John Russell describing Buckingham as "the most untrewe creature lyvyng."[11] The National Archives contain 401 records referring to Richard with dates from January 1483 to December 1485, and these include

- Exchequer receipts
- Acts of Parliament
- Chancery documents
- Family histories
- Letters patent confirming gifts of land, appointments, and other rights and titles
- Legal documents including court rolls, manor rolls, and escheators' files
- Commissions

Among the commissions is one to Sir William Haute, dated September 1483, relating to the sea wall between Faversham and Whitstable, which must have been received only weeks before his part in the rebellion came to Richard's notice.[12]

Anne Neville appears to have accompanied Richard during most of his travels, and so any written evidence she left would also be found in London, Canterbury or York. It is not known whether she was literate; records in the PRO (Public Record Office in Kew, London) and its associated archives only contain one document that mentions her between 1483 and 1485, a petition involving the inheritance left by George, Duke of Clarence. She is known to have owned at least one book, *The Visions of Saint Matilda*.

Elizabeth Wydeville's main residences between July 1483 and her death in 1492 were in Westminster and possibly Gipping Hall, where she and her sons may have stayed after March 1484. She also appears to have lived at Westminster until her retirement to Bermondsey in 1487. She controlled manors that had been bequeathed to her children by her first husband, Sir John Grey, and she also received numerous dower properties from Edward IV. These were restored to her after 1485 until 1487, and so she may have left written evidence concerning her sons' location at any of these places. From her first marriage her properties included the manor of New Bottle, Northamptonshire; the manor of Brington, Northamptonshire, and the manor of Woodham Ferrers, Essex. Dower property from her marriage to Edward IV included the Mote, Maidstone, Kent, and six manors in Essex originally belonging to the Duchy of Lancaster.

It is not known whether she was literate, since records in the PRO and its associated archives only describe her involvement in a number of judicial and financial matters. The Suffolk Record Office also contains no documents referring to her or her sons, and when Gipping Hall was demolished in 1874 its records were lost, if any had been stored in that building.

Elizabeth of York, Edward and Elizabeth's first daughter, lived first in sanctuary at Westminster until March 1483. Her main residence was in London, with her husband, Henry VII, although there are other locations where she might have left written evidence, such as her dower properties, some of which she received from her mother.

Cecily of York was only 14 when her mother went into sanctuary, so she probably lived with her until her own marriage to Ralph Scrope. Subsequently, she lived in Masham, West Yorkshire, Lincolnshire and on the Isle of Wight, in residence with each of her husbands.

After leaving sanctuary in Westminster, it is difficult to say where Anne of York took up residence, although it is probable that she stayed with her mother, since she was only 10 years old at the time of Bosworth. After her marriage at the age of 20, presumably she lived with Howard on one of his Norfolk manors.

Her age at the time of Henry's accession, barely 6, makes it likely Catherine of York was with her mother until her marriage at 16 to William Courtenay. Presumably from 1495 she lived on one of Courtenay's properties in Devon.

Bridget of York died unmarried and does not appear to have lived anywhere but the Dartford priory until her death, so she may have been able to both read and write, in consequence of her clerical associations. No records exist in the National Archives relating to any of Elizabeth Wydeville's female children. Nor is the extent of their education a matter of record, so it is not clear that any of them would have been able to leave a record of what they knew about the fate of their brothers and, at the present time, the complete absence of personal documents written by them relating to their brothers must lend support to this view.

Thomas Gray, Marquess of Dorset, was in France with Henry Tudor for much of the time from July 1483 to August 1485. After Henry's accession he had a number of properties, most notably Bradgate Hall, near Leicester and the manor of Astley in Warwickshire. It is not known whether Dorset was literate, and he does not appear to have left any personal memoranda relating to his half-brothers. Moreover, there are no records in the PRO or the archives associated with his properties that refer to him from 1483 till his death in 1501.

From 1483 until her death in 1503, Margaret of Burgundy seems to have spent most of her time at her court in Mechelin. Some of her estate records are still in existence, as are the records of the city of Mechelen. These city records show at least one entry recording a gift of eight flagons of wine to "the son of Clarence from England,"[13] so there may still be something more to be gleaned from a study of those documents, although this entry probably does not refer to one of Edward's sons, but rather to the son of his brother, George, Duke of Clarence. Margaret was known to be able to both read and write, but there are no records in the PRO and its associated archives referring to her from 1480 to 1495, and she left no personal memoranda describing the arrival of either of her nephews at her court.

Perspectives

In common with many royal dynasties of the period, the family surrounding Edward and Richard does not seem to have been particularly concerned with fostering close and personal relations between its members. Although the boys and their sisters were properly cared for and given all the marks of respect their stations demanded, the two boys in particular seem to have spent relatively little time in the company of their parents and siblings. Consequently it is difficult to evaluate just how concerned the boys' close family would have been to determine what happened to them, especially if it became dangerous for anyone found making such enquiries.

Anne Neville was 27 in 1483 and had less than 2 years left to live when her husband occupied the throne. Her age and closeness to Richard suggest that she might have been in receipt of a certain amount of secret information, although her illness and retiring personality in turn makes this less likely. She was, after all, not another Margaret Beaufort and certainly did not possess that formidable lady's imposing personality.

Eleven. The Family of Edward and Richard

Elizabeth Wydeville, however, was of an entirely different type, and it seems unlikely that with her former contacts in and around Richard's court, she did not know what had happened to her sons. Her failure to leave any record concerned with their disappearance is surprising, as is her failure to reveal their fate, living or dead, before using that information against Richard and for the benefit of her eldest daughter. If, as seems likely, the original intention of the October rebels was to ensure that Elizabeth of York ascended the throne, with Henry Tudor as her ineffectual consort, reliable information about the boys' location, whether living or dead, could have provided a considerable political gain. It was certainly no advantage to her to leave the country uncertain about her sons' fate; that helped nobody, not even her brother-in-law Richard.

Elizabeth of York, Henry Tudor's future queen and Edward and Richard's eldest sister, was 17 when her uncle claimed her brother's throne. She was old enough to be well aware of much that was going on a court, although whether she actually would have been allowed to know what had happened to her two brothers seems doubtful. She was, after all, useful only as a pawn in any lucrative political marriage her uncle might have orchestrated, and she should have had no value as a political figure, unlike her two brothers; although this perception seems to have been ignored by the leaders of the October Rebellion, who seem to have been intent upon crowning a child of Edward IV, whether king or queen being immaterial.

Elizabeth's younger sister Cecily was 14 in 1483, probably too young to have had much perception of the intrigues going on around her. Girls of her age and rank were very carefully sheltered in Tudor times and, like her sister Elizabeth, she would have been regarded more as marriageable breeding stock than a useful political addition to Richard's organization. In those days women had to prove their political worth to a king in the way Margaret Beaufort had to her son, Henry Tudor, and Cecily would have had neither time nor opportunity to make such an impression on her uncle Richard.

Anne, Catherine and Bridget were aged 8, 4 and 3 years, respectively, when their mother entered sanctuary and were probably too young to have any understanding of the significance of their brothers' sudden disappearance from their lives. All three were married young and so left the court before they became acute enough to begin to ask the right questions about their elder brothers.

Although Thomas Grey entered sanctuary in Westminster Abbey with his mother on 1 May 1483, he does not seem to have stayed very long, being known to have joined the October Rebellion soon after it began. After the collapse of the revolt he fled to Brittany, before joining Henry Tudor in France.

Being forced to travel in this way strongly suggests that he would have lost touch with both his mother and events at the English court and so would have been unlikely to be in receipt of information about his young half-brothers. Nor was his situation improved very much when he was allowed to return to England. Henry does not seem to have trusted him particularly, so that even after his arrival in England, which was some time after Bosworth, he was not allowed the same degree of participation in court politics that he had enjoyed under Edward IV. It seems extremely doubtful that he would have been trusted with a secret as potentially explosive as the whereabouts of his half-brothers, if they were still alive.

Despite her support for both Simnel and Warbeck, it is not clear that Margaret of Burgundy actually believed either of the pretenders to be who they claimed to be, and the consensus among historians is that she found them convenient political tools to goad the Tudor regime, rather than believing them to be her long-lost nephews. Her connections within many of the European courts were extensive, and she had cordial relations with James IV of Scotland, so a trip into England for her agents would hardly have been difficult to arrange. Consequently, she could have found out what had happened to her nephews, although she left no record of any such knowledge.

With the obvious exception of their uncle, Richard, none of the members of Edward and Richard's close family had access to them during the period they spent in the Tower and most of them were probably too young or unreceptive to appreciate the significance of anything they learned. Perhaps as a consequence of these conditions, none of the family members appear to have left any sort of informal record in the form of letters or other documents concerned with the boys' time in the Tower, their disappearance, or their whereabouts after the autumn of 1483 when they disappeared.

Table Seven. Possible Location of Documents Left by the Family of Edward and Richard

Witness	Possible locations for documents relating to Edward and Richard	Storage of records from these locations
Richard III	London, during his tenure as king	National Archives, Kew, London
	Canterbury Cathedral, during his tenure as king	Canterbury Cathedral Archives
	Southwest England, during his tenure as king	Bristol Record Office Devon Heritage Centre
	Eastern England, during his tenure as king	Norfolk Record Office

Eleven. The Family of Edward and Richard

Witness	Possible locations for documents relating to Edward and Richard	Storage of records from these locations
	Southeast England, during his tenure as king	Kent County Record Office, Maidstone
	Cumbria, during his tenure as king	Cumbria Archive Centre, Carlisle
	Northern England, during his tenure as king	Doncaster Archives Leeds City Archives
	Wales, during his tenure as king	Archives Wales (various locations)
	Ireland, during his tenure as king	Public Record Office of Northern Ireland
Anne Neville	London, during her tenure as queen (1483–1485)	National Archives, Kew, London
	Canterbury, during her tenure as queen	Canterbury Cathedral Archives Kent County Record Office, Maidstone
Elizabeth Wydeville	Westminster Abbey, 1483–1484, while in sanctuary	National Archives Bermondsey Abbey, 1487–1492, before her death National Archives
	The Mote, Maidstone, one of her dower properties	Kent History and Library Centre
	Her Essex manors	The Essex Record Office
	Gipping Hall, where she may have lived after March 1484	Suffolk Record Office
Elizabeth of York	Westminster Abbey, 1483–1484, during her period in sanctuary	Westminster Abbey Archives
	London, 1486–1503, during her tenure as queen	National Archives, Kew, London
	The Mote, Maidstone, originally her mother's dower property	Kent History and Library Centre
	Her Essex manors, originally part of her mother's dower properties	The Essex Record Office
Cecily of York	Masham, 1483–1486, during her marriage to Ralph Scrope	West Yorkshire Archive Service
	Lincolnshire, 1486–1499, during her marriage to John Welles	Lincolnshire County Council Archives

Section IV: Witnesses

Witness	Possible locations for documents relating to Edward and Richard	Storage of records from these locations
Anne of York	Isle of Wight, c. 1502–1507, during her marriage to John Keme	Isle of Wight Record Office and Archive
	Westminster, 1483–1484, before her marriage	National Archive, Kew
	Norfolk, 1495–1511, after her marriage to Howard	Norfolk Record Office
Catherine of York	Westminster, 1483–1484, before her marriage	National Archives, Kew
	Tiverton Castle, Oakhampton Castle and Colcombe Castle in Devon, 1495–1527, after her marriage to William Courtnay and her subsequent widowhood	Devon County Archives, Exeter
Bridget of York	Dartford, 1486–1517, after her entry to the Dartford Priory	The Dartford Town Archive National Archives, Kew
Thomas Grey, Marquess of Dorset	Before 1483: his estates in Devon, Cornwall, Exeter	Devon County Archive, Exeter
	Rennes, 1483–1485, during his period spent in exile with Henry Tudor	Rennes City Council Archive
	Paris, 1485, after Henry's success at Bosworth and before he was allowed to return to England, 1485	Archives Nationales de France
	Bradgate Hall, Leicester, after 1485, after his return to England	Leicestershire County Council Archive
	Groby, Leicestershire, after 1485	Leicestershire County Council Archive
	Shute, Devon, after 1485	Devon County Archive, Exeter
	Astley, Warwickshire, after 1485	Warwickshire County Record Office
Margaret of York	City of Mechelin, after 1477, as dowager duchess of Burgundy	City Archive of Mechelen
	Antwerp, Belgium, main city in the northern part of what was formerly Burgundy	Archives Générales du Royaume (AGR) (National Archives of Belgium), Brussels

CHAPTER TWELVE

Edward's Council and Servants

Members of the Councils of Edward V

Edward's council (see table 6)[1] was established soon after his birth, and after some additional members were included in 1473, the household was eventually located at Ludlow. Included here are those members of Edward's council who were alive in 1483, with the exception of his mother and uncle Richard, and who might be supposed to have left some record relating to the eventual fate of the boys.[2]

- Cardinal Thomas Bourchier, Archbishop of Canterbury
- Robert Stillington, bishop of Bath and chancellor of England
- Thomas Millyng, abbot of Westminster, bishop of Hereford, king's councilor
- Sir John Fogge, treasurer of the king's household
- Sir John Scott, controller of the king's household
- John Alcock, dean of St. Stephen's Chapel, Westminster, later bishop of Rochester and Winchester
- Edward Storey, bishop of Carlisle, queen's chancellor
- Walter Devereux, Lord Ferrers of Chartley
- Members of the Haute family

Members of Edward's Council from 1471

CARDINAL THOMAS BOURCHIER, ARCHBISHOP OF CANTERBURY (1411–1486: age in 1483: 72)

Thomas Bourchier, later chancellor and Archbishop of Canterbury, was the son of William Bourchier, count of Eu (c. 1374–1420), and Anne of Woodstock, daughter and heir of Thomas of Woodstock, Duke of Gloucester, and granddaughter of Edward III. After the death of his father his mother married

Knole House, Thomas Bourchier's Kent residence (photograph by David Iliff/CC-BY-SA 3.0).

Edmund Stafford, fifth Earl of Stafford, and the links she was able to establish with other members of the English aristocracy through this match were later to prove useful to all her children. The eldest of her sons, Henry Bourchier, was created Earl of Essex by Edward IV, and William and John were summoned to parliament respectively as the lords Fitzwarine and Berners. Their sister Eleanor also married well, becoming the wife of John Mowbray, third Duke of Norfolk (d. 1461). His half brother, from his mother's second marriage, was Humphrey Stafford, first Duke of Buckingham, grandfather of Henry Stafford, second Duke of Buckingham, who was executed for treason by Richard III after the October Rebellion of 1483.

Bourchier was not just well connected but also appears to have been of marked intelligence. He went to Oxford soon after his father's death in 1420, entered holy orders on 24 September 1429 (aged 17) and after a certain amount of negotiation was confirmed as bishop of Worcester on 9 December 1434 (age: 23), even though he was much younger than the minimum age required for consecration as bishop. On 27 February 1444 he was also confirmed as bishop of Ely, despite showing more interest in politics than ecclesiastical matters.

His role during this period seems to have been that of arbitrator, working to resolve violent local disputes between members of the nobility, and this talent may have been a contributory factor in his appointment as chancellor to Henry VI on 7 March 1455, having become Archbishop of Canterbury in the preceding year. He was discharged from office on 11 December 1456, although he still continued his role as peacemaker and was finally able to establish an uneasy truce between all the English factions in the spring of 1458.

Bourchier declared unequivocally for Edward IV and was responsible for crowning the new king on 28 June 1461. After Edward's flight to his sister in 1469, Bourchier worked secretly for the former king, arranging for Clarence to reaffirm his support for his brother and sending Edward secret information. He was appointed to prince Edward's council after the victory of Edward IV at Barnet and the death or murder of Henry VI, and was part of the council left behind in 1475 when Edward took his army to France.

Although he effectively retired in 1480, Bourchier returned to a role in public affairs after the death of Edward IV in 1483. On 2 May 1483 the young Edward V, on his way to London, wrote to him requesting him to see to the safety of the Tower and the treasure there, and five days later Bourchier took official custody of the royal jewels and seals, as the executors of Edward IV's will had hesitated to act in this matter. He saw that Edward's funeral expenses of nearly £1,500 were paid. As the head of a deputation from the Royal Council, he played a crucial part in persuading the king's mother to deliver up her second son, Richard, Duke of York, from sanctuary at Westminster into the keeping of his uncle. He crowned Richard on 6 July, although Mancini claims he was reluctant to perform the ceremony and no record exists of his attendance at any of Richard's council meetings during his reign. After Bosworth, he also crowned Henry VII on 30 October 1485 and married him to Elizabeth of York on 18 January 1486. In 1456 Bourchier had purchased the manor of Knole in Sevenoaks, and it was here that he died on 30 March 1486, aged 75.[3]

ROBERT STILLINGTON, BISHOP OF BATH AND WELLS
(c. 1408–1491; age in 1483: ~75)

Stillington's career followed normal lines for a churchman or diplomat of the period. From some time in November 1442, he acted as proctor for Lincoln College, being already principal of Deep Hall, and by June of 1443 he had graduated from the University of Oxford as a doctor of civil law. He succeeded to the bishopric of Bath and Wells on 30 June 1465, although he does not seem to have been zealous in his duties in this capacity, being recorded in Somerset only once during his twenty-five-year tenure. Having previously undertaken a number of diplomatic missions, Stillington became Keeper of the Privy Seal in July 1460 and was appointed chancellor in 1467, remaining in that post until 1473 when he was replaced, probably due to failing health. He was also present in a supporting role at Richard's coronation.

Stillington had a number of significant difficulties with Edward IV, and it is not clear how these problems can have originated. At some time between 27 February and 5 March 1478 he was arrested and imprisoned in the Tower of London, where he was examined by the king and his council. Fortunately, he was able to satisfy them of his loyalty and was pardoned on 20 June 1478.

This episode is sometimes explained by collusion in Clarence's treason, perhaps by informing the Duke of Gloucester about Edward IV's precontract of marriage, although this seems unlikely, because Stillington was only arrested after the dissolution of the parliament during which Clarence was tried and executed. Moreover, no mention of the precontract had been made at this point; additionally, the allegation that Edward was illegitimate, supposedly repeated by Clarence, can be backdated to as early as 1469. Although Stillington has always been claimed as the author of the precontract story that formed the basis for the Titulius Regius, because he officiated at the "marriage" of Edward and lady Eleanor Butler (whoever she was), Richard did not particularly favor the old bishop. A yearbook of 1488 does, however, contain the claim that it was Stillington who drew up the petition in which the Lords and Commons asked Gloucester to take the crown, suggesting that by then he had become popularly associated with Richard's usurpation.

Stillington spent much of the short remainder of his life in prison after Bosworth, although he was said to have been involved with the plotters who intended to place Lambert Simnel on the throne. He was removed from Oxford, where he had taken refuge, and placed in prison at Windsor in April 1488 until sometime in 1489, dying in April or May 1491, aged 83.[4]

Thomas Millyng, Abbot of Westminster, Bishop of Hereford (c. 1436–1492; age in 1483: 47)

Millyng began his career in the church at Westminster Abbey in 1445, although he was at Oxford University from 1456 until he obtained his doctor of theology degree in 1465. He returned to Westminster Abbey as prior in 1466, was elected abbot in 1469, and stood as godfather to the future Edward V in 1470. Appointed to Prince Edward's council in 1471 and subsequently elected to the papal see of Hereford in 1474, he appears to have spent most of his time at Ludlow with Prince Edward, rather than about the business of his bishopric. The level of his support for Richard is not clear, and he was certainly accepted back into favor at the Tudor court quite rapidly, as he was sent as an envoy to Rome in May 1487. He died at Hereford in 1492, aged 56, and is buried in the Chapel of St. John the Baptist in Westminster Abbey.[5]

Sir John Fogge, Treasurer of the King's Household (1417–1490; age in 1483: 66)

Despite having a number of important posts in the government of Henry VI, including sheriff of Kent in 1453, Fogge also became an important member of the regime of Edward IV. He was head of all the Kent commissions during the early years of Edward's reign and was given custody of Rochester Castle, while also taking possession of the manors of Tonford, Dane and Hothfield. He was appointed treasurer of the royal household in 1468 and probably went into exile with Edward in 1470. Upon Edward's return in 1471, he was rewarded for his loyalty by being granted further landholdings, which included silver and gold workings in Devon.

His association with the royal family was strengthened when he married the queen's first cousin, Alice Haute. He was appointed to Prince Edward's council at Ludlow in 1471, serving as chamberlain jointly with Sir John Scott and acting as administrator of Edward's Devon properties. He was part of the October Rebellion in 1483, being attainted and deprived of his landholding, much of which was granted to Sir Ralph Ashton. Fogge was pardoned by Richard in February 1485, however, and four of his manors were restored. His age probably debarred him from a major role in government under Henry VII, although he does not appear to have been out favor, because his lands were restored to him after Bosworth and he was granted the marriage of the son and heir of Sir Humphrey Stafford. He was dead by November 1490, when he would have been 73, and is buried in Ashford church.[6]

Sir John Scott, Controller of the King's Household (1423–1485; age in 1483: 60)

Scott did well under Edward IV and was well rewarded for his services between 1460 and 1483, with much of the landholding he acquired during this period being in Kent. In addition to fulfilling his duties within the king's household, he undertook several important administrative posts. He was appointed sheriff of Kent in September 1460, was a Kentish commissioner on a number of occasions, and served as a justice of the peace until his death. He represented Kent in the parliament of 1467–8, and probably also in 1461–2, 1463–5, and the first parliament of 1483, as well as sitting for Appleby, Westmorland, in 1472–5. He also sat on the Buckinghamshire bench from 1479 to 1484.

In 1473 he was appointed tutor to the prince of Wales and joint-chamberlain with Sir John Fogge. He remained loyal to Richard III after the usurpation and, more particularly, he seems to have taken no part in the October Rebellion. He died on 17 October 1485, aged 62, apparently from natural causes, Henry having continued to pay him a pension in the period after Bosworth. At his death he held lands in Calais, as well as the manors of St. Cleres, Essex and "la Moote," Sussex, in addition to his properties in Kent.

Those Kentish properties included the manor and advowson of Orlestone and the manors of Capel, Hayton, Hall, and Mead. He also held the manor of Bournewood, near Orlestone, and land in Romney Marsh given to him by Sir John Cheyne in 1457 in settlement of a debt.[7]

John Alcock, Dean of Westminster
(1430–1500; age in 1483: 53)

Having obtained his doctorate in canon law in 1459, Alcock worked in local administration and the law courts until 1470, when he appears to have entered the service of Edward IV as dean of Westminster and keeper of the rolls of chancery. These were very significant appointments and may have been the result of help given to some of the king's family while Edward was in exile. Alcock served successively as assistant to Robert Stillington during his tenure as chancellor (September 1472–June 1473) and then as chancellor from June to September 1475, while Thomas Rotherham, the incumbent chancellor, was in France with the king.

Paralleling his administrative duties, in July 1471, Alcock was appointed administrator of the infant Prince Edward's holdings in Wales, Cornwall, and Cheshire. In November 1473 he was appointed tutor to the prince, then only 3 years old, as well as president of his council. In order to facilitate his role on the council, on 15 July 1476 Alcock was translated to the see of Worcester, which allowed him to participate in diocesan matters there as well as properly discharging his duties at Ludlow.

Little is known of Alcock's reaction to the usurpation of Richard III. Although he was not arrested, it seems unlikely that he was much involved with the new regime; and Henry VII's accession saw Alcock returned to a role in the political center of the kingdom. On 6 October 1486 he was translated to the very rich and easily managed see of Ely, where he was much involved with the University of Cambridge. Despite his age, he also appears to have remained a trusted royal councilor until his death in 1500, aged 70.[8]

Members Added to Edward's Council in 1473

Edward Storey, Bishop of Chicester
(c. 1428–1503; age in 1483: 55)

Academically Storey's attainments are impressive. Admitted to Pembroke College, Cambridge, he was a fellow by 1446, treasurer in 1446, 1448, and

1450, received his MA by 1447 and doctor of theology degree by 1460. Elected master of Michaelhouse in 1466 until 1474, he was also chancellor of the university for two terms, 1468-9 and 1471-1473. A short time after 1464, Storey became confessor to Elizabeth Wydeville and his future seemed assured. Appointed bishop of Carlisle in 1468, he also acted as peace commissioner in a number of counties some distance from his diocese and was subsequently appointed to the see of Chicester, West Sussex, in 1478. He had a place on Edward's council from 1473 but the extent of his involvement is not known; and it is possible that his role was simply that of religious advisor and confessor to the prince's mother. He officiated at the funeral rites of Edward IV, but by 28 July he was back in his diocese of Chicester where he remained, mostly at Aldingbourne, busying himself with diocesan work and avoiding political entanglements until his death in 1503, aged 75.[9]

WALTER DEVEREUX, LORD FERRERS
(1432-1485; age in 1483: 51)

Knighted some time in 1441-42, Devereux was a prominent Herefordshire landowner and county official, involved in attempts by the Duke of York to extend his landholdings from 1450 to 1456. When his father died on 22 or 23 April 1459, Devereux inherited his estates in Herefordshire and Leicestershire, his Lincolnshire lands having been conveyed to him and his wife, Anne (1438-1469), daughter and heir of Sir William Ferrers of Chartley, Staffordshire, when they married in 1446.

He continued his allegiance to the house of York, fighting with York at Ludford Bridge in October 1459 and being appointed to the parliament of 1460-61 after Neville's capture of Henry VI. Upon the accession of Edward IV most of his time was spent in the administration of Wales and Herefordshire on the king's behalf. After the Neville rebellion he was given control of the lordships of Brecon, Hay, and Huntington during the duke of Buckingham's minority, becoming sheriff of Caernarvonshire and master forester of Snowdon for life in July 1470. After Edward's return from exile Ferrers became the prince's tutor and councilor on 20 February 1473. Widowed in 1469, he remarried in 1482 to Joan, widow of Thomas Ilam. Joan who outlived him.

Ferrers is known to have attended Edward IV's funeral at Windsor in April 1483, but his attitude to Richard III is not clear. He did attend the coronation, but when Buckingham rebelled in October, the duke and his family made for Weobley, his ancestral manor in Herefordshire, to raise men, and it was during the period that they were hiding in the neighborhood that the Duke of Buckingham was captured and subsequently executed. This may explain why Richard's treatment of Ferrers was cautious, giving him first an annuity of 100 marks, and subsequently, in August 1484, the manor of Cheshunt, Hertfordshire, perhaps as a bribe to buy Ferrer's aid in opposing Henry Tudor. He was killed fighting for Richard at Bosworth, aged 53, and attainted in Henry VII's first parliament.[10]

Sir Richard Haute (died 1492)

Sir Richard Haute was either the son or the grandson of Nicholas Haute, William Haute's younger brother. He was appointed to the household of the Prince of Wales at Ludlow in 1473, although it is difficult to be sure of this, as both he and his cousin Richard Haute (son of Sir William Haute) were active in South Wales and the Marches during this period. Knighted during Richard of Gloucester's Scottish campaign in 1482, less than a year later he was among those members of the Woodville circle taken at Stony Stratford when Richard of Gloucester began his campaign of usurpation. Unlike his friend Rivers, however, his life was spared, and he lived out Richard III's reign without incident.

After Bosworth, he made a successful return to court life, serving in a

Ightham Mote, home of the Haute family during the reigns of Edward IV and Richard III (photograph by Katie Chan/CC-BY-SA 3.0).

number of capacities both at home and abroad and acquiring estates in Kent, Berkshire, Essex and London. He died in December 1492, possibly while returning from France.

He was married twice: first, in 1474, to Eleanor, daughter of Sir Robert Roos of Northamptonshire; she died about 1486, and between then and 1489 he married Katherine Boston (d. 1493), the widow of Walter Wryttel and of John Green. Katherine was the heir to four of Wryttel's Essex manors. Richard seems to have had literary interests: he may have owned an English version of Christine de Pisan's *Livre du Corps de Policie*, perhaps translated by his friend, Anthony Woodville, while Eleanor was bequeathed a volume of French Grail romances by her uncle, the poet and translator Sir Richard Roos, which she signed, "Thys boke ys myne dame Alyanor Haute."[11]

Servants, Tutors, Priests and Guards

Whatever Mancini may have learned or surmised about the boys being "deprived of their attendants and kept in close confinement," high-born boys of that period could not have been left to their own devices. Someone must have cooked for them, organized their clothing, even guarded them, doing all of the things that were necessary for noble children who had never been used to looking after themselves. Consequently, it follows that those servants must have known, at the very least, when the boys left the Tower and probably could have made a good guess what happened to them. Conversely, it would have been obvious to those servants that if the boys had disappeared without provision being made for a journey or movement to another establishment, that probably they had been murdered.

Unfortunately, such individuals were unlikely to have been literate. More importantly, would probably not have been believed, even if they had come forward. This failure of belief is important, because it would have resulted in a record not being left by some other person who would otherwise have been able to write a credible report. Persons known to have been in the service of Edward or Richard included the following[12]:

- Mrs. Avice Welles, Edward's wet-nurse
- Elizabeth, Lady Darcey, mistress of the royal nursery
- Dr. John Davison, almoner
- Adam Grafton, confessor
- Thomas Bold, MA, confessor
- John Giles, schoolmaster

Mrs. Avice Welles

Mrs. Avice Welles was Edward's wet-nurse from his birth on 2 November 1471 until 12 November 1472.

Elizabeth, Lady Darcey

Elizabeth, Lady Darcey, was mistress of the royal nursery and thus responsible for the care of Edward and his elder sisters, Elizabeth, Mary and Cecily. Later presumably, the same lady took charge of Richard, Anne, George, Catherine and Bridget.

Dr. John Davison

Dr. John Davison was dean of Salisbury and Windsor, Edward's almoner in 1477.

Adam Grafton

Adam Grafton was vicar of St. Alkmund's, Shrewsbury, one of Edward's confessors while he was at Ludlow.

Thomas Bold, MA

Thomas Bold was an absentee rector.

John Giles

John Giles was a professional schoolmaster who taught both Edward and Richard.

Evidence from Edward's Close Associates

From April 1483 until his death in March 1486, Thomas Bourchier probably divided his time between London and his manor of Knole. He was literate, having graduated from Oxford University and become a churchman of high rank. There is a letter in the National Archives to him from Edward V from Northampton, dated 2 May 1483, requesting Bourchier to remain in London until the new king arrived. This letter appears to have been written by Richard himself, and it also includes details of some reservations the king was claimed to have had about the contents of the treasury and the whereabouts of the Great Seal. The archives of Canterbury Cathedral, Westminster Abbey, the County of Kent and the Public Record Office only contain records of various legal, financial and administrative transactions relating to Bourchier during his tenure as archbishop.

In contrast to Bourchier, Robert Stillington probably spent most of his time in London during the years from 1483 to 1485, returning to Oxford after Bosworth. He could read and write, being a churchman of high rank and having graduated as doctor of civil law. However, it is perhaps surprising, considering his involvement with Richard's ascent to the throne, that the only other record in the PRO and its associated archives concerning him is a record of diocesan administration and two legal documents. There are copies of letters sent to him from Oxford University in "Epistolae Academicae Oxon," but these relate to mundane issues addressed to him during his time as chancellor.[13]

Thomas Millyng also probably spent most of his time at Westminster during the period of Richard's reign, having acquired a permanent suffragan for his Hereford see in 1482. He could presumably read and write, being a churchman of high rank with a doctor of theology degree, but surviving documents in the PRO and the Hertfordhire Record Office show only various legal and financial transactions by him in his role as abbot of Westminster.

From 1483 to his death in November 1490, John Fogge was probably living somewhere in Kent, although it is difficult to know exactly where, since his holdings in that county were extensive. Records in the National Archive and Kent County Archive record only details of legal and financial dealings and contain no other records of his life.

Despite also having extensive landholdings in Essex and Sussex, from 1483 to his death in 1485, Scott was another who probably resided at one of his properties in Kent. He and Fogge are known to have been close friends. He was sixty years old when Richard came to the throne in 1483 and so may not have been extensively involved in court life during that period. Records from the National Archives and Kent County Archive reflect this, in that they do not contain any records of his life.

Having little involvement with Richard's government, John Alcock probably spent most of his time in his diocese of Worcester. After Bosworth, he returned to court at Westminster before being granted the see of Ely. The National Archives, Worcestershire County Record Office, City of Westminster Archive Centre, Cambridgeshire Archives and the Cambridge University Manuscripts and University Archive do not contain any records of his life.

Edward Storey lived and worked in his diocese of Chicester, West Sussex, spending little time elsewhere during Richard's reign. Records of his life have not been found either in the National Archives or West Sussex Records Office.

Walter Devereux, Lord Ferrers, probably divided his time between London and his estates in Herefordshire, Hertfordshire and Lincolnshire in the years when Richard was on the throne. He would probably not have neglected the extensive connections he must have developed in Wales. The National Archives contain records of his late marriage to Joan Ilam, his attainder of 1485 and various legal matters, while the other sources listed below do not hold any records that include him. It is not known whether he was literate.

It is difficult to know where Sir Richard Haute was living between October 1483 and August 1485, but it is probable that he was permanently residing at one of his Kentish properties. He is thought to have owned a number of books. The National Archives do contain files relating to him, but these are legal records and do not include documents relating to his personal correspondence, written either by him or a secretary. The Berkshire Record Office and Essex Record Office do not contain any records relating to him.

His uncle, Sir William Haute, and his cousins Richard and James were also important in court circles, both William and Richard being part of the October Rebellion. James refused to participate and was rewarded with the Haute family manor of Ightham Mote, which reverted to Sir Richard Haute after Bosworth.[14] The National Archives contains the usual documents relating to legal matters but no personal correspondence from any of these individuals.

Of the servants—Avice Welles, Elizabeth Darcey, John Davison, Adam Grafton, Thomas Bold and John Giles—no records have been located so far in the most readily available archives.

Perspectives

Edward's council was composed of career politicians intent upon extracting maximum advantage for themselves out of their various royal appointments. Edward IV was probably well aware of this, and his selection of the men who surrounded his son was carefully judged to include men with useful experience whose loyalty could be relied upon just as long as it did not conflict with their own self-interest. They would certainly not have been inclined to follow a lost cause, whatever their previous loyalties may have been, and this will have been reflected in their efforts to locate the sons of their former king.

Thomas Bourchier was over seventy in 1483 and had been retired from any role in public affairs since 1480, although despite his age, he was nevertheless much involved in events at the courts of both Richard III and Henry Tudor. However, he was certainly not one of Richard's closest friends, and it remains doubtful that he would have been trusted with information about the boys that might have been used against the new Yorkist regime. Similar considerations also apply to most of the other members of Prince Edward's council, Fogge, Scott, Alcock, Storey, and even Walter Devereux being older men and long-serving officials of Edward IV, whose service to Richard would have been a matter of expediency rather than choice. Consequently they were probably treated with some reserve by the king and would hardly have been trusted with dangerous secrets. Millyng was a slightly younger man but his previous important position on Edward's council may have cast doubt on his loyalty. His role in Richard's government cannot have been very significant, because he had been reinstated and given an important diplomatic mission by Henry Tudor as early as 1487.

Robert Stillington is perhaps more hopeful as an information source, since he was claimed to have known about the precontract, which he subsequently revealed to Richard, resulting in the "Titulus Regius" and giving Richard the opportunity to depose his nephew. Stillington was also the author of the petition presented to Richard by the Three Estates, asking him to accept the crown, so the king's gratitude to the old cleric should have been considerable and lavishly expressed. This was not the case, however, and Stillington seems to have received little consideration from Richard after he occupied the throne. As an intimate of the king and a useful addition to the regime, of course, Stillington's age (75 in 1483) and previous associations were against him. If he did know anything about the two boys, his secrets died with him.

None of the individuals known to have been employed as servants to either Edward or Richard would have possessed sufficient status to learn anything about the boys from Richard or his associates, although what any of them, council members or servants, might have learned inadvertently is obviously a matter for conjecture. However, if any of the council members or servants did learn anything, no record of that information in the form of personal documents or letters has been located so far.

Table 8. Possible Locations of Documents
Left by the Members of Edward's Council

Witness	Possible locations for documents relating to Edward and Richard	Storage of records from these locations
Thomas Bourchier,	Canterbury Cathedral, 1450–1487, during his	Archive of Canterbury Cathedral

Witness	Possible locations for documents relating to Edward and Richard	Storage of records from these locations
Archbishop of Canterbury	tenure as Archbishop of Canterbury	
	London, 1450–1487, during his tenure as Archbishop of Canterbury	National Archive
	Westminster Abbey, 1450–1487, during his tenure as Archbishop of Canterbury	Westminster Abbey Archives
	Knole House, 1456–1487, a manor house purchased for his private use	Kent History and Library Centre
Robert Stillington, bishop of Bath and Wells	London, 1465–1491, bishop of Bath and Wells	National Archives, Kew
	Oxford, 1488–1491, resident at Lincoln College	Oxfordshire History Centre
Thomas Millyng, abbot of Westminster	Westminster Abbey, 1469–1492, during his tenure as abbot of Westminster	National Archives
	Hereford, 1474–1492, during his tenure as bishop	Herefordshire Record Office
Sir John Fogge	One of his Kentish manors	Kent County Archive Public Record Office
Sir John Scott	His Kentish manors	Kent County Archive Public Record Office
John Alcock, dean of Westminster	Worcester, 1476–1486, during his tenure as bishop	Worcestershire County Record Office
	Westminster, 1475, during his tenure as chancellor	City of Westminster Archive Centre
	Ely, 1486–1500, during his tenure as bishop of Ely	Cambridgeshire Archives
	University of Cambridge, 1486–1500, during his tenure as bishop of Ely	Cambridge University Manuscripts and University Archive
Edward Storey, bishop of Chichester	Aldingbourne, West Sussex, during his tenure as bishop of Chichester	West Sussex Records Office

Twelve. Edward's Council and Servants

Witness	Possible locations for documents relating to Edward and Richard	Storage of records from these locations
Walter Devereux, Lord Ferrers	Herefordshire, 1441–1459, one of his Herefordshire manors	Herefordshire Archive and Record Centre
	Hertfordshire, 1484–1485, his manor of Cheshunt, Hertfordshire	Hertfordshire Archive and Local Studies; National Archive for manorial records
	Lincolnshire, 1483–1485, one of his Lincolnshire manors	Lincolnshire Archives
	Wales, 1483–1485, one of his Welsh holdings from his time serving as an administrator	Archives Wales
Sir Richard Haute	Igtham Mote, Kent, owned in succession by Sir William Haute, Sir Richard Haute, and James Haute (not involved in the 1483 revolt). Reverted to Sir Richard Haute in 1485.	Kent History and Library Centre
	Berkshire manors of Sir Richard Haute	Berkshire Record Office
	Essex manors of Sir Richard Haute	The Essex Record Office

CHAPTER THIRTEEN

Richard's Associates

Close Associates

Richard's close associates between 1483 and 1485 included the following:

- Sir Robert Brackenbury
- Sir James Tyrell
- John Howard, Duke of Norfolk
- William Cateby
- Sir Francis Lovell
- Sir Richard Ratcliffe
- John Russell, bishop of Lincoln and lord chancellor
- Edmund Shaa, lord mayor of London
- John Nesfield

SIR ROBERT BRACKENBURY
(c. 1456–1485: approximate age in 1483: 27)

Brackenbury was the second son of Ralph Brackenbury of Denton in the parish of Gainford, County Durham. Richard III, when Duke of Gloucester, had taken possession of nearby Barnard Castle in 1474 after his marriage to Anne Neville, and Brackenbury had probably entered the duke's service by 1477, when his father granted him land in School Aycliffe, County Durham. This could have marked his coming-of-age, making him 21 in that year, although he may have been younger. By 1479 Brackenbury was treasurer of Gloucester's household and one of the duke's feoffees. Two years later, in 1481, he acquired the manor of Selaby, County Durham.

With Richard's assumption of power in 1483, Brackenbury's loyalty was rewarded appropriately. He was made constable of the Tower on 17 July 1483, only days before Richard began his northern progress, and remained in that post until at least the end of the year. In such a position he must have known what happened to the boys, and his retention of the post of constable after their assumed disappearance confirms that Richard must also have known where the boys were. Those two boys were of the first political importance to the king, and if they were removed without his knowledge or permission, the consequences for Brackenbury would have been swift and permanent. Nothing of the sort happened, however, and Brackenbury went on to die at Bosworth with his friend and king. Consequently, if the boys disappeared from the Tower in the summer or autumn of 1483, Brackenbury and Richard must both have been part of the plot.

After Buckingham's revolt, Brackenbury was given land in Kent and was employed as steward to Thomas Bourchier in March 1484, becoming one of the Kent commissioners of the peace in July 1484 and sheriff of Kent in November 1484, before dying at Bosworth with Richard in August 1485.[1]

SIR JAMES TYRELL (c. 1455–1502; age in 1483: 28)

Tyrell's association with the Yorkists began in May 1471, when he was knighted at the age of 16 by Edward IV after the battle of Tewksbury. By the winter of the same year he had entered the service of the king's brother, Richard, Duke of Gloucester. He was advanced rapidly, becoming ducal councilor and feoffee, and was used by Richard on much of his business that was of a particularly sensitive nature, such as conducting the dowager Countess of Warwick northwards in 1473. He served under Richard in the Scottish campaigns of 1480–82, being made banneret and acting in Gloucester's place as chamberlain of the Exchequer and, in November 1482, acting for him as constable of England. He was also elected to serve in the parliament of Edward V and was later appointed master of the King's Horse and also master of his henchmen.

Tyrell had acquired lands in Cornwall after his marriage to Anne Arundel in 1469 and was awarded the stewardship of the Duchy of Cornwall for his role in the suppression of Buckingham's October Rebellion. He was also given authority to seize and administer Buckingham's forfeited Welsh estates. He is known to have been in London during the first week of September 1483 to collect a large quantity of raiment from the wardrobe, including cloth for himself and the king's henchmen, before taking it to York in preparation for the investiture of the Prince of Wales on 8 September.[2] This would have given him an ideal opportunity to move the boys to a safer location, although he could also have used the visit to have them killed, so his presence in London during that period makes either scenario plausible. On 22 January 1485,

Richard made Tyrell lieutenant of Guînes, one of the Calais fortresses, and awarding him 4,500 marks (about £3,000) as payment for his duties in the post, the equivalent of the entire annual royal budget. Tyrell was still in France when Richard died, so if the boys did escape from Gipping Hall after Bosworth, Tyrell could not have participated, although he may have helped to organize their escape from Henry Tudor. Tyrell's failure to support his former king proved fortunate, as Henry subsequently allowed Tyrell to transfer his services to the new regime and retained him in his post at Guînes.

In January 1486, he was summoned back to England to help clear up a dispute over the Countess of Oxford's lands, allegedly coerced from her by Richard. In February, he was restored as sheriff of Glamorgan and appointed constable of Cardiff Castle. Later that year, he was involved in more controversy. On 16 June, Tyrell was granted a royal pardon, presumably excusing his activities while in the service of Richard III, although the reason for this pardon was not explained in the documents associated with the act. Bizarrely, barely a month later, on 16 July 1486, he received a second pardon, which was also issued without any accompanying explanation. Various explanations have subsequently been supplied for the need to issue two pardons, several understandably associated with the murder of the princes, but the most likely explanation seems to be a simple administrative error associated with the loss of the original paperwork. Certainly, if Henry had ordered Tyrell to murder his brothers-in-law, he would hardly have drawn attention to his act by pardoning the murderer—and he certainly need not have done so twice.

Despite holding on to his position after Bosworth, Tyrell never achieved his previous importance, and on 6 May 1502, he was convicted of treason for an alleged plot to place Edmund de la Pole on the throne and was subsequently executed, aged 47. Thomas More claimed that before he died, Tyrell had confessed to the killing of Edward V and his brother Richard, although no copy of his confession has ever been seen and the only record of its contents comes from the account by Sir Thomas of the crime. Whatever its validity, the dissemination of Tyrell's "confession" finally disposed of claims that the princes were still alive, although if Tyrell's closeness to Richard III made him a plausible murderer, he was also (from the Tudor point of view) a very convenient one.[3]

WILLIAM CATESBY (c. 1446–1485; age in 1483: 37)

Catesby was the son of Sir William Catesby of Asby St. Legers, Northamptonshire (d. 1478–79), but instead of remaining in his father's household and becoming involved in the business of farming, he emulated his uncle Sir

Thirteen. Richard's Associates

Ashby St Ledgers, one of William Catesby's manors (photograph by Ian Robb/CC-BY-SA 3.0).

John Catesby (d. 1487) and embarked upon a career in the law. Between 1470 and 1479 Catesby became legal adviser and estate administrator for a number of landowners near his father's home, among the most influential being Elizabeth Beauchamp (the widow of George Neville, Lord Latimer), the Zouches of Harringworth, and his own wife's stepfather, John, Lord Scrope. Undoubtedly the most important connection he made during this period was with William, Lord Hastings, chamberlain and crony to Edward IV.

He began to attain wider prominence, however, in the events leading up to the usurpation of Richard III in 1483, initially becoming linked with Henry Stafford, the Duke of Buckingham, as chancellor of the earldom of March, although Catesby was already well known to the duke previous to this appointment, having acted for him in a number of legal matters during 1475–79. In June, probably in view of his earlier associations, Richard also selected Catesby to approach Hastings about the possibility of usurpation and Hasting's possible role in supporting such a step. It is possible that it was Catesby's plausible soothing of the fears of Hastings and the Stanleys that allowed Richard to trap and execute the former chamberlain so easily.

Immediately upon Richard's accession, Catesby's loyalty was rewarded with several important appointments: esquire of the king's body, chancellor, and chamberlain of the Exchequer; and in the following year, speaker of the only parliament to assemble during Richard's reign, which met in January 1484. As a reward for his continued loyalty during the October revolt he received a number of further marks of royal favor, including several land grants and a part of the Duke of Buckingham's estates. He was also fully employed in other ways during his time with Richard, being sent to Scotland in September 1484 over a proposed treaty and then later that month traveling to Brittany as part of the delegation negotiating the return of Henry Tudor. Catesby was certainly an influential royal councilor, and along with Ratcliffe, was one of those responsible for dissuading Richard from marrying Elizabeth of York in March 1485, after his wife's death. So influential was he seen to be that William Collingbourne composed what has become a famous poem deriding the association:

> The Cat, the Rat and Lovell our Dog
> Rule all England under the Hog.

However, his duties in and about Richard's court did not prevent him from acquiring substantial landholdings, often by means of threats and coercion, and these activities seem to suggest that he was extremely acquisitive, even avaricious. Sir Thomas More said of him: "Besides his excellent knowledge of [English] Law, he was a man of dignified bearing, handsomely featured and of excellent appearance, not only suitable for carrying out assignments but capable also of handling matters of grave consequence." Later, he added, however, "Indeed you would not wish that a man of so much wit should be of so little faith."

He was taken alive at Bosworth but beheaded three days later in Leicester and buried, in accord with his own wishes, in his family grave at Ashby St. Legers. Catesby married twice. His first marriage, some time before December 1471, was to Margaret, the daughter of William, Lord Zouche, his second wife being Elizabeth St. John. Catesby was thus the brother-in-law of another of Richard III's allies: John, Lord Zouche.[4]

SIR FRANCIS LOVELL (1454–c. 1488; age in 1483: 31)

Lovell's association with Richard, then Duke of Gloucester, began when the pair both lived in the house of Richard Neville, Earl of Warwick. In 1466, Lovell married Anne FitzHugh, cousin of Richard's wife, Anne Neville, and after he and his wife had been pardoned for their apparently unwilling part in the Neville rebellion of 1470 (he was 14, while she was probably younger), Lovell became associated with Richard, Duke of Gloucester. He was with

Thirteen. Richard's Associates

Gloucester during the Scots expedition in 1480 and was knighted by Richard for his part in that campaign.

When Richard ascended to the throne, Lovell was promoted to the office of lord chamberlain and made a knight of the Order of the Garter. He was also instrumental in suppressing the October Rebellion and in June 1485 was given responsibility for guarding the south coast against a possible landing by Tudor's forces. Once aware of Tudor's landing at Milford Haven, Lovell appears to have abandoned his post and hastened to Bosworth, where he is claimed to have fought alongside Richard, two reports of the battle even listing him among those killed on the Yorkist side. He did not, however, die at Bosworth but, escaping from the battlefield, sought sanctuary in Colchester. He stayed in the abbey for approximately six months, before traveling north with his allies Humphrey and Thomas Stafford, where the trio organized an abortive uprising in Worcester, in April–May 1486. Deciding not to risk open war with Henry Tudor because of a lack of support from former Yorkists, Lovell escaped to Burgundy at the end of April. Abandoned by Lovell, the Stafford brothers sought sanctuary 75 miles further south, at Culham in Oxfordshire, where, on the night of 13 May 1486, Humphrey was dragged from the parish church and executed, although his younger brother Thomas was subsequently pardoned. By this time Lovell had made his way to the court of Margaret of York, dowager Duchess of Burgundy, where he was joined in the following spring of 1487 by John, Earl of Lincoln.

In the early summer of 1487 Lovell and Lincoln, with military backing supplied by Margaret, launched an invasion of England from Ireland, with the intention of putting the boy previously crowned "King Edward VI" in Dublin Cathedral on the throne of England. Landing on the Furness peninsula on 4 June near the landholding of one of their allies, Sir Thomas Broughton, the rebel army moved rapidly south. As in the previous year, few former Yorkists joined them, and on 16 June the rebels met the king's army at Stoke and, not unexpectedly, were routed. Lincoln was killed and Lovell, according to the reports that reached York, "was discomfited and fled."

His fate after Stoke remains obscure, although he probably headed north after the battle. It was in that direction his wife sent Edward Franke to look for him, although by the following February he had still not been found. Lovell was still alive, however, and eventually arrived in Scotland, where on 19 June 1488, James IV granted a safe conduct to him and a number of his associates. This is the last known reference to Lovell in any official document and, despite stories to the contrary, it seems unlikely that it was his mummified body that was found in a hidden room in Minster Lovell in 1708. Lovell had hardly spent any time at his family home since starting his rise to power and would not have had a faithful servant there who would have consented to take the risk of hiding him. Additionally, the manor had been granted to Jasper Tudor, Henry Tudor's uncle, and consequently was hardly a safe hiding place for an enemy of the king such as Lovell. Lovell and his wife had no children, and she was granted an annuity of £20 from the exchequer in December 1489. She was still alive in 1495, when her interests were protected in her husband's attainder.[5]

Sir Richard Ratcliffe (c. 1450–1485; age in 1483: ~33)

Ratcliffe came from a landed family in the Lake District, and had become associated with Richard some time before 1475. He was one of Richard's trustees in the lordship of Richmond, before being named constable of Barnard Castle, and was knighted by Richard himself at Berwick in 1481, during the Scottish campaigns. He married Agnes Scrope, daughter of Henry Scrope, fourth Baron Scrope of Bolton, some time after the death of her first husband in 1479. The couple had two children, a daughter, Isabel, and a son, Richard, who succeeded in securing the reversal of his father's attainder in 1495.

Ratcliffe was sent north during the spring of 1483, carrying Gloucester's letters of 10 June requesting military help from the city of York "against the queen's affinity." Known to be present when the northern forces mustered at Pontefract a fortnight later, he apparently also presided over the executions of Rivers, Vaughan, and Grey before accompanying the army south. In September 1484 he received a major grant of land (valued at 1000 marks) in the southwest, much of it once held by the Courtenay earls of Devon, although, despite these holdings, he did not have a significant role in the region. His main interests were always in the north and in 1484, the prior of Durham commented on "the great rule that he beareth under the king's grace in our country." In August 1484, Ratcliffe succeeded his uncle, William Parr, as sheriff of Westmorland, subsequently becoming deeply involved in the negotiations for a truce with Scotland, before also succeeding Humphrey, Lord Dacre, in May 1485, as the king's deputy lieutenant on the West March. He was one of Richard's most influential councilors, and together with Catesby and Lovell he advised against the suggestion that Richard consider marrying his niece, Elizabeth of York, on the grounds that it would alienate the king's northern supporters. Now known to have been killed at Bosworth, there was initially some confusion about his fate, Henry insisting on 23 August that Ratcliffe be arrested and brought before him. He was apparently still thought to be at large on 24 September, when he headed the list of those excluded from pardon, but by then his family knew him to be dead, and he was subsequently attainted in Henry VII's first parliament.[6]

Other Associates

JOHN HOWARD, FIRST DUKE OF NORFOLK
(c. 1425–1485: age in 1483: 58)

Created a baron by Edward IV at some time from December 1469 to February 1470, Howard remained a loyal Yorkist for the rest of his life, serving first Edward and then his brother, Richard. On the death of Edward IV, Howard chose to support Richard and was quickly rewarded with the dukedom of Norfolk and the post of earl marshal on 28 June 1483, two days after Richard accepted the crown. In addition, he was given the East Anglian estates previously granted to Richard, Duke of York, after the death of his betrothed, Anne Mowbray, as well as an additional grant of lands and the offices of chief steward of the duchy of Lancaster south of the Trent (13 May 1483) and admiral of England (25 July 1483). In return Howard remained loyal to Richard III, defending London successfully for him during Buckingham's rebellion and dying in the vanguard of his army at Bosworth, aged 60. Both he and his son, Thomas Howard, Earl of Surrey, were attainted by Henry VII's first parliament, although Surrey was eventually restored as second Duke of Norfolk. John Howard was buried at Thetford Priory, the customary burial place of the dukes of Norfolk.[7]

JOHN RUSSELL, BISHOP OF LINCOLN AND LORD CHANCELLOR (c. 1430–1494; age in 1483: 53)

Admitted as a scholar to Winchester College in 1443, Russell then went to New College, Oxford, in 1447, becoming a fellow there in 1449 and sub-warden in 1461, before leaving Oxford in 1462. He had an impressive academic career, becoming a doctor of canon law in December 1459, aged 29, having passed the requisite inferior degrees (BCL and BCnL) during 1454–59. He was an ordained priest by the time he received his first canonry and prebend in 1461, entering the episcopate as bishop of Rochester in 1476.

Russell deliberately chose to exercise his talents in the service of the king rather than the church and turned early to a career in politics. His early rise is not recorded, but in September 1467 he was one of the envoys who negotiated the marriage of Edward IV's sister, Margaret of York, to Charles,

Duke of Burgundy, and he may have had diplomatic business earlier that year in Bruges, where he is known to have bought a copy of Cicero's *De Officiis*. During Henry VI's readeption in 1470–71, he remained a royal servant, serving as an envoy to negotiate a truce with France in February 1471. After Edward IV's return he continued to be employed in negotiations with various continental powers. In 1474, Russell became Keeper of the Privy Seal and in 1480, he received a further promotion to the prestigious post of bishop of Lincoln, although his administrative duties in government prevented him from making more than occasional visits to his diocese.

He was present when Edward IV died. On 10 May Richard appointed him to replace Archbishop Thomas Rotherham of York as chancellor, following Rotherham's dismissal because of his Wydeville associations. Promotion of the Keeper of the Privy Seal to chancellor was not unusual, representing only a minor change in the existing administration, and there seems to have been little significance attached to the appointment by Richard's closest circle. Between Gloucester's arrival in London and Hasting's execution, Russell was responsible for the administration of the late king's will and for preparations for the coronation and first parliament of Edward V. He seems to have supported Richard against the Wydevilles, and he presided over one half of the council that met at Westminster to discuss coronation arrangements on 13 June, while the other half at the Tower of London were witnesses to the arrest and execution of William, Lord Hastings. He was also present on 16 June when Richard of York was moved to the Tower, and he seems to have accepted his role in the regime quite calmly, being confirmed as chancellor on 27 June, the day after Richard's accession. He also participated in the coronation and attended the banquet, although he may have felt he was left with little real alternative. Russell does not seem to have been a strong supporter of Richard, being an administrator rather than a politician, and he seems to have been more involved in the routine legal and financial matters of government than in any of the more significant political schemes.

He quickly came to terms with Henry Tudor after Bosworth, which argues against significant involvement with the late king, and he was employed on several delicate diplomatic missions after 1485, although he was more active in his diocese than previously. He died at his episcopal manor of Nettleham on 30 December 1494, aged 64.[8]

Sir Edmund Shaa (c. 1438–1488)

Lord mayor of London from 1 October 1482 to 29 September 1483, Shaa (or Shaw) was by trade a goldsmith. He was out of his apprenticeship by 1458, probably aged around 20, and four years later, in 1462, he was appointed engraver to the Tower and a number of other English and Calais mints, which suggests he was good at his job. He was also politically ambitious. After two unsuccessful nominations for the London aldermanry, in September 1470 and June 1471, he was eventually elected alderman of Cripplegate ward in July 1473, becoming sheriff the following year. His first attempt to become lord mayor (in September 1481) was unsuccessful, but he was elected to the post in September 1482.

He is known to have made large loans to Edward IV and was serving as lord mayor of London when Edward IV died and throughout the turbulent period leading up to the usurpation of Richard III. According to Sir Thomas More (writing around 1515) and the sixteenth century London chroniclers, it was his brother Ralph Shaw who preached the sermon at Paul's Cross, insisting that Richard was the only lawful claimant to the throne. Ralph seems to have enjoyed some popularity as a preacher prior to this event, but so hostile was Dr. Shaw's audience on this occasion that his death in the following year was said to have been due to chagrin at the cold reception accorded to his sermon.

Edmund Shaw himself, as mayor, was extensively involved in the ceremonies surrounding the coronation of Richard III, and he was subsequently knighted and became a member of the Privy Council. The value of his commercial dealings with Richard and of the grants he received suggests that, at the very least, the king was keen to secure his support. Shaw survived Richard's downfall, dying on 20 April 1488, and he was sufficiently well liked at the Tudor court to have appointed Sir Reginald Bray as one of his executors.

Shaw held properties in Essex worth over £50 per annum at his death, and he was able to bequeath over £4,000 in cash and plate as well as personal and household effects to his beneficiaries. He was survived by his wife, Juliana, a son, Hugh, who died childless a few years later, daughters Margaret (who was married to mercer Thomas Rich) and Katherine (who later married William Brown, another mercer), and four sisters.[9]

JOHN NESFIELD

Nesfield was responsible for guarding the sanctuary at Westminster while Elizabeth Woodville was resident from April 1483 until March 1484, although his name does not appear in any archived record so far examined.

Evidence from Richard's Associates

Between 1483 and his death at Bosworth, Sir Robert Brackenbury lived first in the Tower, serving as its constable until the end of 1483. Being Bourchier's steward and subsequently a Kentish peace commissioner and then sheriff, he must have spent most of his time in that county. It is not known whether Brackenbury was literate, and records in the National Archives and its associated collections of documents only describe his involvement in a number of judicial and financial matters. Neither the Canterbury Cathedral Archive, Durham County record office or Kent History and Library Centre contain any records of his life in those places or any personal documents.

Sir John Tyrell probably divided his time between Gipping Hall, his wife's Cornish estates and Buckingham's forfeited Welsh lands during the period of Richard's reign. There is said to be a tradition in the Tyrell family that the boys and their mother lived in the Tyrell house, Gipping Hall, but unfortunately Gipping Hall was demolished in 1874, and the location of any records that may have been stored there is not known. Records from one of Tyrell's Arundel estates are still in existence, but they describe only the mundane activities associated with a life on the land during that period. After Bosworth, he appears to have become permanently established at Guînes, until his trial and execution in 1502. Tyrell's educational accomplishments are not a matter of record. The National Archives and its associated collections contain documents describing his appointment as Richard's chamberlain, an account roll from his Cornish estates and a notice relating to the demolition of Gipping Hall, while other documents deal only with his involvement in judicial and financial matters.

Between the time of his appointments within Richard's government and death at Bosworth, William Catesby must have been required to spend most of his time in London. He was trained as a lawyer, not a soldier like most of Richard's closest friends, and so he would have been well educated and literate. This is reflected in the large number of documents referring to him in the National Archives during this period, thirty-one in total. Unfortunately most of these records are only of a legal or financial nature, principally transfers of land or property into his possession, and there does not appear to be anything written in his own hand that clarifies the fate of the boys.

Like Catesby, Francis Lovell could read and write, because he wrote at least two letters to his cousin, Sir William Stonor, urging him in one of them to come and support Richard during the October Rebellion.[10] Between July 1483 and Bosworth, Lovell probably spent most of his time in London, and

Thirteen. Richard's Associates

any writings he left from that period would have been found there. After Bosworth he was either in sanctuary at Colchester or in Worcester, before escaping to Margaret of York in Burgundy. He is next heard of in Ireland and then England, but his movements after the battle of Stoke are obscure, although he is recorded as in Scotland in 1488. Unfortunately, his whereabouts after that and even the place he died remain a complete mystery. Existing records in the National Archives are confined to two letters sent by him to Stonor and descriptions of his attainder after Bosworth, this archive and its related collections of documents from the period containing no other personal correspondence.

Unlike Catesby and Lovell, no record has been left of Richard Ratcliffe's education, and consequently, the extent of his literacy is not known. Between July 1483 and his death at Bosworth, he was usually in the north of England, concerned with keeping the peace in the king's name. He was certainly one of Richard's closest friends and seems to have been a man the king relied upon, as witnessed by his inclusion in Collingbourne's epigram. This close association probably meant he knew what had happened to the boys, although he left no record of their fate in any archived documents so far examined.

In the two years before his death at Bosworth, Thomas Howard spent a significant proportion of his time visiting all the estates he owned in the counties of Norfolk, East Anglia, Suffolk and Surrey, although he appears to have spent most of that period in East Anglia. He was visiting his Sussex properties in the autumn of 1483, and this meant he was able to reach Gravesend without loss of time and organize a successful defense of the river crossings at that point against the Kentish rebels. His presence at Gravesend during the autumn of 1483 placed him only 25 miles from the boys' last residence, so he could have known what happened to them. The extent of Howard's education is not known, and records in the National Archives and its associated collections only describe his involvement in a number of judicial and financial matters, including a record of his household accounts from 1481 to 1491.

From the time of his appointment as lord chancellor and Richard's death at Bosworth, John Russell must have been obliged to spend most of his time in London, although he was not always at court. After Bosworth, he spent a proportionately greater time in Lincoln, although some of his letters were addressed from London, so he must have been there as well. It has been suggested that he was the author of the "civil service" continuation of the Crowland Chronicle, although this claim is now considered to be unlikely. Other records include Chancery pleadings from Russell's tenure as chancellor and other documents of a legal and financial nature.

During his tenure as lord mayor (September 1482 to September 1483) Edmund Shaa would certainly have lived in London, probably in the Cripplegate ward, where he had spent most of his life. Records concerning the lord mayor are held in the London Metropolitan Archives, but unfortunately, these documents only refer to events from 1659 to 1879, although they do include a complete list of lord mayors from the first, Henry Fitz-Ailwyn in 1189, up to the present day. The National Archives only contain records of a number of legal and financial dealings including a number of summonses for debt and a proceeding against the Earl of Kent for the return of a felon, one William Marchall, taken by force from the custody of Shaa and his fellow sheriff of London, Thomas Hill, which is dated some time between 1475 and 1480. It is not known if Shaa was literate, although it would have been unusual for a merchant of that period to be unable to read and write and his accounting skills would have been good, even if he was so unwise as to lend money to Edward IV.

Perspectives

This group contains most of the men likely to have had knowledge of the boys' whereabouts, if they were alive after the autumn of 1483: Brackenbury, the constable; Tyrell, the subtle facilitator; Howard, the loyal retainer and experienced soldier; Catesby, the lawyer; Ratcliffe, the brutal mailed fist; and Lovell, the courtier, loyal and devious in his friend's service.

Each of these men had an important role in Richard's short-lived government, and each would have been necessary for the maintenance of whatever charade Richard was perpetrating around his nephews' disappearance. However, some would have been more important and useful than others. Who could Richard not have done without?

Brackenbury must have had an important role in the plot to organize the boys' disappearance, whatever it was intended that their fate should be. They were in his custody, and their release into any other hand required his willing agreement and probably a signed order. Tyrell seems implicated by the length of his service to Richard as well as his inclusion in More's *Historie* and Henry's persecution. Catesby, Ratcliffe and Lovell were at the core of Richard's organization and had been his friends and associates for many years. If they were not involved, they would have been apprised of developments as soon as possible, because all three were too useful to Richard not to have been asked for advice and help, as they were when marriage to Elizabeth of York was being contemplated. These five were all young men, around thirty

Thirteen. Richard's Associates

in 1483, and were hardly likely to let the deaths of two little boys stand in the way of their own advancement.

Howard is perhaps a different matter. He was older than the rest, fifty-eight in 1483, with grown children of his own. Nor was his association with Richard of long standing, since he had only offered the new king his support after the death of Edward IV. Consequently, Richard may have been reluctant to share his knowledge about the boys with the old duke, although Howard may have discovered some relevant information independently. Russell or Shaa were also new and not particularly close adherents of the king, their rapid acceptance by Tudor after Bosworth in particular implying that this was so; and, like Howard, they would hardly have been trusted with any sort of information that might prove dangerous to the new regime.

With the exception of Catesby, Lovell and Russell, the educational accomplishments of the men in this group are not recorded, and however certain their role as well-informed conspirators, it is equally certain that none of the group left any sort of written record directly concerning the boys in any archive or document examined so far.

Table 9. Possible Locations of Documents
Left by Richard's Associates

Witness	Possible locations of documents	Storage of records from these locations
Sir Robert Brackenbury	Selasby, County Durham	Durham County Record Office
	Canterbury Cathedral during his tenure as Bourchier's steward	Archive of Canterbury Cathedral
	County of Kent, while serving as commissioner of peace and sheriff	Kent History and Library Centre
Sir John Tyrell	Gipping Hall (1455–83)	Suffolk Record Office
	Cornish estates inherited from John Arundel (1483–85)	Cornwall Record Office
	Buckingham's Welsh estates (1483–85)	Glamorgan Record Office
	Guines (1485–1502)	Pas-de-Calais Departmental Archive
John Howard, Duke of Norfolk	Thetford Priory, Norfolk (Duke of Norfolk 1483–85)	Society of Antiquaries of London
	Surrey and Sussex (granted estates in those counties; 1483–85)	West Sussex Record Office

Witness	Possible locations of documents	Storage of records from these locations
William Catesby	London	National Archives, Kew
Francis Lovell	London, during his tenure as lord chamberlain (1483–85)	National Archive
	Colchester Abbey, during his six months in sanctuary	Colchester City Archive
	Worcester, although his brief stay and interest in organizing the rebellion makes it unlikely he wasted time leaving any records.	Worcester City Archive
	Flanders, during his stay with Margaret of York	Mechelin City Archive
	Ireland and England during Simnel/Lincoln rebellion. Record keeping unlikely.	Dublin City Archive Stoke City Archive
Sir Richard Ratcliffe	Westmoreland, during his tenure as sheriff	Cumberland and Westmoreland Archives
	Wales, during his tenure as king's deputy; lieutenant of the Western Marches	Welsh National Archives[11]
	London, while at court as one of Richard's most trusted councilors	National Archives Westminster Abbey Archive
	The north, while serving as Richard's deputy in that region	York City Archives Durham City Archives Durham Cathedral Library Northumberland Archive
John Russell, lord chancellor	London, before Bosworth, during his tenure as chancellor	National Archives
	London, after Bosworth, involved in diplomatic missions for Henry VII	Lincolnshire Archives
	Lincoln Cathedral, after Bosworth	National Archives
Edmund Shaa, lord mayor of London	London, during his tenure as lord mayor	National Archives
	His Essex manors	The Essex Record Office

CHAPTER FOURTEEN

Henry Tudor and His Early Associates

Early Associates

Individuals associated with Henry Tudor who might have been expected to know something about the fate of the boys include the following:

- John Morton, chancellor and Archbishop of Canterbury
- Sir Reginald Bray, chief councilor to Margaret Beaufort
- William Collingbourne, executed by Richard as a spy and traitor
- Margaret Beaufort, mother of Henry Tudor

HENRY TUDOR (1457–1509; age in 1483: 26)

The role of Henry Tudor (later Henry VII) as a witness does not become of major importance until August 1485, when he defeated Richard at the Battle of Bosworth Field. Up to that time, he was living in France, and the circumstances would have ensured that his personal knowledge of the boys and their whereabouts was nothing but superficial, although he may have had knowledge of them from English supporters such as Collingbourne. After Bosworth, however, he quickly began to tighten his hold on England's political establishment, and although he lacked experience with English politics and—particularly—the English court, this did not prove a significant handicap. With the help of associates such as John Morton and Sir Reginald Bray, he was able to establish an efficient regime. His marriage to Elizabeth of York emphasized and consolidated the union of the Houses of York and Lancaster and was intended to heal the centuries-old dynastic wounds that had plagued England since the time of Richard II.

Although Henry was assiduous in introducing talented individuals from both the Yorkist and Lancastrian factions into his government, the early part of his reign was unfortunately marred by a succession of Yorkist-led plots intended to remove him from the throne. Lambert Simnel in February 1487 and Warbeck in 1491 were the most serious, but there were also a number of minor rebellions led by disenchanted Yorkists such as Lovell and Humphrey Stafford, as well as trouble in Ireland from the Kildares and Fitzgeralds. Henry responded to these threats in a number of ways but, significantly, he created a network of spies and informers that not only covered Britain and Ireland but also extended its reach into most of the courts of Europe. This organization helped him to deal effectively with the many threats to his regime and must have provided him, incidentally, with significant information about much that went on in his kingdom, possibly including the previous location of his two brothers-in-law.

By the end of 1497, Henry had Warbeck in secure custody in the Tower. It was at this point, in the final ten years of his reign and after the deaths of many of his more senior advisers such as Morton and Bray, that he began to make a serious attempt to maximize his income. Beginning around 1504, he exploited his legitimate sources of income with a consistent ruthlessness that drew protests from all and sundry, even a young Thomas More, and he even added to his treasury by unsavory means such as the sale of official offices. The king's favor was also available in the law courts … but always at a price.

By the end of his reign in 1509, he had a considerable yearly income, gleaned from land and customs revenue, taxation of both noble landowners and the clergy, and a number of much less savory means. Bacon regarded him as obsessively and consistently avaricious, although later historians considered that his reign exerted a stabilizing influence as well as marking the advent of a more powerful middle class and a concomitant diminution in the influence of the noble landowners. This view has been challenged by recent work on Henry's court, as well as his political and judicial organization and especially his relations with the church; and just how innovative and successful he was during his time on the throne is still a matter for debate among historians.

Henry was often secretive and inscrutable to his contemporaries and even those closest to him, and this feature of his character was never more clearly shown than in his revelations, or rather lack of them, concerning his two young brothers-in-law.[1]

JOHN MORTON (c. 1428–1500; approximate age in 1483: 55)

Morton's early career centered around Oxford and the university, where he practiced law. He became BCL in 1448, which would have made him around twenty years old, gaining his degree of DCL in 1452. However, in 1453 he is recorded as moving to Shellingford, Berkshire, where he had been appointed rector. In 1456, he became chancellor to Edward, Prince of Wales (son of Henry VI), a post he continued to occupy until the battle of Towton put Edward IV on the throne. Although Morton was always Lancastrian in his sympathies, with the death of prince Edward and his father, he finally came to terms with the regime of Edward IV. Having received a royal pardon, he quickly became a valued member of Edward's inner circle and was responsible for several changes in the proceedings of the Courts of Chancery as well as carrying out a number of sensitive diplomatic missions.

When Richard ascended the throne, however, Morton's fortunes changed. He was arrested at the council meeting of 13 June 1483 that led to the summary execution of William, Lord Hastings, and by the end of July had been placed in the custody of the Duke of Buckingham at Brecon, where he may have persuaded the ambitious but vacillating duke to commit himself to open rebellion. He was attainted in January 1484, after the revolt had failed, and eventually escaped to Flanders, where he actively engaged in the consolidation of an anti–Ricardian coalition involving both Henry Tudor, whom he had warned of a plot to deliver him from his refuge in Brittany to Richard, and the family of Queen Elizabeth, widow of Edward IV. Although he was pardoned by King Richard in December 1484, in order to win back his loyalty, Morton ignored this and went to Rome, where he arrived some time before 31 January 1485. His purpose, perhaps, was to secure a dispensation for the marriage of Henry Tudor and Elizabeth of York, and also to prepare the pope for the forthcoming military and political action. If this was the reason for his journey, he was eminently successful, because after the battle of Bosworth, Pope Innocent VIII (1484–92) gave full support to Henry VII's regime. Morton probably did not mastermind the Tudor rebellion, but he was a vital intermediary, securing papal acquiescence for the enterprise as well as taking part in a number of other key enterprises associated with Tudor's victory.

After his return to England, Morton was appointed to the vacant archbishopric of Canterbury in 1486, becoming a member of the King's Council and chancellor on 6 March 1487. Although he was blamed for the high taxation that characterized the first twelve years of the Henry's reign and was said to be responsible for the infamous "Morton's fork," after his death in 1500 at the age of about 80, it became clear to a number of observers, Polydore Virgil in particular, that Morton and his contemporary Reginald Bray had been largely responsible for restraining Henry's harsher fiscal policies, rather than initiating them.

His role in Edward and Richard's story is as an information source rather than active participant, in that it has been claimed that he was responsible for supplying Thomas More with much of the information he subsequently used in his account of the murders of the princes. More describes him very favorably, perceiving him as very learned, honorable in his conduct, and of great natural wit and political skill.²

Sir Reginald Bray (1440–1503; age in 1483: 43)

Sir Reginald Bray was born in Worcestershire and was in service with Henry Tudor's mother, Margaret Beaufort and her second husband, Henry, Lord Stafford, from 1465 until Stafford's death in 1471. He continued in Margaret Beaufort's service after that date and is thought to have acted as liaison between her and John Morton as well as having either recruited or collaborated with Sir Giles Daubney, Sir John Cheney and both the Guildfords. Despite receiving a pardon from Richard in January 1484, Bray is also thought to have been one of the primary conspirators and fundraisers for Henry Tudor's invasion in 1485. His role in the accession seems to have been borne out by Henry's immediate bestowal upon him of a number of significant rewards. He was out of England during the period in which Edward and Richard disappeared, so is unlikely to have been involved as a participant in their disappearance, although he undoubtedly knew or guessed accurately what had happened to them. Consequently, a search for Bray's documents should be concentrated after 1485.³

William Collingbourne (c. 1454–1484; age in 1483: ~29)

William Collingbourne's early history is not absolutely clear. The first record of the man responsible for the famous limerick concerns his activities in Wiltshire and the City of London, during a period when he was buying up properties. During the 1470s, he was involved in legal actions for the collection of debts and against trespassers, most of this litigation involving Kentish residents, so he may have also acquired property in that county as well. He married sometime before 1474, to Margaret, daughter and heiress of John Norwood and widow to Sir James Pykeryng. In common with all the landed gentry he would have married young, so assuming he was approximately 20 at the time of his first marriage, his date of birth would have been around 1454. Margaret Pykeryng had at least two children from her first marriage, Edward and Elen, and she also had two daughters by Collingbourne: Margaret, who later married a George Chaderton, and Jane, who married a James Louder or Lowther, MP for Marlborough in 1491 or 1492.

Collingbourne did well under Edward IV. As well as his financial and legal activities, Collingbourne also held several administrative posts in Wiltshire, serving as sheriff in 1474 and 1481 and commissioner of peace in 1475 and 1478–81. Named in 1475 to "enquire into certain treasons, Lolardries, heresies and errors" in Dorset and Wiltshire, which involved both the dukes of Clarence and Gloucester, he also held a number of other significant appointments until the king's death in 1483, and this included the administration of two manors in Wiltshire.

When Richard became king, however, Collingbourne may have found himself out of favor; and by October, he seems to have decided to side with the southern rebels. At some point from July 1483 to July 1484, he also contacted Tudor, Dorset and a number of other rebels, through an intermediary, Thomas Yate, telling him "to declare unto them that they should very well to return into England with all such power as they might get before the feeat of St Luke the Evangelist [18 October] next ensuring' and furthermore to advise the French king, that negotiations with Richard were useless as the new King meant to make war on France."

This correspondence and the rhyme he is alleged to have written about Lovell, Catesby and Ratcliffe and pinned to the door of St. Paul's Cathedral in July 1484 were sufficient to condemn him for treason. He was executed at Tower Hill, in a public execution as a common criminal, in October or November 1484.[4]

Margaret Beaufort (1443–1509; age in 1483: 40)

Margaret's paternal great-grandfather was John of Gaunt, duke of Lancaster, the fourth son of Edward III, and her family was the illegitimate result of Gaunt's liason with Katherine Swynford. Margaret's first betrothal was to John de la Pole, but this was dissolved in favor of a marriage to Edmund Tudor in 1455, when Margaret was twelve. The marriage appears to have been consummated immediately, although Tudor paid for his brutality, succumbing to the plague in November 1456. Margaret gave birth to her son, Henry Tudor, on 28 January 1457 and this early experience of childbirth may have damaged her mentally as well as physically, because she bore no more children.

In January 1458, aged fifteen, she married her second husband, Henry Stafford. Edward IV assumed the throne in 1461 and the wardship of her son was given to William, Lord Herbert. Although he was still under Herbert's wardship, Henry Tudor's position become more hazardous in 1471, when he became a significant Lancastrian claimant for the throne after the deaths of Henry VI and his son Edward. This was a particularly dangerous position for him in the England of Edward IV, and Margaret acted quickly to distance Tudor from the court, sending her son to France out of Edward's reach and subsequently marrying an influential courtier, Thomas Stanley, when her second husband died in 1471. These actions protected her position with the king and subsequently allowed her to establish herself on a secure financial basis.[5]

Upon Richard's usurpation, Margaret sought an accommodation that would allow her son to return and marry into the royal family. However, when the rumors of the deaths of Edward and Richard began to be accepted, she aligned herself with the rebels and may even have been part of the plot to gain access to the boys in July 1483. Certainly, by the autumn of 1483, she had opened negotiations with Elizabeth Wydeville to arrange a marriage between her son and Elizabeth of York. Unfortunately, with the collapse of the October revolt she was dangerously placed and only her marriage to Stanley, who had remained loyal to Richard, saved her. She was not attainted in the parliament of 1484, but all her property was made over to her husband, and provisions for Henry Tudor's inheritance were canceled. Stanley was also made responsible for her secure custody, without household servants to wait upon her. These conditions did not prevent her communicating with her son both in France and when he landed in Wales, and it was Richard's betrayal by her in-laws, the Stanley family, at Bosworth that helped Henry Tudor to the throne.

After Tudor's ascent to the throne, Margaret came to have a significant role in the affairs of government. She was declared "femme sole" at Henry's first parliament and thus became responsible for her own actions at law, independent of her husband, and her inherited properties were subsequently redistributed between Margaret and her husband. She received land from the Crown in Devon, Lincolnshire, Cambridgeshire and Kendal, which had formerly belonged to Henry Holland, Duke of Exeter, and her position at court and in local government eventually became second only to that of her son. She was as acquisitive and ruthless as her son, in one instance acquiring properties in Wiltshire and Somerset as heir of her great-uncle, Cardinal Henry Beaufort, by depriving Edward Plantagenet of his inheritance of them as Earl of Warwick and Salisbury in 1492. She died aged 66 in 1509, two months after her son.[6]

Evidence from Henry Tudor's Associates

Although he traveled widely during his reign, Henry Tudor's permanent base was London, and it is in that city's records that personal documents such as memoranda or letters relating to Edward and Richard will probably be found, among the 11,000 documents in the National Archive that are listed as pertaining to Henry Tudor.

The National Archives of Great Britain and its associated collections hold a large collection relating also to Henry's chancellor. Over 4,500 entries are associated with John Morton as either Archbishop of Canterbury or chancellor, and the Canterbury Cathedral archive contains, in addition, twenty-nine original documents concerning him. Since he was a highly respected churchman, he was certainly both literate and probably numerate and was thus capable of leaving some sort of written record, although so far such a document has not been located.

Reginald Bray is much less well known, the National Archives containing no records of his life, nor any that describe his education, either in terms of his literacy or numeracy, although his position in the Stafford house argues that he was competent in both those skills from an early age.

By contrast, William Collingbourne is known to have been literate. From July 1483 to his execution in 1484, he was probably dividing his time between London and one of his Wiltshire manors. There are no records in the National Archives referring to him during this period, although there is a single, earlier Chancery writ endorsed by him as sheriff of Wiltshire, dated 1470.

For a woman with such a direct role in government, Margaret Beaufort appears to be the subject of relatively few documents. Records in the National Archives and Canterbury Cathedral archive describe only a number of financial and legal transactions including a Papal Bull confirming the foundation of Christ's College, Cambridge.

Perspectives

Although there have been times in the past when revisionists have turned in desperation to Henry Tudor as the one responsible for the boys' murder, there is very little to implicate him or any of his associates in the disappearance of Edward and Richard. The most damning evidence against Henry is that he did not take the obvious course of revealing the location of the bodies of his brothers-in-law nor their murderer, if he knew them, when confronted with Simnel and Warbeck. That omission has led to the frequently repeated suggestion that this joint failure meant he knew they were alive, although not where they were living, and consequently was concerned that one of the boys might actually have reappeared as one of these pretenders. However, if he did have information about their whereabouts he does not appear to have shared it with anyone else. It is only his actions that some authors feel point to secret knowledge, and those actions are open to other interpretations. Most obviously, he may have refrained from revealing the whereabouts of the boy's bodies or accusing their murderer because he felt that he would not have been believed and that such a revelation would have been seen by many as a little too convenient, if presented without overwhelming corroborative evidence. Henry, after all, was not a well-loved king, nor was he a figure to inspire trust in those he ruled.

It does seem unlikely, however, that he was directly responsible for their deaths. If he had found them living somewhere in England it is extremely doubtful that the boys would have survived their first meeting with their brother-in-law, for the most obvious of reasons. Consequently, if he had arranged to have them killed, displaying their bodies and affixing the blame to their wicked uncle Richard (who was already implicated) would have been a relatively simple matter and, moreover, would have avoided any of the complications he suffered from the Simnel and Warbeck conspiracies. It is equally difficult to accept, however, that he knew absolutely nothing about their fate after July 1483, because of the efficiency of his countrywide network of agents and informers. Henry either knew they were dead but did not feel that the evidence he could present was conclusive; or he knew they were alive but could not arrange for their removal because either (a) his organization had lost sight of them completely or (b) he knew their location but for some reason could not deal with them summarily. Either one of these scenarios would explain his subsequent difficulties with the pretenders and with Warbeck, in particular.

Morton and Bray may both have known something about the boys' disappearance, but if they did, neither man has left any record, although they would have certainly revealed such knowledge to Tudor. Unfortunately, neither was in a very good position to be the recipient of secret knowledge about Edward and Richard's movements during the critical period from July to December 1483. Morton was imprisoned in Brecon, probably until October, after which time he was running for his life until the end of the year, while Bray spent the whole period with Margaret Beaufort in France. After 1485 and their return to power, such men certainly could have discovered the details of the boys' disappearance, but if they did, their discovery has not become common knowledge.

Collingbourne and his associates seem more hopeful as witnesses. Collingbourne himself could have been in London during the summer and autumn of 1483 and discovered something about the boys' disappearance. Once again, however, no record remains in his personal correspondence,

Fourteen. Henry Tudor and His Early Associates

although he survived until sometime in the autumn of 1484 and so could have left a document containing relevant information about the boys, either as a letter or diary entry.

Margaret Beaufort as a witness presents something of an enigma. This was a lady of powerful intellect with formidable organizational skills. She had initially tried to interest Richard in allowing her son to return to England. It is interesting that after the rumors of the boys' death began to spread, she wholly abandoned Richard and concentrated her efforts on negotiating a marriage for her son to the eldest daughter of Edward IV. In this context, it also seems significant that she was never claimed to have suggested alternative arrangements for her son if the boys were found alive. The Tudor sources are not wholly reliable about this period, their claim being that the October Rebellion was based on the assumptions that the boys were dead and that Henry Tudor was the sole candidate for the crown. Consequently, any suggestion that Margaret Beaufort might have been unsure about the fate of the boys and was keeping her options open while negotiating with Elizabeth Wydeville would probably have been disregarded by her son's chroniclers. Upon her return to England, her private information sources would have been considerable, and presumably anything she discovered would have been passed on to her son, with the same, inevitable result for the sons of Edward IV.

Unfortunately, despite the huge numbers of documents in the National Archives that refer to some members of this group, none of these records include any reference to Edward, either as Prince Edward or Edward V; and nor do any refer to his younger brother, either as Prince Richard or Richard, Duke of York.

Table 10. Possible Locations of Documents Left by Henry Tudor's Associates

Witness	Possible locations of documents	Storage of records from these locations
Henry Tudor	London, 1485–1509, the Tudor court	National Archives, Kew Westminster Abbey Archives
	Flanders (January 1484–October 1485)	The relevant archive is the State Archive of Belgium, which unfortunately only contains documents from 16th century onwards.
John Morton, Chancellor	Brecon, July 1483–January 1484, during his period as a prisoner	National Archives
	Flanders, January 1484–October 1485, while in exile	The relevant archive is the State Archive of Belgium, which

Section IV: Witnesses

Witness	Possible locations of documents with Henry Tudor	Storage of records from these locations unfortunately only contains documents from 16th century onwards.
	Canterbury, 1485–1500, during his tenure as archbishop	Archives of Canterbury Cathedral
	London, 1485–1500, during his tenure as chancellor	National Archives, Kew
Sir Reginald Bray	London, 1485–1503, during his service as advisor to both Margaret Beaufort and Henry Tudor	National Archives, Kew
William Collingbourne	London, 1483–84, while trying to foment rebellion against Richard, both before and after the October Rebellion	National Archives, Kew
	Wiltshire, August 1483– November 1483, during the October Rebellion	National Archives, Kew Wiltshire County Archives
Margaret Beaufort	Estates in Devon and Somerset 1472	National Archives, Kew Devon County archives
	Stanley estates in Cheshire, Lancashire and North Wales, 1473, after her marriage	National Archives Welsh National Archives
	Grant of land, 1486, Devon, Lincolnshire Cambridge and Kendal	National Archives Cambridgeshire archives
	Wiltshire and Somerset, law suit, 1492	National Archives Devon County archives

Chapter Fifteen

The October Rebels

Although Croyland claims that there was no rumor of the boys' death until October 1483, many of the leaders of the rebellion must have known or suspected what had happened to them before this date. The rebels were almost exclusively moderately prosperous southern landowners who had done well under Edward IV and probably raised their insurrection because of resentment generated by the favoritism Richard had shown to his northern retainers. Although it has been claimed that the initial cause of the rebellion was the rumor that was spread about Edward and Richard having been killed by their uncle, in fact, the Croyland writer says specifically that the rumor about their death was spread *after* Buckingham had accepted nominal leadership of the rebellion. Altruism was not a strong factor with these minor landowners, and current historical thought has begun to favor the suggestion that, after rumors of the boys' death had been spread, the rebels were intent upon placing Elizabeth of York on the throne with Henry Tudor as her ineffectual, powerless consort. Having regard to the nature of the men involved in the rebellion, this seems a much more likely scenario than a pointless revolt resulting from an outburst of loyalty to the outgoing regime. The contention that Tudor was viewed as a prospective candidate for the throne from as early as October 1483 now seems more likely to be wishful thinking on the part of later writers whom Tudor was paying to write what he wanted to read.

A number of these rebels were probably capable of leaving some written record, and these men included the following:

- Henry Stafford, Duke of Buckingham
- Sir William Stonor, who is known to have corresponded with his wife
- Richard Hill, bishop of London, 1489–96
- Peter Courtenay, who was bishop of Exeter in 1478 and later appointed bishop of Winchester

The Rebels

HENRY STAFFORD, DUKE OF BUCKINGHAM
(1455–83; age in 1483: 28)

Born on 4 September 1455, Henry Stafford was the son of Humphrey Stafford, Earl of Stafford, and was related via his grandmother to the Nevilles of Westmorland. His mother was Margaret Beaufort, daughter of Edmund Beaufort, Duke of Somerset, and Eleanor Beauchamp, daughter of the Earl of Warwick. Consequently, as Stafford's oldest son, Henry was both rich and well connected, although this did not save him when Edward decided to marry him into the royal family and monopolise the wealth from his land-holdings.

The deaths of both his father and grandfather saw him enter into his inheritance at the age of four, and sometime before May 1465, at the insistence of the king, he was married to Katherine Wydeville, the new queen's sister. This was a match that Buckingham is said to have detested because of his bride's humble origins and her lack of any dowry. His treatment after Edward's return to the throne in 1471 was not consistent with his place as husband of the queen's sister, and there appears to have been some trouble between the pair during the 1475 expedition to France, which was sufficient to keep Buckingham out of any important public office during the rest of Edward's reign.

However, this situation changed with the king's death in 1483. Buckingham quickly allied himself with the new protector, Richard, Duke of Gloucester, and together the two men intercepted the new king at Stoney Stratford. They secured his escort, which included Earl Rivers, Richard Wydeville, and Thomas Vaughan, whom they sent north under guard, while the two dukes escorted Edward to London.

Buckingham became Gloucester's most important ally during the next three months. On 15 May 1483, he was given overall control of Wales and the Marches, becoming chief justice and chamberlain of both north and south Wales for life, and being granted the supervision and governance of the king's subjects there, with the control of royal castles, nomination to offices, and the right to raise troops. He was also given the oversight of Shropshire, Herefordshire, Somerset, Wiltshire, and Dorset, which again included powers to raise troops. Most importantly and as a sign of Richard's faith in his new friend, he was excused from rendering financial accounts for all these new holdings.

Richard went even further, proclaiming on 10 June that the queen and her adherents were plotting the murder of himself and Buckingham "and the old royal blood of the realm" and demanding that his northern allies send troops to the capital. Hasting's death on 13 June allowed Buckingham to reestablish his family's power in the north midlands, from which it had been largely excluded by Edward IV's promotion of Hastings, and the late chamberlain's retinue was now reported to have "become my lord of Buckingham's." Buckingham was part of the delegation headed by Cardinal Bourchier that persuaded the queen to hand over Richard, Duke of York, from sanctuary on 16 June. He also addressed the lord mayor and his councilors at the Guildhall on 24 June, setting out Gloucester's claim to the throne. His involvement began to be increasingly important to Richard's regime, seeing him given the "chief rule and devising" of Richard's coronation on 6 July, followed by appointment to the office of constable (which was hereditary to his Bohun ancestors) and chamberlain on 15 July. Along with these titles he was also given life custody of the castle at Tutbury, Staffordshire, which was a key strategic outpost in the north Midlands; this post was previously occupied by Lord Hastings. Clearly, up to this point Richard was treating him as a trusted servant, despite their association being of only a short duration, and his rewards, in fact, were considerably more than Richard had given the northerners who had supported him for much longer.

Some time in the summer of 1483, Buckingham made his catastrophic decision to rebel against his new king. His reasons for this course of action have never been clear, although he may have been persuaded to act so impulsively by his captive, John Morton. Richard showed his resentment and anger when he heard about Buckingham's conduct in a letter to his chancellor, John Russell, in which he described Buckingham as "the most untrewe creature lyving." Whatever his motivation, disaster soon overtook Buckingham and he was executed at Salisbury on 2 November 1483.

Little information is available about the duke away from the intrigues of court. He probably supported Richard's usurpation because he resented his exclusion from political power by Edward IV, although his subsequent rebellion suggests an inherent instability, which Edward may have suspected as early as the French trip in 1475. He seems to have been an unintelligent, superficial young man without any political acumen and particularly lacking the ability in local politics so necessary in a major landowner of that period. His rhetorical talents may have been slightly more impressive, although nothing is known specifically about his religious or cultural interests.[1]

Sir William Stonor (1449–1494; age in 1483: 34)

Stonor's rise as part of the regime of Edward IV began in 1478 and his involvement was mostly within the political and economic environment of the Thames Valley, where he held important local offices in Oxfordshire. His rise within Edward's hierarchy was steady rather than spectacular, but he made the mistake of joining the October Rebellion of 1483, for which he was attainted and his lands given to Francis Lovell. His location after October of that year is not known for certain, but he may have escaped to Brittany with Thomas Gray. His estates were restored, and in 1487, he fought for Tudor at the battle of Stoke. His relationship with the king is thought to have been close as evidenced by his appointment as steward to Oxford University in 1492, two years before his death in 1494. He was married three times, and his wives brought him property in London, Devon and Cornwall.[2]

RICHARD HILL (c. 1443–96; age in 1483: 40)

Hill is thought to have been born in Cricklade, Wiltshire, and he appears to have been related to Owain ap Maredudd, the royal attorney in south Wales from 1487 to 1509, although how extensive these Welsh connections were is not clear.

He appears to have studied at Oxford, graduating with a BCnL. He did reasonably well under Edward IV in a small way, being granted the wardenship of St. John's Hospital, Dorchester, in 1477. However, Richard dispossessed him in December 1483 and also ordered the seizure of his goods, presumably as a result of his involvement with the October rebels. He may have joined Henry Tudor for a period in France, but he was back 31 May 1485, because he acted as proctor for the institution of a parson to Holy Trinity Church, Dorchester.

His prospects improved after Bosworth, Tudor appointing him dean of the Chapel Royal and confirming his wardenship of St. John's Hospital at the November Parliament. He was also granted custody of a manor in Dorset and given a number of lucrative ecclesiastical appointments in Salisbury, Dorset, Swansea and London, eventually being consecrated bishop of London on 15 November 1489. This seems to have marked the end of his useful service with Henry, although Hill was involved in several confrontations with John Morton, from 1494 until just prior to his death.

He seems to have been an able, aggressive churchmen, content to divide his time between ecclesiastical and lay matters. He certainly formed a close relationship with Henry VII, being described on his death as "parrain" or spiritual father to the king.[3]

Fifteen. The October Rebels 179

Powderham Castle, home of the Courtenay dukes of Devon during the reign of Richard III (Wikipedia).

PETER COURTENAY (1432–92; age in 1483: 51)

Courtenay was the third son of Sir Phillip Courtenay of Powderham, who was head of a junior branch of the family of the earls of Devon. He was also related to the barons of Hungerford via his mother, Elizabeth. Courtenay spent a significant part of his youth in study, spending six years at Oxford between 1451 and 1457, where he graduated with a degree in civil law, then a short period at Cologne, before moving on to Padua where he remained until April 1461.

Prior to his enrollment at Oxford he had received a number of ecclesiastical appointments, and after returning from Padua this trend continued, culminating in his consecration as bishop of Exeter on 8 November 1478. He was also an able politician and is recorded as a royal councilor in 1477–78.

With the death of Edward IV, Courtenay was initially seen as an ally by the new king, being commissioned to deliver Richard's niece, the young Anne of Exeter, to the custody of the Duke of Buckingham in May of that year. On 27 June (the day after Richard's assumption of the throne), Courtenay was also present when Richard gave the great seal to John Russell, bishop of Lincoln. Subsequently, however, he reconsidered his allegiance and with his younger brother Walter and a number of his cathedral clergy, joined the October Rebellion, escaping to Brittany when the revolt collapsed. He was attainted and his temporalities forfeited in Richard III's parliament of January 1484.

After Bosworth, his loyalty to Tudor was rewarded by appointment as keeper of the Privy Seal and consecration as bishop of Winchester in 1487. He continued to participate in life at Henry's court, being present at the ratification of the treaty with Spain on 23 September 1490, and was a witness to the creation of Arthur as Prince of Wales on 29 November 1491. He died on 23 September 1492 and is buried in Exeter cathedral.[4]

Evidence from the October Rebels

Like so much else about Henry Stafford, it is not known whether he was literate. Records during the period from April, when he took control of Edward's landholdings, to his death on 2 November 1483 would have probably been left in London or his usual residence in Brecon. The four documents in the National Archives referring to him from 1480 to 1483 only concern minor legal and financial matters. However, there are also twenty-nine other documents referring to the Duke of Buckingham covering the same period and these include the Act of Attainder from the parliament of 1484.

William Stonor is known to have been literate because letters he wrote to his wife are still in existence. His landholdings included manors in Devon and Cornwall and he had property in London, so personal records may have been stored in any of those locations. He is also thought to have spent the period from November 1483 to August 1485 in Brittany, and so there may be documentary evidence to be found in one of the local French archives. The National Archives contain 456 entries relating to the Stonor family, including an extensive collection of personal correspondence and papers.

Although Richard Hill had property and several lucrative appointments in Dorset, he seems to have spent much of his time after Henry Tudor's coronation in London; consequently, this is where any personal correspondence is likely to be found. Documents in the National Archive, however, only include his will and a number of legal and financial documents.

Peter Courtenay is also poorly represented in the National Archive, only his will and some other documents of little significance being stored there, including his recommendation for the post of bishop of Winchester from the pope to Henry Tudor. Despite holding the sees of Exeter and Winchester, Courtenay—like most churchmen and politicians of the period—seems to have spent much of his time in London, although he appears to have been zealous about matters concerning his diocese.

Perspectives

The men involved in the October Rebellion do not really seem likely to have been in receipt of very detailed information about the eventual whereabouts of Edward and Richard, despite the rumors Croyland claims were spread about the boys' deaths. Apart from Henry Stafford, none were ever part of the inner hierarchy of Richard's court, although initially, Peter Courtenay does seem to have been trying to develop a relationship with Richard, probably because he wanted to retain his Exeter bishopric. After 2 November, all these individuals were intent upon escape to France and the flimsy shelter provided by Henry Tudor, so information sources during what was probably the most significant period with regard to the princes' disappearance would have been completely closed to them. After Bosworth, Stonor, Hill and Courtenay became influential figures in Tudor England, but if they did know anything about the disappearance of Richard's nephews, it has never appeared in any of the major archives. Nor have any letters or other informal communications appeared that included any mention of the boys. Even the documents held in the National Archives that refer to members of this group are not an extensive collection, and none of these scanty records include any reference to Edward, either as Prince Edward or Edward V; nor do any refer to his younger brother, as Prince Richard nor as Richard of York.

Table 11. Possible Location of Documents Left by the October Rebels

Witness	Possible locations of documents	Storage of records from these locations
Henry Stafford, Duke of Buckingham	London Brecon	National Archives, Kew National Archive of Wales
Sir William Stonor	London Devon and Cornwall	National Archives, Kew Devon County Archives, Exeter
Richard Hill	London Dorset	National Archives, Kew
Peter Courtenay	London Winchester	National Archives, Kew

Chapter Sixteen

The July Rescuers

Some time between Richard's coronation and 29 July 1483, an attempt was made to gain access to Edward and Richard by a body of men who claimed to be in communication with Henry Tudor (described as the Earl of Richmond) and the Earl of Pembroke. Stow claims that the original plan was to start fires in various parts of London, presumably away from the vicinity of the Tower, and, while attention was consequently focused elsewhere, to extract the boys from their prison.[1] The plan failed, and Richard's letter of 29 July to his chancellor, John Russell, ordering the appointment of a commission to try unnamed men arrested for an "enterprise," appears to refer to this plot.[2] Stow gives some more details of later events, describing how four of the plotters were condemned to death at Westminster. He writes of the plot:

> When he [Richard] had begun his reign in July, after this mocking election, then was he crowned the first or rather the sevebth day of the same month. And that solemnitie was furnished for the most part by the self same provision that was appointed for the coronation of his nephew.
>
> After this were taken for rebels against the king Robert Ruffe sergeant of London, William Davy pardoner of Hounslow, John Smith groom of king Edwards stirrup and Stephen Ireland wardrober in the Tower, with many others, that they should have sent writings into parts of Britaine to the earles of Richmond and of Pembrooke, and the other lords: and how they purposed to have set fire on divers parts of London, which fire, whilst men had been quenching, they would have stolen out of the tower, the prince Edward, and his brother the duke of Yorke, etc. Robert Ruffe, William Davy, John Smith, and Stephen Ireland were at Westminster judged to death, and thence drawne to Tower hill, and there beheaded, and their heads set on London bridge."

Although Russe and his friends appear to have been the only ones punished for participation in the plot, there were almost certainly more senior figures involved. John Cheyne, master of the King's Horse, was Smith's immediate superior, and the accusation that the men were sending letters to Henry Tudor, then Earl of Richmond, strongly suggests that both Tudor and his mother may have been involved. At that point, Margaret Beaufort cannot

Sixteen. The July Rescuers

Early picture of the Tower of London depicting the imprisonment of Charles, Duke of Orleans. The White Tower, St. Thomas' Tower (which included Traitors' Gate), and the river Thames are shown. The area in front of the Tower is shown reinforced by a substantial stone wall, with the ground behind grassed over. This would have differed from the marshland on the other side of the river, a good environment for the ubiquitous malarial mosquitoes (Wikipedia).

have envisioned her son as eligible for the crown, and her involvement in the rescue may have been simply an attempt to buy her way back into favor with the sons of Edward IV.[3] Stow, however, is careful to say that the plot "would have stolen" the boys out of the Tower. Rescue is not mentioned and it is possible that, if Margaret Beaufort was involved, the abstraction of the boys

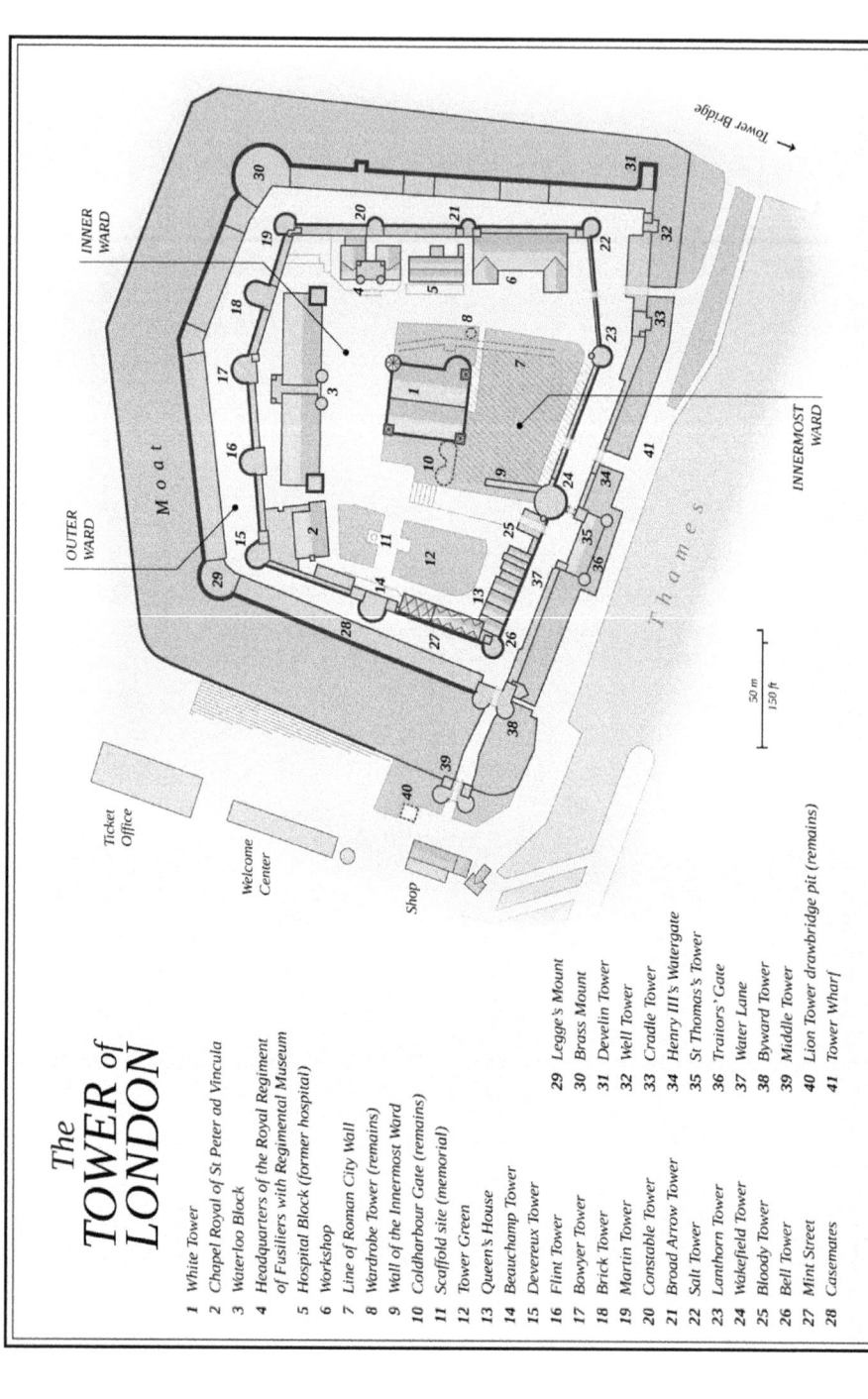

The TOWER of LONDON

1. White Tower
2. Chapel Royal of St Peter ad Vincula
3. Waterloo Block
4. Headquarters of the Royal Regiment of Fusiliers with Regimental Museum
5. Hospital Block (former hospital)
6. Workshop
7. Line of Roman City Wall
8. Wardrobe Tower (remains)
9. Wall of the Innermost Ward
10. Coldharbour Gate (remains)
11. Scaffold site (memorial)
12. Tower Green
13. Queen's House
14. Beauchamp Tower
15. Devereux Tower
16. Flint Tower
17. Bowyer Tower
18. Brick Tower
19. Martin Tower
20. Constable Tower
21. Broad Arrow Tower
22. Salt Tower
23. Lanthorn Tower
24. Wakefield Tower
25. Bloody Tower
26. Bell Tower
27. Mint Street
28. Casemates
29. Legge's Mount
30. Brass Mount
31. Develin Tower
32. Well Tower
33. Cradle Tower
34. Henry III's Watergate
35. St Thomas's Tower
36. Traitors' Gate
37. Water Lane
38. Byward Tower
39. Middle Tower
40. Lion Tower drawbridge pit (remains)
41. Tower Wharf

Sixteen. The July Rescuers

The White Tower, where the boys may have been imprisoned, viewed from the river Thames.

might have been an attempt at assassination, rather than rescue. Henry's mother cannot have been unaware that the deaths of the two boys would have moved her son to within reach of the throne, and she was almost certainly ambitious and avaricious enough not to hesitate over the murder of two children, if by killing them she improved her chance of becoming the mother of the king of England.

The Rescuers

Four men were named by Stow:

- Richard Russe, a sergeant of London
- Stephen Ireland, wardrober in the Tower
- William Davy, a pardoner of Hounslow
- John Smith, groom of stirrup to Edward IV

Of these four, only Smith can be traced with any certainty.[4] Stow's account is confirmed by a French contemporary, Louis Basin, who suggests that a total of fifty citizens of London were involved, but that they failed to achieve their objective because the rest of the City refused to join them.

Opposite: **Map of the Tower of London (map by Thoroe/CC-BY-SA 3.0).**

Section IV: Witnesses

Richard Russe, a Sergeant of London

Richard Russe is described by Stow as a "sergeant," a term that, in the fifteenth century, usually referred to a man who was some sort of superior servant or official. More specifically he was often a military servant, an officer whose duty it was to enforce the judgments of a tribunal or legislative body, and when operating in this role, he could also have beeen referred to as a "sergeant-at-arms," a term whose use had began to be seen as early as the late thirteenth century. "Sergeant" is the spelling used in Stow's original text, although there is an alternative spelling, "Serjeant," which was applied during the same period to a superior order of barristers. The two spellings, in fact, seem to be largely interchangeable, and so it is not really clear whether Russe was a superior sort of soldier or policeman, or a lawyer.

Stephen Ireland: Wardrober of the Tower

Stephen Ireland, the "wardrober in the Tower," occupied a privileged position within the royal household of Edward IV, which makes his participation in a plot of this sort rather curious. Richard seems to have transferred his brother's servants wholesale to his own service, and so Ireland would probably not have been affected by any of the changes that were at the heart of the October Rebellion. Moreover, his position would have been a very senior one, and what such a man could have hoped to gain by entering into a conspiracy to free the boys is difficult to understand. A wardrober in medieval England was not simply concerned with clothes and their storage or distribution. The king's wardrobe or wardrober, along with the chamberlain, made up the personal part of medieval English governmental organization usually referred to as the king's household. Although originally referring only to the room where the king's clothes, armor and treasure were stored, the term was expanded subsequently to include the contents of the wardrobe and eventu-

The outer curtain wall of the tower of London from the landward side (Wikimedia Commons/CC-BY-SA 3.0).

ally the department of clerks who administered it. The contents of the wardrobe, effectively the king's treasure, was originally provided by the treasury but was neither controlled nor audited by that department nor even by Parliament. It was the exclusive property of the king and used by him for any purpose he felt appropriate or necessary, but in particular to make rapid, secret payments for his diplomatic and military operations.

For the earlier period between 1200 and the end of the fourteenth century, there were two wardrobes: the Great Wardrobe and the Household Wardrobe. The Great Wardrobe was responsible only for such everyday necessities as clothing, textiles, wine and other foodstuffs, and from 1200 this treasury was split from the Household Wardrobe. The Household Wardrobe, which was traditionally the more senior, remained responsible for financing the king's personal expenditure and his military operations, although the two departments were once again reunited for administrative purposes in 1399. In addition, there were smaller privy wardrobes at the Tower and various royal palaces. These were separate funds used for the general maintenance

The White Tower, earliest part of the Tower of London, where it is claimed the remains of the princes were found (photograph by Bernard Gagnon/CC-BY-SA 3.0).

of each building and administered by bodies of senior clerks and accountants who were responsible for all aspects of finance involving these establishments.

Ireland is listed as wardrober in the Tower by Stow. This position would have involved him in all the details of financial expenditure for that establishment, which was a royal palace rather than a prison during the period of Richard's reign. In reality, he was only a fairly high-level accountant, certainly not a noble or even a landowner, but he must have been trusted by his superiors and would have had a sound knowledge of the place where he was employed. More significantly, such a responsible position would have called for a good deal of experience, suggesting he was fairly advanced in years when the plot was hatched. It is difficult to perceive what use such a man, elderly and certainly not in the best of health from years of working at a desk, would have been in a desperate attempt to rescue his former master's children from a fortress as formidable as the Tower of London. Perhaps he supplied a map or directions that allowed the group of younger, more agile plotters to locate the boys. He must also have been both literate and numerate, and these skills may have meant that he was selected to act as liaison between his colleagues and the original noble instigators of the plot.

William Davy: Pardoner of Hounslow

A pardoner was originally a man who collected money on behalf of a religious foundation by importuning the congregation of a church to contribute to a cause approved by the diocesan bishop. Pardoners, or questors, as they were first called, were always employed by the local bishop. Part of the pardoner's role was to issue "indulgences," or pardons, although not being ordained, a pardoner was not supposed to hear confessions or preach to any of the congregations from whom he collected money.

Perhaps inevitably, the role became subject to considerable abuse, especially relating to misappropriation of the monies collected in the bishop's name and the sale of pardons. Even before the the period of Richard's reign, pardoners were almost invariably perceived to be criminals by the general population,[5] and it may have been Davy's connections with the criminal underworld of Yorkist London which made him seem a good recruit when the original plotters were formulating their plans. Certainly, it is curious that he should have been mentioned by name in the indictment if his role was only that of a minor conspirator.[6]

The Bloody Tower, viewed from the river approach.

JOHN SMITH: GROOM OF THE STIRRUP TO EDWARD IV

Smith's role in the plot is perhaps a little clearer than those others mentioned by Stow. As one of their father's grooms, Smith would probably have been well known to Edward and Richard, and they may have felt reassured at the sight of a familiar face when their rescuers arrived unexpectedly in the middle of night. It is conceivable that Smith was included in the group for this purpose. A man who was also used to handling horses quietly and efficiently would certainly have been useful after leaving the Tower, in order to get the boys away in the least possible time.

Below St. Thomas' Tower is the water gate access (see lower arrow) emblazoned "Entry to the Traitors' Gate." The archway above (see upper arrow), partially hidden by the crowd, is the closest entrance to the Bloody Tower.

Evidence from the Rescuers

Ireland would have been able to both read and write, although the literacy of the other three seems doubtful. The pardoner, with his ecclesiastical connections, may have been able to read, but the work of neither Russe (if he was a soldier/ policeman) nor Smith necessitated any level of literacy, and it is no surprise that records have not been located from any of these men named by Stow.

Perspectives

Exactly how feasible it would have been to extract the boys in the way Russe and his companions appeared to have planned is difficult to estimate. Presumably, Ireland was sufficiently well known to get one or two companions past the guards, either as his guests or possibly disguised as Tower workers. Alternatively, it may have been easier for him to simply bring the boys to the main gate of the Tower himself, whereupon his companions could deal with the guards, take the boys and slip away, with no one any the wiser.

All the men named as involved in the plot appear to have been long-serving, trusted servants of Edward IV, except the pardoner, whose criminal connections may have been the reason for his inclusion. These connections would have been especially important to ensure a covert exit from England after escaping the Tower, perhaps via the Port of London, which would have been an absolute necessity if the boys were to survive. Both Smith and Ireland would have been well known to the boys and were probably included to ensure that the children went willingly with their rescuers, although any violent participation in the plot by a man of Ireland's age and occupation seems unlikely. If Russe was a soldier or policeman it would have been his military expertise, knowledge of London and ability to recruit similarly qualified individuals that recommended him. This seems to suggest he was a sergeant in the military sense, since a lawyer would hardly have been qualified for such a desperate enterprise.

Despite the superficial nature of Stow's original account, it does contain a number of peculiar inconsistencies. Stow records specifically that the plotters, whoever they may have been, were in contact with both the Earl of Richmond and the Earl of Pembroke. Tudor was Earl of Richmond, so his involvement in the plot may have been significant, but identifying the Earl of Pembroke is more problematic. William Herbert, second Earl of Pembroke, had surrendered the earldom in 1479, accepting the lesser honor of the earldom of Huntingdon and marrying Elizabeth Wydeville's sister, Mary, during the same period. The title was immediately conferred on Edward, Prince of Wales, and he held it until he was deprived of all his landholdings in Wales on 15 May 1483, in favor of Henry Stafford, Duke of Buckingham. Stafford, however, does not appear to have taken up this title, and consequently, in July 1483, Prince Edward was still Earl of Pembroke, his title presumably not having been revoked, despite his alleged illegitimacy.

If the "Earl of Pembroke" noted in Stow's text was either Edward or Stafford, why were they referred to in that obscure way and not by their usual titles? However, suggesting the participation of William Herbert, who had not held the title since 1479, seems to make a little more sense. After the October Rebellion, he received the post of chief justice of South Wales, superseding the Duke of Buckingham and, his first wife having died, he subsequently married Richard's illegitimate daughter, Katherine, in 1484. An annuity of £600 a year went with Katherine, and such a promotion and marriage indicates that Richard cannot have doubted his loyalty.[7] This would surely not have been the case if he had participated in a plot to remove the boys from the Tower, and it is possible that, if he was the one in receipt of the plotter's initial communication, Herbert immediately informed the king and was given Richard's daughter and the post of chief justice as rewards for his loyalty. This may also account for the rapidity that which the plot was both detected and circumvented.

One or two points about the trial and subsequent executions are also peculiar. There exists no record of the proceedings against these four men in any of the Chancery records of the period. The only records describing the existence of a plot are the letter from Richard to John Russell and the warrants issued under the Great Seal for the execution of the men involved. This may be because Russe and his colleagues were dealt with under martial law, which would have meant no trial and a summary death sentence, such a proceeding being deemed necessary because their activities were a threat to the realm and they needed to be disposed of quickly. However, although the matter may have proceeded quickly to the imposition of a sentence, the authorities do not appear to have been in any hurry to have these men executed. Stow implies that they were captured very soon after the plot was discovered and tried almost immediately, but the record of confirmed executions at the Tower show that the four men, who are named in that record, were not executed until 26 February 1484 and that their crime was treason.[8]

Moreover, all are listed as beheaded, and Stow adds that their heads were then placed on spikes on London Bridge, both practices that were unusual when the executions in question were those of commoners. Status in that period even extended to the way a person was executed, and it seems very strange—almost unheard of—for four commoners to be accorded the sort of death that was a privilege of the noble classes. The only other execution of a commoner recorded at the Tower before then was in 1475 and that was John Goose, a Lollardist, burned at the stake for his religious beliefs. Men such as Russe and his friends would usually have been taken to Tyburn and hanged there as a form of public entertainment, even though they were traitors. This is also particularly well demonstrated when considering the different fates of the Earl of Warwick and others involved in the final conspiracy that resulted in the execution of Perkin Warbeck. All involved in the conspiracy were accused of treason, for which the punishment was public hanging, drawing and quartering. However, of the fourteen sentenced to death only Edward Plantagenet, Earl of Warwick, was eventually beheaded at the Tower. All the rest were executed at Tyburn, even Warbeck, although he was spared the degradation of the full treatment, being simply and, with luck, speedily hanged at Tyburn.

Perhaps the most problematic inconsistency in this episode is the behavior of Richard himself. More's account of the boys' death has Richard convinced of the need to murder his nephews almost from the time of his

Sixteen. The July Rescuers

Detail of one of the windows of the St. Thomas' Tower. The windows of both the Bloody Tower and Wakefield Tower are similar and indicate how difficult a surreptitious entry would have been for the boys' rescuers.

Tower Wharf. In this picture, taken in 2015, the original grass has been replaced by cobblestones.

The walkway of the Bloody Tower, between the battlements and the exterior wall, where many of the prisoners incarcerated here would have taken their daily exercise.

coronation. He says that Richard began to make plans for the murder while on his way to Gloucester, which makes the original genesis of the plot some time before 2 August,[9] and Richard's letter demanding the establishment of a commission to try the unnamed men is only slightly earlier, dated 29 July 1483. Consequently, if, as some have claimed, Richard was intent upon murdering his nephews almost from the time of his initial moves towards the usurpation, this botched attempt to remove the princes from the Tower would have been a perfect solution for him. Such an attempt, even if it was thwarted, could have easily been used to cover the murders of the boys by one of Richard's trusted confederates. The resulting discovery of the two little corpses could have been bewailed as the result of assassination by an individual intent upon their uncle's throne, whose identity was as yet unknown. Even if Tudor was not seriously considered as an aspirant to the throne at that time, the October Rebellion threw up Buckingham and Tudor as very believable candidates for an attempted assassination, and Richard would hardly have needed to exert himself to convince his subjects, with hindsight, that either or both of them were behind the murder of his innocent nephews. Why did he not seize such a convenient opportunity?

Table 12. Possible Location of Documents Left by the July Rescuers

Witnesses	Possible locations of documents	Storage of records from these locations
Richard Russe	London	National Archive, Kew
William Davy	London	National Archive, Kew
John Smith	London	National Archive, Kew
Stephen Ireland	London	National Archive, Kew

Chapter Seventeen

Where from Here?

The role of Richard III as the murderer of his nephews has become accepted fact for many of those interested in the late medieval period. Richard, so the story goes, having usurped the throne, then took the decision to have his nephews murdered because, left alive, they represented a nucleus for rebellion that would be an overwhelming threat to his own rule, a threat that came to fruition in the autumn of 1483 and saw its final flowering at Bosworth Field in August 1485. Unfortunately, one glaring incongruity arises within this neat solution that has been either ignored or minimized by many who have written about him.

Up to the period after his coronation, Richard's usurpation of the monarchy had been a model of subtle planning and effective execution. He had isolated and demonized the Woodvilles, replaced or arrested the closest councilors and personal servants of the boy king, and then rid himself of Hastings, his brother's friend and confidante, who might have opposed Richard's actions for the sake of Edward's children and his own interests. With the field clear of adult opposition, Edward, Richard and their sisters were disposed of as competitors by the sworn evidence presented to the Lords Spiritual and Temporal questioning their parentage and their father's morality, before that august body was coerced into declaring them illegitimate and leaving Richard, Duke of Gloucester and Lord Protector, as the only remaining acceptable candidate for the crown. More importantly, Richard had brought this about by portraying himself, with the help of the Rolle, as saving the country from those who had been a bad influence upon his easily swayed elder brother, and that idea had caused the previous regime, and anyone connected with it, to be viewed as wholly unsuitable for the responsibilities of government. This gave all his actions a superficial veneer of respectability, because no one could accuse him of seizing the crown, since it was officially Parliament who offered it to him, even though he had so engineered the situation that they were left without any choice in the matter. Consequently, although there were clearly misgivings about his methods, particularly the summary executions of Hastings, Anthony Wydeville, Grey and Vaughan, the usurpation had retained its unstable veneer of respectability when he was crowned as Richard III on 6 July 1483. Edward, although he had been appointed successor by his father was, after all, an unknown quantity, while the former Duke of Gloucester had been his brother's right-hand man in the north and had a good reputation as a soldier and administrator. More importantly, at that time most of the country seems to have thought the boys were still alive and were probably waiting to see what exactly Richard had in store for them.

So, by the time of his coronation in July, things seemed to be going smoothly for Richard and the picture of him as a subtle, deliberate, even sophisticated schemer, well able to manipulate both public and private opinion for his own ends, seems sufficiently clear and coherent. However, soon after his departure from London for the north during 18–20 July, this vision of Richard is completely shattered. Despite his surely being able to predict what the public reaction would be to the murder of two children, more especially his nephews whom he had sworn to protect and to whom he had also sworn an oath of allegiance, it is claimed he had them killed. Not content with that, he compounds the stupidity of the act by offering no explanation of their disappearance, when he had several likely candidates to whom the blame could have been shifted, including Buckingham, dead by 2 November, and Henry Tudor, still cowering in France. Even death by natural causes would have been a better solution, whatever conclusions may have been drawn by some, especially if the boys died some months apart. Moreover, even if Richard had given no thought to the potentially disastrous consequences of his actions, those around him would surely have done. Catesby and Francis Lovell would certainly have described the effects on public opinion of the boys' unexplained disappearance to him, in the same way as they advised against his remarriage to his niece, Elizabeth of York.

However, because he adopted none of the apparently more sensible courses open to him, inevitably, trial by rumor found him guilty of the boys' murder and, as a direct result of this smearing of a previously almost spotless reputation, he found himself demonized, isolated and subsequently destroyed at Bosworth. Why, after all the careful planning and the care to ensure the veneer of legality to his actions, would he throw it all away by one ill-conceived, thoughtlessly savage act? That, of course, is where the inconsistency at the heart of this account of Richard lies: the tale insists that he was the clever schemer, subtle and devious as a snake, who is suddenly transformed into a mindless butcher, intent only upon the eradication of his nephews, whatever it cost him.

No one with any knowledge of the period or Richard's personality could reasonably deny that he was capable of this pair of very convenient murders. He may have had qualms, he might have hesitated even, but eventually, whether they were his nephews or not, he would have acted in his own best interests. It is not the act or even the possibility of the act that is in question, but the ineptitude with which it was carried out and total disregard of its consequences that makes it so difficult to reconcile with Richard's character. Why leave himself so openly exposed to blame, especially when it was so easily avoided?

The actions of Elizabeth Wydeville are equally inconsistent. She cannot have been ignorant of the boys' fate; the friends and connections she still had at court would have kept her informed, especially on such an important subject as the location of her sons. Knowing them to be alive and free, she had no reason to support Tudor, and conversely, knowing them to be dead for certain meant she could have used their deaths as a rallying point to bolster her daughter's claim to the throne, with Tudor forced to accept the role of consort. The forced accession of Elizabeth of York seems to have been the real reason behind the October Rebellion, and Elizabeth Wydeville, in giving her support to the rebels, would have made herself dowager queen mother, with a daughter on the throne as queen in her own right. This would have placed her in a far better position than being simply the mother of a girl who was effectively only the wife of Henry VII, which is what she finally became. What was her reason for supporting Tudor with promises of her daughter's hand while still within sanctuary, then apparently deciding to support Richard soon after leaving, by sanctioning his arrangement of her daughters' marriages and all but ordering her son Thomas Grey to return to court?

Henry Tudor's actions with regard to the boys also require some explanation. The only reference he makes to his young brothers-in-law after Bosworth is in the Act of Attainter against Richard of Gloucester, whom he simply accuses of "shedding infants' blood." When he came to the throne he had no necessity to offer any sort of explanation about the fate of the boys, but within months he found himself faced with a pretender who initially claimed to be Richard of York. Surely, his easiest option then was to produce the evidence of Richard's death, even if that evidence was faked. The trouble he had with Warbeck would have justified any sort of subterfuge. His spy system in England was too efficient for him not to have known what had happened to them; and even if they had been buried in secret and he could not produce the actual bodies, two convenient corpses of the same age and gender could easily have been found to use as substitutes.

If Richard's actions did not result from a simple act of misjudgment, whereby he ignored the advice of his councilors and close friends by sanctioning the secret murder and, more importantly, the unexplained disappearance of two royal heirs, there is at least one explanation that seems to fit all the facts. He allowed the story of the boys' disappearance to spread and gain acceptance, with its damaging implications for himself, because he had no other choice—or rather, any other choice was worse than popular condemnation as a murderer, especially if such a label was only intended to be a temporary encumbrance. He may have had no other choice because the boys were alive and safely hidden away somewhere, until Richard could reintroduce one or both at court, not as his illegitimate, dispossessed nephews but as accepted members of his own hierarchy, in the same way that Henry V had reestablished one of the Mortimer heirs. Alternatively, although less likely, they may have been rescued and hidden by a group of their father's adherents, intent upon fielding one or both of the boys as rivals opposing Richard in a contest for the monarchy.

Some historians of the medieval period have insisted that for the safety of Richard's regime, he had no choice but to remove the boys. However, it was not absolutely necessary for the new king to murder the children to ensure his own political survival; he needed only to have them under his control and sufficiently out of the way so that they could not become a focus for any more plots, such as the July rescue attempt and October Rebellion. As recently as the reign of Henry IV, Edmund and Roger Mortimer, the two young heirs to the previous king, Richard II, had been not only kept alive but actually brought up with Henry's children. Significantly, the Mortimer boys were not threatened by another candidate for the crown, so there was no necessity for their whereabouts to be kept secret, as was the case with Edward and Richard—but, just like Edward's sons, they were also the focus of a number of plots against the reigning monarch, in particular the conspiracy led by Henry "Hotspur" Percy in 1403. Despite the considerable inconvenience occasioned by his action, Henry did not execute his rivals but rather imprisoned them under close supervision in Pevensey Castle until his death in 1413, whereupon the new king, Henry V, released both young men and made them Knights of the Bath. Roger is thought to have died young, but Edmund Mortimer subsequently served under Henry V during his French wars and was appointed by Henry VI as king's lieutenant in Ireland. So Richard may have felt he had good reasons and even a convenient precedent for both keeping his nephews alive and also assuming that eventually he might even be able to involve them profitably in the administration of the kingdom. In this context, it may also be indicative that Vergil claims he invited their half brother, the Marquess of Dorset, to return soon after Elizabeth

Wydeville left sanctuary, especially if Richard was intent upon bolstering his regime with family members, much as his elder brother had done before the unfortunate circumstances that had forced Clarence's trial and execution. Whatever he may have claimed during the period of the usurpation, his relations with the Wydevilles had been good before his brother's death; and Elizabeth Wydeville may have been enough of a realist to accept the deaths of her son, Richard Grey, and her brother, Anthony, Earl Rivers, if it meant her younger sons could occupy positions of power in a regime whose future revolved around Richard's sickly ten-year old son, Edward of Middleham, whose health and eventual survival were in question. This may also explain her curious behavior during the period of autumn 1483 and March 1484. *If* she agreed to the marriage between her daughter and Henry Tudor while in sanctuary because she thought that the disappearance of the boys meant that they were dead, and then upon leaving sanctuary found they were alive, she might have decided to change sides again. This would be particularly to her advantage if her brother-in-law Richard had promised her surviving sons significant roles in the new regime and her daughters good marriages. These circumstances could also be the reason she wrote to Dorset, telling him to return to England.

This scenario would also explain why Richard could not clear himself of his nephews' murders. If the boys were in hiding with friends of their father, Richard would not have been able to produce two convenient bodies who had died either of natural causes or from murder by persons known or unknown, because the identification of the bodies would have been repudiated by the men who had them hidden. Alternatively, if he had hidden the boys from view himself because he needed them alive for later employment, clearly they, or rather two substitutes, could not be given a convenient state funeral at this point. It also explains the problems Henry VII encountered when faced with his two imposters, Simnel and Warbeck, especially if his mother-in-law suspected that one or both of the boys were still alive and had been taken abroad out of his reach after Bosworth. Tudor could not simply deny either claim, because he could not prove they were not valid by producing two dead princes. Nor could he simply concoct a tale of murder blaming either Richard or Buckingham, because he was not sure how many witnesses, perhaps including his mother-in-law, were still alive and could repudiate his fictions.

Sir James Tyrell's suspected involvement in the boys' rescue and subsequent disappearance would also explain Henry's interest in questioning and then executing him. Given Tudor's shaky title, it also explains the alleged Tyrell confession admitting to the murder, no copy of which has ever been found and the existence of which is known only from More's history. Once Tyrell was saddled with the murder, the boys' deaths were explained and any further aspirants to the throne had to be proven imposters. Moreover, Tyrell's implication would invalidate any story about his involvement in their rescue and concealment because it could be interpreted by the Tudor regime as an implausible attempt on the part of Sir James's family to clear his name. Perhaps most importantly, if Tyrell was the last survivor of the plotters who rescued the boys on Richard's orders and he really knew and perhaps could *prove* what had happened to the king's brothers-in-law, his death was the perfect opportunity for Tudor to concoct a suitable story that could not be challenged now by anyone living, since the last witness who knew the truth had been executed. Tyrell's involvement in the boys' removal or rescue may also have been the reason for Lovell's journey to Colchester after Bosworth. Gipping Hall, Tyrell's family home, where it is suggested that one or both of the boys may have been hiding, was only a short day's ride from Colchester; and Richard could have ordered his old friend Lovell to ensure his nephews had news of the result of the battle in time to escape. Gipping Hall would also have been convenient both as a hiding place and as a point from which to conduct an escape to Burgundy and Aunt Margaret, being away from the main roads running north or east and within easy reach of the Channel ports of Harwich, Felixstowe and Lowestoft.

So if this mass of theory and speculation is correct, how might the story have gone? And, more importantly, where are there places where it could be checked?

Another Version

Edward and Richard were moved to the Tower and remained there while their uncle was crowned on 6 July. Richard began his progress through the Midlands and northern regions on 20 July. While he was away, there was an attempt to either murder the boys or remove them from the Tower, organized either by Tudor or former adherents of Edward IV. Richard had already approached his nephews about becoming part of his new regime and perhaps felt that the signs were hopeful; but he realized that if they ever get out of his control, instead of being the acquiescent, well-trained assets he intended them to be, they would immediately become the focus for rebellion, whether willing or otherwise. He sent Sir James Tyrell south, on the pretext of collecting some goods that were needed on the royal progress, but in reality Tyrell carried a message for Brackenbury, instructing him to release the boys into Tyrell's custody. Tyrell immediately arranged for them to be moved secretly to Gipping Hall or a similar convenient residence, where they were to remain hidden. A pretense was maintained that the boys were still in the Tower, and this became more immediately necessary when the October Rebellion erupted, because the rumor about the boys' deaths clearly showed the real intentions of Buckingham and Henry Tudor.

The rebellion was settled, but there was still considerable unrest in the country. Richard, knowing the caliber of Henry Tudor's associates, in particular John Morton and Sir Reginald Bray, was concerned that the boys might be discovered and murdered, since Edward's two live heirs were all that stood between Henry Tudor and the throne, assuming he intended to reestablish the legitimacy of his prospective bride, Elizabeth of York. Consequently, Richard decided that they should remain hidden, but gave them the assurance of powerful places in his new administration, because he felt that the family ties he had with his two nephews would make them more loyal assistants than any of his other associates, whose motives for helping him were, not unreasonably, wholly selfish. Moreover, with their illegitimacy established, Edward and Richard did not have many options left. Association with their uncle might have seemed the best of a lot of difficult choices, both to them and to their mother when she joined them from her Westminster sanctuary.

Elizabeth Wydeville was persuaded to leave sanctuary in March 1484. Upon being given evidence of Richard's good faith by a reunion with her sons, she wrote to Dorset, telling him to come home, as his uncle wished to offer both him and his half-brothers places at court. Dorset attempted to return but was blocked by Tudor's men. Tudor, Morton and Bray learned that the boys were alive and begin to spread further rumors of their deaths through their agents, associating Richard with the stories to weaken his hold on the loyalty of his subjects. Richard was now caught in a trap of his own devising. It was too dangerous for the boys to bring them back to London and show them alive and well to the populace, but the rumor that he was responsible for their murder made his position increasingly difficult and tenuous, the more so since any arrangements he made had to be done in absolute secrecy. His son's death on 9 April 1484 also gave impetus to his decision to recruit his nephews to positions of trust in the new regime, as did his wife's death on 16 March 1485.

This was the position when Richard met his death at Bosworth. On the previous evening he ordered Lovell to bring news of the result of this final battle to the boys and then either move them to London, where they could once again appear safely, or if the fight went against him, send them abroad, probably to their aunt, Margaret. Lovell made the journey to Colchester and then went secretly to Gipping Hall where he arranged for the boys to escape to safety, either to Aunt Margaret, Ireland or some other secure hiding place. Within weeks of Edward and Richard's escape, Henry Tudor learned that they had disappeared from the Tower during the summer of 1483. Although their final whereabouts were unknown, he was forced to assume that one or both of the boys were still alive and hence a threat to his security. Consequently, he was obliged to treat both the Simnel and Warbeck plots seriously, because he could not be certain that either of the main protagonists were not one of his lost brothers-in-law, and because there were a number of surviving witnesses who knew about their escape. Perhaps it was only much later, in the wake of Warbeck's execution, that he finally traced them as far as Gipping Hall, which precipitated the arrest and trial of Sir John Tyrell and his destruction of all the relevant documents.

Obviously, there are objections to this theory. Most importantly, apart from the rather nebulous and wholly unconfirmed Tyrell family legend, the only support for it is circumstantial. The major question about the idea of Richard as rescuer is obviously this: If the boys were taken from the Tower and hidden at his orders in a more secure and secluded place, why did they not reappear after the rebellion had been quelled and take their places in his hierarchy, thus avoiding all the accusations of murder to which he was subjected? That is clearly a significant problem but—danger of assassination by Tudor's associates apart—another factor forcing their seclusion may have been the possibility that, despite their early conditioning, one or both boys had proven unreceptive to Richard's offer. This sort of reaction would have obliged him to keep them imprisoned somewhere out of the way until they became more amenable. Returning to Henry IV and the Mortimers, there was a precedent for this. After Edmund and Roger's abduction from Windsor Castle on 13 February 1409 and their subsequent recapture, Henry had them imprisoned in Pevensey Castle under the supervision of Sir John Pelham and later Henry, Prince of Wales (later Henry V) for a period of four years, until 1413, when Henry became king upon the death of his father. This fits neatly with the story of the princes, because it was soon after the rescue attempt by Russe and his confederates that stories of the boys' disappearance began to circulate. Richard may also have been concerned about the activities of Henry Tudor's associates. Men such as Reginald Bray and John Morton must have still have had channels of communication into England, because *someone* was continually encouraging the dissident Yorkist factions to undermine Richard's position during his reign, and he may well have felt that the boys were best hidden to prevent an assassination attempt by one of Tudor's adherents, such as William Collingbourne. By 1484, whatever Richard's problems, there was no ambiguity about Henry Tudor's position. Two live heirs to the English throne with better title than his were an obstacle that would have to be removed, whatever their relation to his prospective bride. Tudor needed Edward and Richard dead, either before or after he got rid of their uncle, if he ever managed that.

Their failure to appear makes even more sense if they had been spirited away by former members of their father's regime. In that case, they would have needed to remain in hiding, to escape the consequences if Richard or Henry Tudor's agents located them. Although Richard may have felt that they could still serve a useful function within his own regime and so kept them alive until a more appropriate time, it is doubtful that the boys' rescuers would have accepted or trusted this view. Henry Tudor would have had no good reason for preserving them alive, because his claim to the throne, although strengthened by his marriage to Elizabeth of York, was void if either of Edward's heirs turned up. Moreover, even if they had been moved and then imprisoned at Richard's command, nobody familiar with the character of Henry Tudor or his mother, Margaret Beaufort, would have given much for their chances if they had been taken by the new king, considering the unsatisfactory basis for his claim to the throne.

Unfortunately, although a theory like this one may be convincing and even fits most of the facts, without hard evidence its validity remains impossible to demonstrate. Consequently, it is reasonable to consider, as one way forward, what documents would have had to be exchanged to make such a scenario plausible and where such evidence might be found.

Relevant documents would include these:

- Letters between Edward and his uncle confirming Richard's plans for the boys' future within his new government and Edward's acceptace of his altered status.
- A series of public proclamations designed to show the country that the boys were safe in their uncle's custody and outlining their future. Incidentally, if such a proclamation *was* made, this would explain Croyland's contention that the boys were known to be safe, since they were in "certain deputed custody."
- Letters to Elizabeth Wydeville, confirming Richard's offer to the boys and promising good husbands for her daughters. Richard actually made this offer about his brother's daughters, according to Vergil, but the letter giving details of his suggestions is lost.
- Written instructions to both Tyrell and Brackenbury ordering the boys' removal from the Tower and giving the location of their new home. At

the very least, Tyrell must have carried a written order from Richard to Brackenbury, because the constable of the Tower would have been most unlikely to release two prisoners of such political importance without his sovereign's express permission.

- Letters, placards or other documentation listing the grievances of the October rebels.
- Entries in Exchequer documents and manorial accounts detailing the boys' expenses, even if they were not specifically named.

No documents of this sort have ever been found, although from what is known about Henry Tudor's disposal of all but one copy of the Titulus Regius, it is not implausible to suggest that the absence of this paper trail may be due to deliberate suppression or destruction by Tudor or one of his subordinates, rather than because it never existed.

Perspectives

Whatever ingenious suggestions may be made about the fate of Edward and his little brother, based on the current evidence, further speculation about what happened to the boys is largely pointless. Yes; Richard, Buckingham or Henry could have killed them, or they could have escaped and died on the road to wherever they were going. Or they could have gotten away and lived their lives out quietly after Richard's defeat at Bosworth, avoiding any further entanglements with the deadly business of insurrection. Or they could have just died, of a simple accident or from any one of a dozen fatal, infectious diseases that children were subject to in those times.

What is needed now is not speculation but more evidence; and that requires someone to go looking for it. The facts may well be available, hidden in a collection of documents no one has thought to investigate. In this context, it is significant that Dominic Mancini's report of Richard's reign remained unexamined in the Municipal Library at Lille until 1934. And who could have possibly foreseen that Richard himself would have been found, over 500 years after his death, under a municipal parking lot in Leicester? Moreover, he would still be there if Ms. Phillipa Langley of the Richard III Society had not initiated the project and the University of Leicester undertaken the excavation, with funding from a number of interested parties, which included the Leicester City Council.

Unfortunately, a search of the most readily available archives for documents originating from the people closest to Edward and Richard has produced no new evidence of their fate. This is not wholly unexpected. The main problem with such a search is that these archives contain mostly legal and financial documents, not diaries or chatty letters about the day-to-day happenings in the manors or great houses where these people spent their time. Letters from the Stonor, Cely and Paxton families contain a wealth of detail about the daily lives of these well-to-do merchants, but they were not much involved at court, and their knowledge of the internal workings of Richard's political machine appears to have been minimal. Or perhaps more accurately, the degree of knowledge they felt it safe to commit to paper was minimal. With such a proviso in mind, the type of source that might include details of the boys' eventual fate will probably not be included in any archive to which there is either easy access or a simple protocol for searching. Almost certainly, if there is documentary evidence still in existence that reveals what happened to the boys, it is stored in some obscure collection that has not been considered worth troubling with in a search for the sons of Edward IV. Then, like so many of the documents from this and earlier periods, only time and luck will reveal their existence. Hopefully, if such a document is in existence, its discovery will not take too long.

APPENDIX 1

Chronology of Edward and Richard, 1470–1483

1470

November

2—Edward of York born in sanctuary at Westminster during his father's exile.

He was baptized in the Abbey itself, the abbot and prior standing sponsor, along with Lady Scrope, one of the queen's ladies-in-waiting.

1471

March

Edward IV returns to England

June

26—Prince Edward created Prince of Wales and Earl of Chester.

July

3—Lords "Spiritual and Temporal" take oath of allegiance to Prince Edward in Parliament Chamber.

8—Rule of Prince Edward's household and lands is entrusted to a council headed by his mother, his paternal uncles, the dukes of Clarence and Gloucester, and his maternal uncle Anthony Woodville, Earl Rivers. This arrangement is originally intended to last until he reaches the age of 14 (2 November 1484).

1472

November

Revenues from the Principality of Wales and the counties of Chester and Flint are made available to Prince Edward.

1473

February

20—Edward's council is enlarged and given full powers to act in Prince Edward's name.

August

17—Richard of York born at Shrewsbury.

November

10—John Alcock, bishop of Rochester, appointed president of Edward's council and given responsibility for his education. Earl Rivers is appointed his governor.

209

1474

May

28—Richard created Duke of York.

1475

March

Welles and Willoughby lands settled on Richard.

April

18—Princes Edward and Richard knighted.

May

15—Edward and Richard both made Knights of the Garter.

June

20—Edward named keeper of the realm during the king's absence in France.

1476

Prince Edward's council begins to develop into the main agent of royal authority in Wales and the Marches. Marriage between Prince Edward and the Spanish infanta, Isabella, daughter of Ferdinand and Isabella, is discussed.

January

Negotiations begun to arrange marriage of Richard, Duke of York, to Anne Mowbray.

June

12—Richard made Earl of Nottingham.

1477

February

7—Richard made Duke of Norfolk, Earl Warenne and Lord of Seagrave, Mowbray and Gower.

1478

January

15—Marriage of Richard (5 years old) and Anne Mowbray (4 years old).

1479

May

Richard appointed lord lieutenant of Ireland.

July

8—Edward has the title Earl of Pembroke conferred by his father.

1480

Negotiations begun to arrange Prince Edward's marriage to Anne, daughter of the Duke of Brittany and heir to the duchy.

Officers appointed to Richard, including his chamberlain, Thomas Grey.

1481

Negotiations to arrange Edward's marriage to Anne of Brittany.

In Sandwich, Kent with his father to review fleet sent against Scotland.

November

19—Anne Mowbray, Richard's wife, dies at Greenwich.

1483

April

9—Edward IV dies.
Edward is twelve. Richard is ten.

APPENDIX 2

Chronology of Richard III and the Princes

Introduction

Henry VI was expelled from Normandy in 1450, so ending any pretensions he had to the French throne. Impractical and unworldly, Henry was removed from the throne by Edward, son of Richard, Duke of York, who became Edward IV, after his father was treacherously killed at Battle of Wakefield by men of Margaret of Anjous (wife of Henry VI).

NB: Yorkists would probably have reopened the claim for the French throne.

Warwick, known as the king-maker, was instrumental in Edward's accession but became estranged after Edward's marriage to Elizabeth Woodville, the "gilt haired widow," and fomented rebellion. Warwick's daughter Isabel married Clarence. Warwick was defeated by Edward and killed at the battle of Barnet.

Woodville influence came to dominate court and realm, with Elizabeth Woodville's sons and brothers holding many positions of power, and Woodville greed became a byword. Prince Edward was sent to live under this influence, which explains the concern of Richard and others, notably Hastings, that after Edward IVs' death, the realm would be dominated by the dowager queen and her family, using her son as a pawn.

1452

October

2—Richard, Duke of Gloucester, born at Fotheringay Castle, twelfth of thirteen children born to Richard, third Duke of York and Cecily Neville (daughter of Ralph Neville, first Earl of Westmoreland).

1460

July

10—Edward and Richard Neville,

Earl of Warwick, capture Henry VI and rule in his name, after defeating Henry's forces at the Battle of Northampton. Richard, Duke of York (Edward's father) to succeed Henry VI after the king's death, rather than Henry's son.

October

31—Agreement reached whereby Richard, Duke of York, will succeed Henry VI to the throne.

December

30—York and his son Edmund killed at Battle of Wakefield. Richard and George, Duke of Clarence, sent by their mother, Cecily Neville, to Flanders for safety.

1461

March

4—Edward begins his reign as Edward IV.

29—Battle of Towton. Edward defeats force of Lancastrians, despite being outnumbered. Richard and George return to England in time to be present at Edward's coronation.

June

28—Coronation of Edward IV.

1464

May

1—Edward IV marries Elizabeth Wydeville.

1465

July

Henry VI captured and confined to the Tower.

1467

Beginning of estrangement between Edward and Warwick.

1468

July

3—Margaret of York marries Charles, Duke of Burgundy, becoming Margaret of Burgundy.

1469

Beginning of Neville rebellion, which included George, Duke of Clarence.

July

Edward captured.

September

7-14—Edward freed.

Before 30—Edward able to defeat and execute Sir Humphrey Neville and his brother.

1470

Henry VI temporarily regains power only to lose it, and his life, in 1471.

September

Edward, Richard of Gloucester, and a group of followers escape to Burgundy.

October

Henry VI released from the Tower.

November

2—Birth of Edward V.

1471

March

Edward lands in Yorkshire at Ravenspur.

April

11—Henry VI returned to the Tower.
14—Battle of Barnet: Edward defeats Warwick's army.

May

4—Battle of Tewksbury: Death of Henry VI's only son, Edward of Lancaster, thought to have been killed while fleeing the battle.

Henry VI dies while resident in the Tower, after Edward's return to London, probably killed on his orders. Official stance is that Henry died of "pure displeasure and melencoly" brought about by the death of his son.

Sir James Tyrell knighted after Tewksbury.

December

Tyrell in service with Richard, Duke of Gloucester.

1472

March—July (exact date uncertain)

Richard, then Duke of Gloucester, marries Anne Neville after death of her original husband Edward, Prince of Wales (son of Henry VI), at battle of Tewksbury.

1475

Stillington (source of the precontract information), now chancellor, is sent to Burgundy on a diplomatic mission for Edward, to persuade the duke, his brother-in-law, to give up Henry Tudor.

1478

January

George, Duke of Clarence, attainted for treason by Parliament and executed.

1480

Margaret of Burgundy visits England and has a meeting with her brother, Richard of Gloucester.

1483

April

9—Edward IV dies of natural causes. No evidence found that he was murdered by Richard or anyone else. His eldest son is considered to be the next king, Edward V, at 12 years of age.

11—Edward, still at Ludlow Castle 200 miles from London, is proclaimed Edward V in London, the council setting his coronation date for May 4. A 2,000-man escort for the king is agreed upon.

Not trusting the Woodvilles, William Hastings, the late king's best friend and lord chamberlain, writes to Richard, Duke of Gloucester, to tell him of his brother's death and to suggest that he come to the capital with a large force and intercept the young king. The Croyland Chronicler says that Hastings also wrote to Buckingham. That evening, William Hastings and John Howard have supper together.

14—Edward hears news of his father's death while at Ludlow castle, and preparations begin for his journey to London. Stafford also learned of Edward IV's death while on his estates at Brecon on the Welsh Marches.

15—Richard of Gloucester, the new king's uncle, receives the letter from Lord Hastings, his brother's chamberlain. He travels to York where he swears an oath of fealty to the new king, making the local nobility swear the same oath.

This is significant because Richard was known to be religious, almost puritanical, and to him such an oath would be hugely binding and not something to be broken lightly. His personal motto "Loyaultie me lie" ("loyalty binds me") was important to him as well.

It is suggested that this means, by his later actions, that he must have been convinced of the spuriousness of Prince Edward's claim. However, he may have also simply seen it as a convenient opportunity.

20—Having asked his followers to meet him in York, Richard leaves Middleham Castle, taking 300 men with him. The Royal Council is still in session; Croyland writes that it was "the most urgent desire of all present that the Prince should succeed his father in all his glory." The council argues over the type of government that should be established during the king's minority, and the nature of the protectorate, which would naturally go to Richard, as only living brother of Edward IV. The council also appoints Edward Woodville admiral of the fleet to assemble a navy that would confront French and Breton pirates.

24—Edward V and his household officers leave Ludlow.

While in route to Nottingham, Richard receives word from Rivers that they will meet in Northampton on 29 April. Richard spends the night at Pontefract Castle.

26—Buckingham leaves Brecon with 300 men. Richard arrives in Nottingham, where he is met by Buckingham's servant.

29—Edward V and his party arrive at Northampton, but Rivers remains behind to intercept Richard and the Duke of Buckingham while Edward and his other household officers ride on ahead to Stony Stratford. Richard and Buckingham arrive in Northampton separately.

According to Vergil, Richard tells the Duke of Buckingham that he intends to seize the throne.

Sir Edward Woodville takes his ships to sea.

30—Edward V's ministers (Rivers, Grey, Vaughan and Haute) are arrested at Stony Strattford and imprisoned separately, the king being placed under Richard's protection. Richard then writes a letter to the council explaining his actions. Richard, Edward and Henry Stafford (the Duke of Buckingham) proceed to London and a rapturous reception. The weapons cache is found at this time; it is claimed by traditionalists to have been stored for the Scottish war and used as an excuse to implicate innocent Woodvilles.

May

1—Elizabeth Woodville and Dorset try to raise support to rescue Edward, but nobles reject them. Elizabeth Woodville, Richard, the five princesses, Elizabeth's brother Lionel, and Thomas Grey, Duke of Dorset, flee to sanctuary in Westminster during the early hours. At dawn, Thomas Rotherham, the Archbishop of York, gives the queen the Great Seal of England in his capacity as chancellor.

2—Richard writes to the City Corporation and the Royal Council, and a copy of his letter is also sent for public proclamation. In it, he declares his loyalty to the new king, saying that the actions he has taken were to remove the Woodvilles from power and deploring the Wydeville theft of his brother's treasure.

4—Richard escorts his nephew into London, showing him to people as their new king. The date for Edward's coronation is fixed for 22 June. Edward is housed in the Bishop of London's palace.

9—Edward's instructions are issued under his own seal and "sign manual."

10—A council meeting is held at which Richard is made protector, under terms of Edward's will, the appointment seen as being effective from the date of the king's death (although this is disputed and no copies of the will were ever available for subsequent examination). Thus, he has no need to assume any rights; they become his upon his brother's death. At the same meeting, the decision is taken to transfer Edward to the Tower. Coins are ordered to be minted in the name of Edward V.

Despite giving their support to Richard, the council does not agree that Rivers, Grey, Vaughan and Haute should be accused of treason. They further criticize Richard for not taking proper concern for the dignity and safety of the queen, although they join with Richard in denouncing Edward Woodville and asking him to disband his fleet, although it was the council who had authorized his actions initially. All but two ships return after the crews of the other vessels mutiny.

11–23—During this period, Richard sends an envoy to the French pirate Lord Cordes as a prelude to a truce. Committees of councilors meet in the Star Chamber of Westminster, in the Tower of London, and in each other's homes. During this period Richard is still working diplomatically, appointing people to try to persuade the queen and her children to leave sanctuary, although he also seizes the lands of Rivers, Grey, Dorset, and other members of the family.

13—Writing in the name of Edward V, Richard issues writs to summon all the peers of the realm to London for a parliament three days after the coronation, now scheduled for 22 June. When he asks the council to extend his protectorate until Edward V reached his majority, its members rule that this is a matter for Parliament.

15—Much of the power of Edward's council is transferred to Henry Stafford, Duke of Buckingham. He is also given access to all the revenues from Edward's Welsh estates, including the castle at Ludlow.

19—Grants and proclamations are still being issued in Edward's name and around this time (16–19) he is moved to the Tower of London. The Tower during this period is just another royal palace, and it is the usual place for kings to stay prior to their coronation.

Between this date and the council meeting of 8 or 9 June, Richard possibly decides or is persuaded to usurp the crown, although there is good evidence that he has already made that decision before leaving the north and intercepting his nephew's party at Stoney Stratford. Suspicions of Richard are certainly growing. Croyland states that, in spite of Richard's public gestures of loyalty and the setting of a date for the coronation, there are those who wonder why the king's relatives and servants were still being held in prison.

June

During the early part of June, Richard (it is claimed) meets in private with his supporters at Crosby Place, while the rest, Hastings, Rotherham, Morton and others loyal to Edward V, meet at Baynard's Castle and Westminster to plan the coronation and discuss routine business. Mancini and Thomas More both report that Edward's supporters meet in each other's homes to discuss the situation away from Richard's influence.

8 or 9 (date uncertain)—"Council" meeting called, possibly informal, since it apparently took place in Richard's council chamber but is attended by all "lords spiritual and temporal." It is at this meeting that Stillingtom is claimed to have revealed Edward IV's association with Eleanor Butler.

9—Edward's own servants paid off, presumably replaced by men loyal to Richard.

10—Richard writes to York for reinforcements, claiming the queen, Elizabeth Woodville, is about to "murder and utterly destroy us and our cousin the Duke of Buckingham and **the old royal blood of this realm**."

Possible significance of this: Would Elizabeth Woodville have murdered her own children to seize power?

NB: Claimed that Richard had already arranged for these forces to be available, which means that he had plans to usurp the throne before the ceremony swearing allegiance to his nephew in York.

Last known document bearing Edward's signature is dated this day.

13—A council meeting is held at which Hastings is arrested and immediately executed for treason. Lord Stanley, Archbishop Rotherham and Bishop Morton are also imprisoned as traitors (although they are pardoned later). Richard's real reason for executing Hastings may have been that Hastings would not agree to support him in assuming the crown. Hastings may have felt his best chance for retaining his former power was a 12-year-old king, who could be influenced, rather than Richard. Morton is released into Buckinghams' custody, it is claimed at the duke's request, and subsequently imprisoned at Brecknock. Morton is believed to be the instigator of the later Buckingham rebellion.

16—Westminster, where Elizabeth Woodville, Dorset, and her youngest son, Richard of York, had sought sanctuary, is surrounded. Thomas Bourchier, Archbishop of Canturbury, persuades Elizabeth Woodville to give up Richard.

Richard is removed to the Tower with his brother.

17 or 18—Coronation of Edward V is canceled.

21—Stonor letter received from Simon Stallworth describing Hasting's execution and naming two others placed in prison at the same time as Morton and Stanley.

22—Shaa gives sermon revealing the results of the council meeting on 9th and detailing the boy's illegitimacy. During this sermon, Shaa (or Shaw) is also said to have accused Edward's (and Richard's) mother of infidelity, but this seems unlikely since Richard maintains good relations with his mother for whole of his life. The sermon is based on evidence from the bishop of Bath and Wells, Robert Stillington, who disclosed knowledge of a pre-contract, predating Edward IV's marriage to Elizabeth Woodville. Stillington claimed that, in 1461, Edward had entered into a precontract to marry Lady Eleanor Butler. This was a form of marriage in which the man promised to marry the woman concerned before they had sexual intercourse. It was considered to be as legally binding as a formal marriage. If this precontract story was true, Edward's marriage to Elizabeth Woodville was legally invalid and their children thus illegitimate.

Richards' acceptance of this story was his basis for claiming the throne, although he may have been aware of the story from his brother, the Duke of Clarence, and simply bided his time before exploiting it.

There is no record of the complete text of the Shaa sermon in existence, the only accounts of what was said being contemporary reports.

23-25—Some time after Shaa delivers his sermon, Buckingham addresses the mayor and leading citizens of London at the Guildhall, enlarging upon Richard's credentials as a future king.

25—"Parliament" (i.e., the three estates) is convened, and its members examine Stillington's proofs, which they find "good and sufficient." ODNB: These proofs have not survived, in line with many other documents that Henry VII might have found inconvenient.

The council decides that Edward's sons were illegitimate. They produce a "Rolle," later formalized as the "Titulus Regius," detailing their findings and calling upon Richard to accept the crown.

Rivers, Grey and Vaughn are executed in Pontefract.

26—Members of the "Parliament," the lord mayor and other leading citizens wait upon Richard and offer him the crown, stating that they will not have Edward's sons to rule over them and that if Richard refuses, they will choose another (possibly Buckingham). Witnesses record that Richard accepts with an appearance of considerable reluctance.

July

6—Richard is crowned king at a coronation in Westminster. The Wardrobe account appears to show Edward V still alive, although this may be spurious.

18-20—Richard leaves London for a progress through the north country, accompanied by the Duke of Buckingham and Tyrell.

23—Progress reaches Reading.

End of July (exact date not known): An attempt is made to liberate the princes from Tower and later also the princesses from Westminster. The plot is foiled and the plotters are executed. It may be significant that commands to execute the plotters are recorded but orders for the death of the princes are not.

29—Richard sends letter to his chancellor, ordering the appointment of a commission to try unnamed men arrested for an "enterprise." This appears to refer to the plot to remove the princes from the Tower.

August

2—Progress reaches Gloucester.

8—Progress reaches Warwick.

Tyrell leaves the progress at Warwick and returns to London to collect coronation cloth. He may have been ordered to murder the princes or perhaps to arrange for them to be moved for their own safety, especially if Richard suspected Buckingham.

13—Land of John Welles, half-brother of Margaret Beaufort, is put into the custody of John, Lord Scrope of Bolton.

27—Progress reaches Pontefract.

28—A commission of "oyer and terminer," headed by Henry Stafford, Duke of Buckingham, is appointed to enquire into treasons and felonies in London, Surrey, Sussex, Kent, Middlesex, Oxfordshire, Berkshire, Essex and Hertfordshire.

29—Progress reaches York. Richard's son, Edward of Middleham, is created Prince of Wales at York Minster during the company's stay here. Buckingham leaves the progress some time during 27–29 August.

September

15—News reaches Richard of Buckingham's rebellion (this date is contested).

19–21—Richard leaves York and moves towards Gainsborough and then Leicester.

24—Leaders of the October Rebellion launch their enterprise (according to Parliamentary rolls). Buckingham is now at his castle in Brecon; from there he sends a letter inviting Henry Tudor to invade and become the consort of Elizabeth of York.

October

10—Risings begin in Kent, spreading west to southern counties.

Richard spends the night at Gainsborough.

(Did Richard move the boys during this period because of danger from Buckingham?)

11—Richard arrives in Lincoln, where he learns that a rebellion has broken out in the southern counties and that Buckingham has risen in revolt against him.

Letter is sent from Sir Francis Lovell to Sir William Stonor, all but demanding his attendance upon Richard with forces to fight against Buckingham.

21—Richard reviews his troops at Leicester.

November

2—Buckingham is executed and the rebellion loses direction, although a rising occurs at Bodmin "on behalf of the New King." It is not clear who this refers to, Buckingham or Henry Tudor.

Buckingham is claimed to have instigated the revolt because of his abhorrence of Richard's crime in killing the princes. Given the character of the man, this appears to be unlikely. He may really have been supporting Henry, but more likely he was using the Tudor heir as a "stalking horse," ready to claim the crown if a convenient "accident" should claim Henry on the battlefield. Buckingham was constable of England at the time and so had easy access to the boys. Also, it was apparently his suggestion that they be lodged in the Tower; although this may not be significant, since the Tower was traditionally the place kings left from for their coronation and the pre-contract had not come to light when the suggestion was made, so Edward was still going to be crowned. It may be significant that it was at about the time of the abortive Tudor/Buckingham invasion that Croyland claims "rumours were spread of the Princes' death," although he implies that these were only rumors, and the text suggests that they were spread after Buckingham's decision to lead the rebellion, perhaps to weaken Richard's standing with the country and help Henry's first attempt at invasion.

Tyrell delivers Buckingham into Richard's hands for execution. Buckingham demands to speak to the king but is denied. One of Buckingham's sons claims that he had a concealed dagger to attempt assassination.

The claim that John Kendall, Richard's secretary, was appointed "Keeper of Princes' wardrobe," thus showing one or both of boys must be alive, is spurious. Actually Kendall was simply authorized to "have the keeping of the place *called* the 'Prince's wardrobe' and … to dwell in the same." Clearly, there is no evidence that the boys are still alive.

8—Richard and his army arrive at Exeter.

13—Thomas St. Leger executed at Exeter.

25—Richard is back in London, with the rebellion apparently crushed.

December

25—Henry Tudor is proclaimed king of England at Rennes Cathedral, promising to marry Elizabeth of York, Edward IV's daughter, when he secures the throne.

1484

January

23—Parliament is convened and passes the Titulus Regius, an act confirming that the Eleanor Butler pre-contract invalidated the Woodville marriage, thus making all the children of that marriage illegitimate and confirming Richard as next in line and Edward IV's rightful heir.

Richard is seen as "a good lawmaker for the ease and solace of the common people."

February

26—Execution of July rescuers at the Tower of London; Russe, Davy, Smith and Ireland.

March

Elizabeth Woodville leaves sanctuary with the promise of husbands and lands for her daughters, possibly in the charge of John Nesfield, who had previously been responsible for guarding the Westminster sanctuary. Meanwhile, she has been plotting with Henry Tudor's mother, Margaret Beaufort, to arrange a marriage between Elizabeth of York (Edward IV's oldest daughter) and Henry. Henry Tudor's claim to throne is weak so this will strengthen it, but only if Elizabeth of York is declared legitimate. Unfortunately for Henry, any act legitimizing her has the same effect on her brothers. Since their claim to the throne is much better than Henry's, they would represent a significant threat to his bid for the throne if they were found alive.

April

9—Richard and Anne's son Edward (Prince of Wales) dies suddenly. King and queen appear to be distraught, although the boy was known to have been sickly.

Richard's nephew, the Earl of Lincoln, is named as his heir.

(After the death of his son, did Richard consider reinstating Edward and Richard? Did he send Kendall to Rome, in December, to seek a papal dispensation to reverse the Titulus Regius, so he could appoint one of the boys as his heir?)

December

25—Christmas: Anne Neville and Elizabeth of York appear in similar dresses. There is a huge, ornate celebration at court to show Richard's power.

1485

January

13—Tyrell receives appointment to Guînes, a castle guarding the port of Calais, perhaps as a reward for his role in guarding the princes. He is paid 3,000 marks, equivalent to one year's income for Richard's kingdom.

March

16—Richards' wife, Anne Neville, dies, probably of consumption.

Elizabeth of York is anxious to marry her uncle (aided and abetted by her mother), but Richard issues a public denial of his intention to do this, having been told by Sir Richard Ratcliffe and William Catesby that the country, especially the North, would not accept what would be seen as an incestuous marriage.

August

22—Battle of Bosworth Field. Richard is betrayed by Stanley and the Earl of Northumberland and dies fighting. His body is later stripped and degraded, then buried in the Church of St. Mary at Leicester.

THE PRETENDERS

1487

May

24—Simnel is crowned in Christ Church Cathedral, Dublin, as Edward VI.

June

4—Simnel lands in England.

16—Battle of Stoke; the Earl of Lincoln is killed and Simnel is captured.

1491

December
Warbeck lands in Cork and is persuaded to adopt his role as Richard, Duke of York.

1492

March
Warbeck moves from Cork to Harfleur under the patronage of the French king, Charles VIII.

June
8—Elizabeth Wydeville dies at Bermondsey Abbey.

November
Warbeck escapes to Mechelin and the protection of Margaret of Burgundy.

1495

November
20—Warbeck is welcomed at Scottish court by James IV.

1496

January
13-14—Warbeck marries Lady Katherine Gordon.

November
21—Warbeck invades England from Scotland, but retreats almost immediately.

1497

September
7—Warbeck lands at Whitesands Bay, Cornwall.

October
5—Warbeck is captured and brought to Taunton castle, where (it is claimed) he confesses his imposture.

1499

November
23—Warbeck is executed at Tyburn.

1502

May
6—Tyrell is executed for treason as the result of his alleged involvement in a plot to put Edmund de la Pole on the throne.

1505

Polydore Vergil begins his *Anglica Historia*, which is the first text to accuse Richard of killing his nephews.

Appendix 3

The Titulus Regius

To the High and Mighty Prince Richard, Duc of Gloucester.

Please it youre Noble Grace to understande the consideracon, election, and petition of us the lords spiritual and temporal and commons of this reame of England, and thereunto agreably to geve your assent, to the common and public wele of this lande, to the comforts and gladnesse of all the people of the same.

First, we considre how that heretofore in tyme passed this lande many years stode in great prosperite, honoure, and tranquillite, which was caused, foresomuch as the kings then reignyng used and followed the advice and counsaill of certaine lords speulx and temporelx, and othre personnes of approved sadnesse, prudence, policie, and experience, dreading God, and havyng tendre zele and affection to indifferent ministration of justice, and to the comon and politique wele of the land; then our Lord God was dred, luffed, and honoured; then within the land was peace and tranquillite, and among neghbors concorde and charite; then the malice of outward enemyes was mightily repressed and resisted, and the land honourably defended with many grete and glorious victories; then the entrecourse of merchandizes was largely used and exercised; by ehich things above remembered, the land was greatly enriched soo that as wele the merchants and artificers as other poor people, laboryng for their lyvyng in diverse occupations, had competent gayne to the sustentation of thaym and their households, livyng without miserable and intolerable povertie. But afterward, when that such as had the rule and governaunce of this land, deliting in adulation and flattery and lede by sensuality and concupiscence, followed the counsaill of persons insolent, vicious, and of inordinate avarice, despising the counsaill of good, vertuous, and prudent personnes such as above be remembred, the prosperite of this land dailie decreased soo that felicite was turned into miserie, and prosperite into adversite, and the ordre of polecye, and of the law of God and man, confounded; whereby it is likely this reame to falle into extreme miserie and desolation,—which God defende,—without due provision of convenable remedie bee had in this behalfe in all godly hast.

Over this, amonges other things, more specifially we consider howe that the tyme of the raigne of King Edward IV, late decessed, after the ungracious pretensed marriage, as all England hath cause to say, made betwitx the said King Edward IV and Elizabeth, sometyme wife to Sir John Grey, Knight, late nameing herself and many years heretofore Queene of England, the ordre of all politeque rule was perverted, the laws of God and of Gode's church, and also the lawes of nature, and of England, and also the laudable customes and liberties of the same, wherein every Englishman is inheritor, broken, subverted, and contempned, against all reason and justice, so that this land was ruled by self-will and pleasure, feare and drede, all manner of equite and lawes layd apart and despised, whereof ensued many inconvenients and mischiefs, as murdres, estortions, and oppressions, namely of pooe and impotent people, so that no man was sure of his lif, land, ne lyuvelode, ne of his wif, doughter, no servannt, every good maiden and woman standing in drede to be ravished and defouled. And besides this, what discords, inward battailes, effusion of Christian men's blode, and namely, by the destruction of the noble blode of this lond, was had and comitted within the same, it is evident and notarie through all this reaume unto the grete sorrowe and heavynesse of all true Englishmen. And here also we considre howe the said pretensed marriage, betwitx the above named King Edward the Elizabeth Grey, was made of grete presumption, without the knowyng or assent of the lords of this londe, and alsoe by sorcerie and wichecrafte, committed by the said Elizabeth and her moder, Jacquett Duchess of Bedford, as the common opinion of the peole and the publique voice, and fame is through all this land; and hereafter, if and as the case shall require, shall bee proved sufficiently intyme and place convenient. And here also we considre how that the said pretenced marriage was made privately and secretly, with edition of banns, in a private chamber, a profane place, and not openly in the face of the church, aftre the laws of Godd's churche, but contrarie thereunto, and the laudable custome of the Churche of England. And how also, that at the tyme of the contract of the same pretensed marriage, and bifore and longe tyme after, the saide King Edw was and stood marryed and troth plyght to oone Dame Elianor Butteler, doughter of the old Earl of Shrewsbury, with whom the said King Edward had made a precontracte of matronie, long tyme bifore he made the said pretensed mariage with the said Elizabeth Grey in manner and fourme aforesaid. Which premises being true, as in veray trouth they been true, it appeareth and followeth evidently, that the said King Edward duryng his lyfe and the said Elizabeth lived together sinfully and dampnably in adultery, against the lawe of God and his church; and therefore noe marvaile that the souverain lord and head of this londe, being of such ungodly disposicion, and provokyng the ire and indignation of oure Lorde God, such haynous mischiefs and inconvenients as is above remember, were used and committed in the reame among the subjects. Also it appeareth evidently and followeth that all th'issue and children of the said king been bastards, and unable to inherite or to clayme anything by inheritance, by the lawe and custome of England.

Moreover we consider howe that afterward, by the thre estates of this reame assembled in a parliament holden at Westminster the 17th yere of the regne of the said King Edward the iiijth, he than being in possession of the coroune and roiall estate, by an acte made in the same parliament, George Duc of Clarence, brother to the said King Edward now decessed, was convicted and attainted of high treason; as in the same acte is conteigned more at large. Because and by treason whereof all the issue of the said George was and is disables and barred of all right and clayme that in any wise they might have or challenge by inheritance to the crowne and roiall dignitie of this reame, by the auncien lawe and custome of this same reame.

Over this we consider howe that ye be the undoubted sonne and heire Richard late Duke of Yorke verray enheritour to the said crowne and dignitie roiall and as in right Kyng of Englond by way to enheritaunce and that at this time the premisses duelly considered there is noon other peron lyving but ye only, that by right may clayme the said coroune and dignitie roiall, by way of enhertiaunce, and how that ye be born within this lande, by reason whereof, as we deme in our myndes, ye be more naturally enclyned to the prosperitie and comen weal of the same: and all the three estates of the land have, and may have more certain knowledge of your birth and filiation above said. Wee considre also, the greate wytte, prudence, justice, princely courage, and the memorable and laudable acts in diverse battalls which we by experience know ye heretofore have done for the salvacion and defence of this same reame, and also the great noblesse and excellence of your byrth and blode as of hym that is descended of the thre most royal houses in Christendom, that is to say, England, Fraunce, and Hispaine.

Wherefore these premisses by us diligently considered, we desyring affectuously the peas, tranquilitie and wele publique of this lande, and the reduction of the same to the auncien honourable estate, and prosperite, and havyng in your greate prudence, justice, princely courage and excellent virtue, singular confidence, have chosen in all that is in us is and by this our wrytyng choise you, high and myghty Prynce into our Kyng and souveraine lord &c., to whom we know for certayn it appertaneth of enheritaunce so to be choosen. And hereupon we humbly desire, pray, and require your said noble grace, that accordynge to this election of us the three estates of this lande, as by your true enheritaunce ye will accept and take upon you the said crowne and royall dignitie with all things thereunto annexed and apperteyning as to you of right belongyng as well by enheritaunce as by lawful election, and in case ye do so we promitte to serve and to assist your highnesse, as true and faithfull subjietz and liegemen and to lyve and dye with you in this matter and every other just quarrel. For certainly we bee determined rather to adventure and comitte us to the perill of our lyfs and jopardye of death, than to lyve in such thraldome and bondage as we have lyved long tyme heretofore, oppressed and injured by new extorcos and imposicons, agenst the lawes of God and man, and the liberte, old polce and lawes of this reame wherein every Englishman is inherited. Our Lorde God Kyng of all Kynges by whose infynyte goodnesse and eternall providence all thyngs have been pryncypally gouverned in this worlde lighten your soule, and graunt you grace to do, as well in this matter as in all other, all that may be accordyng to his will and pleasure, and to the comen and publique wele of this land, so that after great cloudes, troubles, stormes, and tempests, the son of justice and of grace may shyne uppon us, to the comforte and gladnesse of all true Englishmen.

Albeit that the right, title, and estate, whiche our souverain lorde the Kynge Richard III hath to and in the crown and roiall dignite of this reame of England, with all things thereunto annexed and appertynyng, have been juste and lawefull, as grounded upon the lawes of God and of nature and also upon the auncien lawes and laudable customes of this said reame, and so taken and reputeed by all such personnes as ben lerned in the above-saide laws and custumes. Yet, neverthelesse, forasmoche as it is considred that the most parte of the people of this lande is not suffisiantly lerned in the abovesaid lawes and customes whereby the trueth and right in this behalf of liklyhode may be hyd, and not clerely knowen to all the people and thereupon put in doubt and question: And over this howe that the courte of Parliament is of suche autorite, and the people of this lande of suche nature and disposicion, as experience teacheth that maifestation and declaration of any trueth or right made by the thre estats of this reame assembled in parliament, and by auctorite of the same maketh before all other thyng, moost faith and certaintie; and quietyng men's myndes, remoweth the occasion of all doubts and seditious language:

Therefore at the request, and by the assent of the three estates of this reame, that is to say, the lords spuelx and temporalx and comens of this lande, assembled in this present parliament by auctorite of the same, bee it pronounced, decreed and declared, that our said souveraign lorde the kinge was and is veray and undoubted kyng of this reame of Englond; with all thyngs thereunto within this same reame, and without it annexed unite and apperteynyng, as well by right of consanguinite and enheritance as by lawful election, consecration and coronacion. And over this, that at the request, and by the assent and autorite abovesaide bee it ordeigned, enacted and established that the said crowne and roiall dignite of this reame, and the inheritaunce of the same, and other thyngs thereunto within the same reame or without it annexed, unite, and now apperteigning, rest and abyde in the person of our said souveraign lord the kyng during his lyfe, and after his decesse in his heires of his body begotten. And in especiall, at the request and by the assent and auctorite abovesaid, bee it ordeigned, enacted, established, pronounced, decreed and declared that the high and excellent Prince Edward, sone of our said souveraign lorde the Kyng, be heire apparent of our said souveraign lorde the kyng, to succeed hym in the abovesaid crown and roiall dignite, with all thyngs as is aforesaid thereunto unite annexed and apperteignyng, to have them after the decease of our saide souveraign lorde the kyng to hym and to his heires of his body lawfully begotten.

(To this bill the Commons gave their assent, and it consequently passed.)

APPENDIX 4

Sir Thomas More's Account of the Princes' Deaths

When he hadde begonne his reygne the [twenty sixth] day of Iune, after this mockishe selccion, than was he Crowned the [sixte] day of Iuly. And that solemnitie was furnished for the most part, with the selfe same prouision that was appointed for the Coronacion of his nephew.

Now fell ther mischieues thick. And as the thinge euill gotten is neuer well kept: through all the time of his reygne, neuer ceased there cruel death & slaughter, till his owne destrucccion ended it. But as he finished his time with the beste death, and the most righteous, that is to wyt his own: so began he with the most piteous and wicked, I meane the lamentable murther of his innoocent nephewes, the young king and his tender brother. Whose death and final infortune hathe natheles so far comen in question, that some remain yet in doubt, whither they wer in his dayes destroyde or no. Not for that onely that.

Perken Warbecke, by many folkes malice, and mooe folkes foly, so long space abusyng the worlde, was aswel with princes as the porer people, reputed and taken for the yonger of those two, but for that also that all thynges wer in late daies so couertly demeaned, one thing pretended and an other ment, that there was nothyng so plaine and openly proued, but that yet for the comen custome of close & couert dealing, men had it euer inwardly suspect, as many well counterfaited iewels make the true mistrusted. Howbeit concerning that opinion, with the occasions mouing either partie, we shall haue place more at large to entreate, yf we hereafter happen to write the time of the late noble prince of famous memory king Henry the seuenth, or parcase that history of Perkin in any compendious processe by it selfe. But in the meane time for this present matter, I shall rehearse you the dolorous end of those babes, not after euery way that I haue heard, but after that way thay I haue so hard by such men & by such meanes, as me thinketh it wer hard but it should be true.

King Richarde after his coronacion, takyng his way to Gloucester to visit in his newe honor, the towne of which he bare the name of his old, deuised as he roode, to fulfil that thing which he before had intended. And forasmuch as his minde gaue him, that his nephewes liuing, men woulde not recken that hee could haue right to the realm, he thought therfore without delay to rid them, as though the killing of his kinsmen, could amend his cause, and make him a kindly king. Whereuppon he sent one Iohn Grene whom he specially trusted, vnto sir Robert Brakenbery constable of the Tower, with a letter and credence also, that the same sir Robert shoulde in any wise put the two children to death. This Iohn Grene did his errande vnto Brakenbery kneling before our Lady in the Tower, who plainely answered that he would neuer putte them to death to dye therfore, with which answer Ihon Grene returning recounted the same to Kynge Richarde at Warwick yet in his way. Wherwith he toke such displeasure and thought, that the same night, he said vnto a secret page of his: Ah whome shall a man trust? those that I haue brought vp my selfe, those that I had went would most surely serue me, euen those fayle me, and at my commaundemente wyll do nothyng for me. Sir quod his page there lyeth one on your paylet without, that I dare well say to do your grace pleasure, the thyng were right harde that he wold refuse, meaning this by sir Iames Tyrell, which was a man of right goodlye parsonage, and for natures gyftes, woorthy to haue serued a muche better prince, if he had well serued god, and by grace obtayned asmuche trouthe & good will as he had strength and witte. The man had an high heart, and sore longed vpwarde, not rising yet so fast as he had hoped, being hindered and kept vnder by the meanes of sir Richard Ratcliffe and sir William Catesby, which longing for no moo parteners of the princes fauour, and namely not for hym, whose pride thei wist would beare no pere, kept him by secrete driftes out of all secrete trust. Whiche thyng this page wel had marked and knowen. Wherefore thys occasion offered, of very speciall frendship he toke his time to put him forward, & by such wise doe him good, that al the enemies he had except the deuil, could neuer haue done him so muche hurte. For vpon this pages wordes king Richard arose.

(For this communicacion had he sitting at the draught, a conuenient carpet for such a counsaile) and came out in to the pailet chamber, on which he found in bed sir Iames and sir Thomas Tyrels, of parson like and brethren of blood, but nothing of kin in condicions. Then said the king merely to them: What sirs be ye in bed so soone, and calling vp syr Iames, brake to him secretely his mind in this mischieuous matter. In whiche he founde him nothing strange. Wherfore on the morrow he sente him to Brakenbury with a letter, by which he was commaunded to deliuer sir Iames all the kayes of the Tower for one nyght, to the ende he might there accomplish the kinges pleasure, in such thing as he had geuen him commaundement. After which letter deliuered and the kayes receiued, sir Iames appointed the night nexte ensuing to destroy them, deuysing before and preparing the meanes. The prince as soone as the protector left that name and toke himself as king, had it shewed vnto him, that he should not reigne, but his vncle should haue the crowne. At which worde the prince sore abashed, began to sigh and said: Alas I woulde my vncle woulde lette me haue my lyfe yet, though I lese my kingdome. Then he that tolde him the tale, vsed him with good wordes, and put him in the best comfort he could. But forthwith was the prince and his brother bothe shet vp, and all other remoued from them, onely one called black wil or William slaughter except, set to serue them and see them sure. After whiche time the prince neuer tyed his pointes, nor ought rought of himselfe, but with that young babe hys brother, lingered in thought and heauines til this tratorous death, deliuered them of that wretchednes. For Sir Iames Tirel deuised that thei shold be murthered in their beddes. To the execucion wherof, he appointed Miles Forest one of the foure that kept them, a felowe fleshed in murther before time. To him he ioyned one Iohn Dighton his own horsekeper, a big brode square strong knaue. Then al the other beeing remoued from them, thys Miles Forest and Iohn Dighton, about midnight (the sely children lying in their beddes) came into the chamber, and sodainly lapped them vp among the clothes so be wrapped them and entangled them keping down by force the fetherbed and pillowes hard vnto their mouthes, that within a while smored and stifled, theyr breath failing, thei gaue vp to god their innocent soules into the ioyes of heauen, leauing to the tormentors their bodyes dead in the bed. Whiche after that the wretches parceiued, first by the strugling with the paines of death, and after long lying styll, to be throughly dead: they laide their bodies naked out vppon the bed, and fetched sir Iames to see them. Which vpon the sight of them, caused those murtherers to burye them at the stayre foote, metely depe in the grounde vnder a great heape of stones. Than rode sir Iames in geat haste to king Richarde, and shewed him al the maner of the murther, who gaue hym gret thanks, and as som say there made him knight. But he allowed not as I have heard, the burying in so vile a corner, saying that he woulde haue them buried in a better place, because thei wer a kinges sonnes. Wherupon thei say that a prieste of syr Robert Brakenbury toke vp the bodyes again, and secretely entered them in such place, as by the occasion of his deathe, whiche onely knew it could neuer synce come to light. Very trouthe is it & well knowen, that at such time as syr Iames Tirell was in the Tower, for Treason committed agaynste the moste famous prince king Henry the seuenth, bothe Dighton an he were examined, & confessed the murther in maner aboue writen, but whither the bodies were remoued thei could nothing tel. And thus as I haue learned of them that much knew and litle cause had to lye, wer these two noble princes, these innocent tender children, borne of moste royall bloode, brought vp in great wealth, likely long to liue to reigne and rule in the realme, by traitorous tiranny taken, depryued of their estate, shortly shitte vp in prison, and priuily slaine and murthered, theyr bodies cast god wote where by the cruel ambicion of their vnnaturall vncle and his dispiteous tormentors. Which thinges on euery part wel pondered: god neuer gaue this world a more notable example, neither in what vnsuretie standeth this worldy wel, or what mischief worketh the prowde enterprise of an hyghe heart, or finally what wretched end ensueth such dispiteous crueltie. For first to beginne with the ministers, Miles Forest at sainct Martens pecemele rotted away. Dighton in ded walketh on a liue in good possibilitie to bee hanged ere he dye. But sir Iames Tirel dyed at Tower hill, beheaded for treason. King Richarde himselfe as ye shal herafter here, slain in the field, hacked and hewed of his enemies handes, haryed on horsebacke dead, his here in despite torn and togged lyke a cur dogge. And the mischief that he tooke, within lesse then thre yeares of the mischiefe that he dyd. And yet all the meane time spente in much pain and trouble outward, much feare anguish and sorow within. For I haue heard by credible report of such as wer secrete with his chamberers, that after this abhominable deede done, he neuer hadde quiet in his minde, hee neuer thought himself sure. Where he went abrode, his eyen whirled about, his body priuily fenced, his hand euer on his dager, his countenance and maner like one alway ready to strike againe, he toke ill rest a nightes, lay long wakyng and musing, sore weried with care & watch, rather slumbred then slept, troubled wyth fearful dreames, sodainly sommetyme sterte vp, leape out of his bed & runne about the chamber, so was his restles herte continually tossed & tumbled with the tedious impression & stormy remembrance of his abominable dede. Nowe hadde he outward no long time in rest. For hereupon sone after began the conspiracy or rather good confederacion, betwene the Duke of Buckingham and many other gentlemen against him.

APPENDIX 5

Perkin Warbeck's Confession

It is first to be known that I was born in the town of Tourney in Flanders, and my father's name was John Osbeck, which said John Osbeck was controller of the said town of Tourney and my mother's name is Katherine de Faro. And one of my grandsires on my father's side was named Diricke Osbecke, which died. After whose death my grandmother was married unto Peter Flamin, that was receiver of the forenamed town of Tourney and dean of the boatmen that row upon the water or river called the Schelt. And my grandsire upon my mother's side was Peter de Faro, which had in his keeping the keys of the gate of St. John's within the same town of Tourney. Also I had an uncle called Master John Stalin, dwelling in the parish of Saint Pias within the same town which had married my father's sister whose name was Johne Jane with whom I dwelt a certain season. And after I was led by by my mother to Antwerp for to learn Flemish in a house of a cousin of mine, an officer of the town called John Stienbeck, with whom I was the space of half a year. After that I returned again to Tourney by reason of wars that were in Flanders. And within a year following I was sent with a merchant of the said town of Tourney named Berlo, to the mart of Antwerp were I fell sick, which sickness continued upon me five months. And then the said Berlo sent me to board in a skinner's house that dwelled beside the house of the English nation. And by him I was thence carried to Barrow mart and I lodged at the "Sign of the Old Man" where I abode for the space of two months.

After this said Berlo sent me with a merchant of Middlesborough to service for to learn the language, whose name was John Strew, with whom I dwelt from Christmas to Easter, and then I went into Portugal in company of Sir Edward Brampton's wife in a ship which was called the queen's ship. And when I was come thither, then was I put in service to a knight that dwelled in Lushborne, which was called Peter Vacz de Cogna, with whom I dwelt an whole year, which said knight had only one eye. And because I desired to see other countries I took licence of him and then I put myself in service with a Breton called Pregent Meno, who brought me with him to Ireland. Now when we were there arrived in the town of Cork, they of the town (because I was arrayed with some cloths of silk of my said master's) came unto me and threatened upon me that I should be the Duke of Clarence's son that was before time at Dublin.

But forasmuch as I denied it, there was brought unto me the holy evangelists and the cross, by the mayor of the town which was called John Llellewyn, and there in the presence of him and others I took mine oath (as truth was) that I was not the foresaid duke's son nor none of his blood. And after this came unto me an English man whose name was Stephen Poitron and one John Water, and laid to me, in swearing great oaths, that they knew well that I was King Richard's bastard son, to whom I answered with like oaths that I was not. Then they advised me not to be afeared but that I should take upon me boldly, and if I would do so they would aid and assist me with all their power against the King of England, and not only they, but they were well assured that the Earl of Desmond and Kildare should do the same.

So they forced not what they took, so they might be revenged upon the King of England, and so against my will made me learn English and taught me what I should do and say. And after this they called me the Duke of York, second son of King Edward the fourth, because King Richard's bastard son was in the hands of the King of England. And upon this the said Water, Stephen Poitron, John Tiler, Hughburt Burgh with many others, as the aforesaid earls, entered into this false quarrel, and within short time others. The French King sent an ambassador into Ireland whose name was Loit Lucas and master Stephen Friham to advertise me to come into France. And then I went into France and from thence into Flanders, and from Flanders into Ireland, and from Ireland into Scotland, and so into England.

Glossary

Advowson: the right in English law of a patron to present to the diocesan bishop a nominee for appointment to a vacant ecclesiastical benefice or church living, a process known as presentation.

Escheat: a common law doctrine (law in which decisions are governed by precedents, rather than statutes derived from the crown or similar executive body) that transfers the property of a person who dies without heirs to the crown or state. It serves to ensure that property is not left in "limbo" without recognized ownership.

Feoffee: a trustee who holds a fief (or "fee"), that is, an estate in land, for the use of a beneficial owner. The term is more fully stated as a feoffee to uses of the beneficial owner. This system came into being to serve two purposes: to avoid feudal relief, a form of taxation to the king that had to be paid before a man could inherit his property, and to allow the landholder to bequeath his land to an heir of his choice, rather than his eldest son.

The modern equivalent is a trustee, and like a modern-day trustee, in medieval times a feoffee would have been a person in whom the owner of an estate could have felt able to place absolute trust. Appointment as a feoffee to someone like Richard, Duke of Gloucester, would have important implications about the duke's perception of the loyalty of the one appointed.

Messuage: (property law) a dwelling house together with its outbuildings, curtilage, and the adjacent land appropriated to its use.

Oyer and terminer, court or commission of: A court for the trial of cases of treason and felony. The commissioners of assize and *nisi prius* are judges selected by the king and appointed and authorized under the Great Seal. The commission of oyer and terminer gives them authority for the trial of treasons and felonies; that of general jail delivery empowers them to try every prisoner then in jail for whatever offense; so that, altogether, they possess full criminal jurisdiction.

Seisin (or seizin): the legal possession of a feudal fiefdom (i.e., an estate in land). It was used in the form of "the son and heir of X has obtained seisin [possession] of his inheritance," and thus is effectively a term concerned with conveyancing in the feudal era. In the feudal age, the king alone "owned" all the land of England by his allodial right; all his subjects merely held tenures in fiefs, that is to say estates-in-land.

Chapter Notes

Abbreviations

ODNB: Oxford Dictionary of National Biography

Introduction

1. Sir Winston Churchill, *A History of the English-Speaking Peoples, Vol. 1* (New York: Skyhorse, 2011), 383–84.

Chapter One

1. M. Hicks, *Richard III* (Gloucestershire: Tempus, 1991), 91; P.W. Hammond and Sutton, *Richard III: The Road to Bosworth Field* (London: Constable, 1985), 94.
2. Hicks, *Richard III*, 91; A. Cheetham, *The Life and Times of Richard III* (London: Weidenfeld and Nicholson, 1972).
3. Hicks, *Richard III*, 108; P.W. Hammond and A.F. Sutton, *Richard III: The Road to Bosworth Field* (London: Constable, 1985), 95.
4. Charles Ross, *Richard III* (California: University of California Press, 1981), 81.
5. Hicks, *Richard III*, 119–24, for detailed discussion of Richard's propaganda coup.
6. P.W. Hammond and A.F. Sutton, *Richard III: The Road to Bosworth Field* (London: Constable, 1985), 94.
7. M. Hicks, *The Prince in the Tower* (Gloucestershire: Tempus, 2003), 139–42; P.W. Hammond and A.F. Sutton, *Richard III: The Road to Bosworth Field* (London: Constable, 1985), 94–98.
8. Hicks, *Richard III*, 109.
9. Ibid.
10. Ross, *Richard III*, 73.
11. ODNB, s.v. "Thomas Gray, First Marquess of Dorset (1455–1501)."
12. P.W. Hammond and A.F. Sutton, *Richard III: The Road to Bosworth Field* (London: Constable, 1985), 99.
13. Ross, *Richard III*, 74; Hicks, *Richard III*, 110; A. Cheetham, *The Life and Times of Richard III* (London: Weidenfeld and Nicholson, 1972), 110.
14. Hicks, *Richard III*, 111.
15. Ibid.
16. Ibid., 117.
17. Ibid., 126.
18. Cheetham, *Life and Times*, 118.
19. Hicks, *Richard III*, 108, 112.
20. Ross, *Richard III*, 74.
21. Ross, *Richard III*, 76–77; M. Hicks, *The Prince in the Tower* (Gloucestershire: Tempus, 2003), 154–56.
22. Ross, *Richard III*, 74–75.
23. Hicks, *Richard III*, 112.
24. Ibid., 130–33.
25. Hammond and Sutton, *Richard III*, 102.
26. Hicks, *Richard III*, 125; Hammond and Sutton, *Richard III*, 103–04.
27. Ross, *Richard III*, 80–84; Sir Thomas More gives the original account, including Catesby's approaches to Hastings.
28. Ross, *Richard III*, 93; Hicks, *Richard III*, 117.
29. Ross, *Richard III*, 89–91; appendix 3.
30. Appendix 3.
31. Ross, *Richard III*, 89–95: this is an excellent, balanced discussion of Richard's motives and the pressures that aided his usurpation.

Chapter Two

1. A.J. Pollard, *Richard III and the Princes in the Tower* (Gloucestershire: Sutton, 1991), 105–08.
2. Rosemary Horrox, *Richard III: A Study in Service* (Cambridge: Cambridge University Press, 1991).
3. Hicks, *Richard III*, 157.

4. Pollard, *Richard III and the Princes in the Tower*, 109.
5. P.W. Hammond and A.F. Sutton, *Richard III: The Road to Bosworth Field* (London: Constable, 1985), 141; Ross, *Richard III*, appendix 4.
6. Charles Ross, *Richard III* (Berkeley: University of California Press, 1981), 111.
7. Ibid., 112.
8. Ibid.; Hicks, *Richard III*, 154–55.
9. Ross, *Richard III*, 113–14.
10. Ross, *Richard III*, 114; Hicks, *Richard III*, 157–58.
11. Hammond and Sutton, *Richard III*, 141–42.
12. Hicks, *Richard III*, 157.
13. ODNB, s.v. "Henry Stafford, Second Duke of Buckingham (1455–1483)."
14. Ross, *Richard III*, 109–11.
15. Ibid., 116.
16. Ibid.; Hammond and Sutton, *Richard III*, 142.
17. Hicks, *Richard III*, 168.
18. Cheetham, *Life and Times*, 140
19. Louise Gill, *Richard III and Buckingham's Rebellion* (Gloucestershire: Sutton, 2000), 147.
20. Ibid.

Chapter Three

1. Charles Ross, *Richard III* (California: University of California Press, 1981), 147–50.
2. A.J. Pollard, *Richard III and the Princes in the Tower* (Gloucestershire: Sutton, 1991), 145–47.
3. Pollard, *Richard III*, 146–47.
4. Ibid., 145.
5. Ibid., 150.
6. Ross, *Richard III*, 123–24.
7. Ibid., 186; Pollard, *Richard III*, 150–51.
8. Pollard, *Richard III*, 153–57.
9. Ibid., 157–60.
10. Ibid., 132.
11. Ibid., 132–35.
12. Bernard Fields, *Royal Blood* (Gloucestershire: Sutton, 2000), 157.
13. Ross, *Richard III*, 145.
14. Ibid., 145–46.
15. Pollard, *Richard III*, 159; ODNB, s.v. "Henry VII."
16. Ross, *Richard III*; a full account of the battle of Bosworth is given in chapter 11.
17. David Baldwin, *The Lost Prince: The Survival of Richard of York* (Gloucestershire: Sutton, 2007), 90.
18. M. Hicks, *Richard III* (Gloucestershire: Tempus, 1991), 108.
19. Ibid., 110.
20. Ibid., 130–34.
21. Ibid., 133–34.
22. Ross, *Richard III*, chapter 9: "The Government of the Realm."
23. Ibid., introduction, liii.
24. Ross, *Richard III*, 158–62.
25. Hicks, *Richard III*, 158.
26. ODNB, s.v. "Henry Stafford, Second Duke of Buckingham (1455–1483)."

Chapter Four

1. Rosemary Horrox, *Richard III: A Study in Service* (Cambridge: Cambridge University Press, 1991), 2–10.
2. Charles Ross, *Richard III* (California: University of California Press, 1981), 30.
3. Charles Ross, *Edward IV* (Yale: Yale University Press, 1997), 11.
4. R. Grassby, *The Business Community of Seventeenth-Century England* (Cambridge: Press Syndicate of the University of Cambridge, 2002), 3.
5. Tim Lambert, personal Web site, "Daily Life in the Middle Ages," http://www.local histories.org/middle.
6. Grassby, *Business Community*, 85.
7. "Health and Medicine in Medieval England," The History Learning Site, www.historylearningsite.co.uk/medieval-england/health-and-medicine-in-medieval-england; W.W. MacArthur, "A Brief Story of English Malaria," *British Medical Bulletin* 8 (1951): 76–79.
8. Author not recorded, *Life in Medieval Britain*, chapter 6: "Medieval British Society," lyceumbooks.com/pdf/histvol1_chapter_06.pdf.
9. "Popular print," Wikipedia, https://en.wikipedia.org/wiki/Popular_print.
10. S.H. Rigby, *Britain in the Later Middle Ages* (London: Wiley, 2002), 466.

Chapter Five

1. M. Hicks, *The Prince in the Tower* (Gloucestershire, Tempus, 2003), 58.
2. Hicks, *Prince in the Tower*, 83–90.
3. Ibid., 156–57; ODNB, s.v. "Edward V."
4. ODNB, s.v. "Richard of York."
5. Hicks, *Prince in the Tower*, 74.
6. Ibid., 75.
7. Ibid., 75–78.
8. Ibid., 78.
9. David Baldwin, *The Lost Prince: The Survival of Richard of York* (Gloucestershire: Sutton, 2007), 49.

10. M. Hicks, *Richard III* (Gloucestershire: Tempus, 1991), 97; Hicks, *Prince in the Tower*, 79.
11. Hicks, *Prince in the Tower*, 70.
12. Ibid., 80.
13. Ibid., 82.
14. Ibid., 79; ODNB, s.v. "Edward V."
15. ODNB, s.v. "Richard of York."
16. Hicks, *Prince in the Tower*, 144.
17. Ibid., 145.
18. Ibid.
19. Ibid., 148–49.
20. Ibid., 150–51.
21. Ibid., 151.
22. Ibid., 93.
23. Ibid., 94.

Chapter Six

1. Domonic Mancini, *De Occupatione Regni Anglie per Riccardum Tercium* (The Occupation of the Throne of England by Richard III), trans. C.A.J. Armstrong (London: Sutton, 1984), 50–120
2. Robert Fabyan, *Great Chronicles of London* (Oxford: Clarendon, 1905), 515–16.
3. Caroline Halstead, *Richard III: As Duke of Gloucester and King of England* (London: Longman, Brown, Green and Longmans, 1844), 178.
4. David Baldwin, *The Lost Prince: The Survival of Richard of York* (Gloucestershire: Sutton, 2007), 2.
5. A. Hanham, ed., *The Cely Letters, 1472–1488* (Early English Text Society, 1975), 147.
6. J. Ashdown-Hill, *The Dublin King: The True Story of Edward Earl of Warwick, Lambert Simnel and the "Princes in the Tower"* (Gloucestershire: History Press, 2015), 48 .
7. Hanham, ed., *The Cely Letters*, 147; A.J. Pollard, *Richard III and the Princes in the Tower* (Gloucestershire: Sutton, 1991), 121.
8. Nigel Saul, *The Three Richards: Richard I, Richard II, and Richard III* (London: A. and C. Black, 2006), 221.
9. Pollard, *Richard III*, 122.
10. Ibid.
11. Ibid., 123.
12. Ibid.
13. Ibid., 115–25. This is a good summary of the more obscure writings related to the princes.
14. Halstead, *Richard III*, 181.
15. Ibid.
16. Sir Thomas More, *The History of King Richard the Third (Unfinished)* (Renascence e-publishing, www.luminarium.org, 128.

17. Halstead, *Richard III*, 181.
18. ODNB, s.v. "Edward Mortimer."
19. P.W. Hammond and A.F. Sutton, *Richard III: The Road to Bosworth Field* (London: Constable, 1985), 95.

Section III

1. Timeline 1.
2. A.J. Pollard, *Richard III and the Princes in the Tower* (Gloucestershire: Sutton, 1991), 132–35.

Chapter Seven

1. Table 4.
2. Chapter 4.
3. W.W. MacArthur, "A Brief Story of English Malaria," *British Medical Bulletin* 8 (1951): 76–79.
4. Table 4.
5. Lawrence E. Tanner and William Wright, "Recent Investigations Regarding the Fate of the Princes in the Tower," *Archaeologia* 34 (1934): 9–10; F. Sandford, A Genealogical History of the Kings and Queens of England: and Monarchs of Great Britain, from the Conquest, Anno 1066. to the Year 1707 … (London: Tho. Newcomb for the author, 1677. Ann Arbor, Michigan: University of Michigan, Digital Library Production Service, 2011), 411.
6. Tanner and Wright, "Recent Investigations," 9–10.
7. Charles Ross, *Richard III* (California: University of California Press, 1981), 97 and appendix 1.
8. Ross, *Richard III*, 97.
9. Geoffrey Parnell, "The Roman and Medieval Defences and the Later Development, of the Inmost Ward, Tower of London: Excavations 1955–77," Transactions of the London and Middlesex Archaeological Society 36 (1985): 5–7.

Chapter Eight

1. M. Hicks, *Richard III* (Gloucestershire: Tempus, 1991), 130.
2. Charles Ross, *Richard III* (California: University of California Press, 1981), 113.
3. Hicks, *Richard III*, 131.
4. Caroline Halstead, *Richard III: As Duke of Gloucester and King of England* (London: Longman, Brown, Green and Longmans, 1844), 193.
5. Ibid., 231.

6. Ross, *Richard III*, 145–46.
7. Table 4.
8. A.J. Pollard, *Richard III and the Princes in the Tower* (Gloucestershire: Sutton, 1991), 123.
9. Ibid.
10. Ibid., 127.
11. Ibid., 129–30.
12. ODNB, s.v. "Henry VII."

Chapter Nine

1. Charles Ross, *Richard III* (California: University of California Press, 1981), 145.
2. P.W. Hammond and A.F. Sutton, *Richard III: The Road to Bosworth Field* (London: Constable, 1985), 142.
3. P.M. Kendall, *King Richard the Third* (New York: W.W. Norton, 1955), 345.
4. David Baldwin, *The Lost Prince: The Survival of Richard of York* (Gloucestershire: Sutton, 2007), 81.
5. Audrey Williamson, *The Mystery of the Princes* (Gloucestershire: Amberly, 2010), 3; the story of the princes living at Gipping Hall was related to Williamson by Mrs. Kathleen Margaret Drewe, a descendent of a Tyrell son adopted into the family in the 18th century.
6. Baldwin, *Lost Prince*, 87–97.
7. Caroline Halstead, *Richard III: As Duke of Gloucester and King of England* (London: Longman, Brown, Green and Longmans, 1844), 126.
8. J. Ashdown-Hill, *The Dublin King: The True Story of Edward Earl of Warwick, Lambert Simnel and the "Princes in the Tower"* (Gloucestershire: History Press, 2015), 75.
9. ODNB, s.v. "Henry VII."
10. J. Ashdown-Hill, *The Dublin King: The True Story of Edward Earl of Warwick, Lambert Simnel and the "Princes in the Tower"* (Gloucestershire: History Press, 2015), 86.
11. ODNB, s.v. "Margaret of Burgundy."
12. Sir George Buck, *History of King Richard III*, 1619, ed. A.N. Kincaid (Gloucestershire: Sutton, 1979), 84.
13. Ashdown-Hill, *Dublin King*, 57.
14. ODNB, s.v. "Lambert Simnel."
15. Ibid.
16. Ibid.
17. ODNB, s.v. "Perkin Warbeck."

Chapter Ten

1. Charles Ross, *Richard III* (California: University of California Press, 1981), 99; M. Hicks, *The Prince in the Tower* (Gloucestershire, Tempus, 2003), 175.
2. Hicks, *Prince in the Tower*, 179.
3. Chapter 4.
4. Rosemary Horrox, *Richard III: A Study in Service* (Cambridge: Cambridge University Press, 1991), 149.
5. M. Hicks, *Richard III* (Gloucestershire: Tempus, 1991), 155–56.
6. Ian Arthurson, *The Perkin Warbeck Conspiracy* (Gloucestershire: History Press, 1994, 2009), 13–14; 2009 edition.
7. Records relating to most of the individuals described in the succeeding chapters are located at a number of sites, but the facilities now available at the National Archives Web site shows the location of such records available in most British archives, not just those documents in storage at Kew. Consequently, although the National Archives may appear as the only source for records in the tables, this refers to their location as found by the PRO's "Discovery" search engine, not necessarily the site of the archive itself.

Chapter Eleven

1. ODNB, s.v. "Anne Neville."
2. ODNB, s.v. "Elizabeth Woodville."
3. Table 5.
4. ODNB, s.v. "Elizabeth of York."
5. ODNB, s.v. "Cecily of York."
6. ODNB, s.v. "Anne of York."
7. ODNB, s.v. "Catherine of York."
8. ODNB, s.v. "Bridget of York."
9. ODNB, s.v. "Thomas Grey, Marquess of Dorset."
10. ODNB, s.v. "Margaret of York and Burgundy."
11. P.W. Hammond and A.F. Sutton, *Richard III: The Road to Bosworth Field* (London: Constable, 1985), 144.
12. Richard Haute, Kent, 22 August 1487–21 August 1488, E 150/458/1, Public Record Office, Kew.
13. ODNB, s.v. "Margaret of York and Burgundy."

Chapter Twelve

1. M. Hicks, *The Prince in the Tower* (Gloucestershire, Tempus, 2003), 93.
2. M. Hicks, *The Prince in the Tower* (Gloucestershire, Tempus, 2003), 94.
3. ODNB, s.v. "Cardinal Thomas Bourchier."
4. ODNB, s.v. "Robert Stillington, Bishop of Bath and Wells."
5. ODNB, s.v. "Thomas Millyng."

6. ODNB, s.v. "Sir John Fogge."
7. ODNB, s.v. "Sir John Scott."
8. ODNB, s.v. "John Alcock."
9. ODNB, s.v. "Edward Storey."
10. ODNB, s.v. "Walter Devereux."
11. ODNB, s.v. "Sir Richard Haute."
12. Hicks, *Prince in the Tower*, 71.
13. Henry Anstey, ed., Epistolae Academicae Oxon, vols. 35 and 36 (Oxford: Oxford Historical Society, 1898).
14. ODNB, s.v. "The Haute Family."

Chapter Thirteen

1. ODNB, s.v. "Sir Robert Brackenbury."
2. P.M. Kendall, *King Richard the Third* (New York: W.W. Norton, 1955), 470.
3. ODNB, s.v. "Sir James Tyrell."
4. ODNB, s.v. "William Catesby."
5. ODNB, s.v. "Sir Francis Lovell."
6. ODNB, s.v. "Sir Richard Ratcliffe."
7. ODNB, s.v. "John Howard, First Duke of Norfolk."
8. ODNB, s.v. "John Russell."
9. ODNB, s.v. "Sir Edmund Shaa."
10. Charles Lethbridge Kingsford, The Stonor Letters and Papers (1290–1483) (London: Royal Historical Society, 1919), 162–63.
11. Access availaible via PRO "Discovery" search engine.

Chapter Fourteen

1. ODNB, s.v. "Henry VII."
2. ODNB, s.v. "John Morton."
3. ODNB, s.v. "Sir Reginald Bray."
4. ODNB, s.v. "William Collingbourne."

5. ODNB, s.v. "Margaret Beaufort."
6. Ibid.

Chapter Fifteen

1. ODNB, s.v. "Henry Stafford, Second Duke of Buckingham."
2. ODNB, s.v. "Sir William Stonor."
3. ODNB, s.v. "Richard Hill."
4. ODNB, s.v. "Peter Courtenay."

Chapter Sixteen

1. Rosemary Horrox, *Richard III: A Study in Service* (Cambridge: Cambridge University Press, 1991), 149.
2. PRO C81/1392/1; "Warrants made under The Great Seal: for trial,", Public Record Office, Kew; Rosemary Horrox, *Richard III: A Study in Service* (Cambridge: Cambridge University Press, 1991), 149.
3. Rosemary Horrox, *Richard III: A Study in Service* (Cambridge: Cambridge University Press, 1991), 149.
4. Ibid., 150.
5. Geoffrey Chaucer, "The Pardoner's Tale," in *The Canterbury Tales* (London: Penguin Classics, 2005), 151.
6. Rosemary Horrox, *Richard III: A Study in Service* (Cambridge: Cambridge University Press, 1991), 149–50.
7. ODNB, s.v. "William Herbert, Earl of Pembroke."
8. Capital Punishment UK, "Confirmed Executions at the Tower of London," www.capitalpunishmentuk.org/tower.html.
9. Chapter 2.

Bibliography

Books and Articles

Anstey, Henry, ed. *Epistolae Academicae Oxon.* Vols. 35 and 36. Oxford: Oxford Historical Society, 1898.

Arthurson, Ian. *The Perkin Warbeck Conspiracy.* Gloucestershire: History Press, 1994, 2009.

Ashdown-Hill, J. *The Dublin King: The True Story of Edward Earl of Warwick, Lambert Simnel and the "Princes in the Tower."* Gloucestershire: History Press, 2015.

Baldwin, D. *The Lost Prince: The Survival of Richard of York.* Gloucestershire: Sutton, 2007.

Buck, Sir George. *History of King Richard III.* 1619. Edited by A.N. Kincaid. Gloucestershire: Sutton, 1979.

Chaucer, Geoffrey. *The Canterbury Tales.* London: Penguin Classics, 2005.

Cheetham, A. *The Life and Times of Richard III.* London: Weidenfeld and Nicholson, 1972.

Churchill, Sir Winston. *A History of the English-Speaking Peoples, Vol. 1.* New York: Skyhorse, 2011.

Fabyan, Robert. *Great Chronicles of London.* Oxford: Clarendon, 1905.

Fields, B. *Royal Blood.* Gloucestershire: Sutton, 2000.

Gill, Louise. *Richard III and Buckingham's Rebellion.* Gloucestershire: Sutton, 2000.

Grassby, R. *The Business Community of Seventeenth-Century England.* Cambridge: Press Syndicate of the University of Cambridge, 2002.

Halstead, Caroline. *Richard III: As Duke of Gloucester and King of England.* London: Longman, Brown, and Green, 1844.

Hammond, P.W., and A.F. Sutton. *Richard III: The Road to Bosworth Field.* London: Constable, 1985.

Hanham, A., ed. *The Cely Letters, 1472–1488.* London: Early English Text Society, 1975.

Hicks, M. *The Prince in the Tower.* Gloucestershire: Tempus, 2003.

———. *Richard III.* Gloucestershire: Tempus, 1991.

Horrox, Rosemary. *Richard III: A Study in Service.* Cambridge: Cambridge University Press, 1991.

———, and M.W. Ormrod, eds. *A Social History of England, 1200–1500.* Cambridge: Cambridge University Press, 2006.

Kendall, P.M. *King Richard the Third.* New York: W.W. Norton, 1955.

Kingsford, Charles Lethbridge. *The Stonor Letters and Papers (1290–1483).* London: Royal Historical Society, 1919.

Lamb, V.B. *The Betrayal of Richard III: An Introduction to the Controversy.* London: Sutton, 1990.

MacArthur, W. "A Brief Story of English Malaria." *British Medical Bulletin* 8 (1951): 76–79.

Mancini, Domonic. *De Occupatione Regni Anglie per Riccardum Tercium (The Occupation of the Throne of England by Richard III).* Trans. C.A.J. Armstrong. London: Sutton, 1984.

More, Sir Thomas. *The History of King Richard the Third (Unfinished).* Renascence e-publishing. http://www.luminarium.org/renascence-editions/r3.html

Parnell, Geoffrey. "The Roman and Medieval Defences and the Later Development, of the Inmost Ward, Tower of London: Excavations 1955–77." *Transactions of the London and Middlesex Archaeological Society* 36 (1985).

Pollard, A.J. *Richard III and the Princes in the Tower.* Gloucestershire: Sutton, 1991.

Rigby, S.H. *Britain in the Later Middle Ages.* London: Wiley, 2002.

Ross, C. D. *Richard III.* Berkeley: University of California Press, 1981.

———. *Edward IV.* New Haven [Conn.]: Yale University Press, 1997.

Sandford, F. *A Genealogical History of the Kings and Queens of England: and Monarchs of Great Britain, from the Conquest, Anno 1066 to the Year 1707. [London] In the Savoy: Printed by Tho. Newcomb, for the author, 1677.* Ann Arbor, Michigan: University of Michigan, Digital Library Production Service, 2011.

Saul, Nigel. *The Three Richards: Richard I, Richard II, Richard III.* London: Hambledon Continuum, 2006.

Tanner, Lawrence E., and William Wright. "Recent Investigations Regarding the Fate of the Princes in the Tower." *Archaeologia* 34 (1934): 9–10.

Williamson, Audrey. *The Mystery of the Princes.* Gloucestershire: Amberly, 2010.

Archival Documents

Canterbury Cathedral Archives

Richard III, King of England. Letter to William Haute, knight; John Brumston, esq.; John Dygges, esq.; John Isaak, esq.; John Alfegh; John Fyneux; Roger Brent; John Nethirsole; and Robert Billysdon. 4 September 1483. CCA-DCC-CHANTT/S/365.

Cornwall Record Office

"Account Roll Cornish Estate General Receiver of Manors, Etc., of Thomas Arundell, Knight, in Cornwall ... Arundell of Lanherne and Trerice." AR/2/925.

"Indented Receipt, 18 May 1485, by Thomas Southwode from Thomas Tregoys, for Sir James Tyrell, Knight, of the Revenues of His Lands in Cornwall and Devon. 1484–1485."

Public Record Office, Kew

Catesby, William. Will. 31 January 1486. PROB 11/7/290.

"Deputy Chamberlain of the Lower Exchequer ... of Sir James Tyrell as Chamberlain Under Letters Patent of Richard, Duke of Gloucester. (ii) With: Sir James Tyrell's Appointment of Thomas Salle as His Deputy: Black Book of the Exchequer, f. 48B." SP 46/139/fo167.

"Exchequer, 26 June 1484–25; June 1485." E 154/2/4.

"Extracts from Wardrobe Accounts Concerning Robes Given at Coronations of Edward IV, Henry IV and Richard III. 1483–1509." LC 9/50.

Hastings, William. "kt Counties: Yorks Chancery: Inquisitions Post Mortem, series 1, Richard III. 26 June 1483–25; June 1484." C 141/1/11.

Haute, Richard. "Kent. 22 August 1487–21; August 1488." E 150/458/1.

Howard, John, Duke of Norfolk. Northampton 22 August 1485–21; August 1486. E 150/668/1.

"Inventory of certain clothes and furniture of William Catesby at London."

Stonor Family. "Barons Camoy, Henley-on-Thames, correspondence and papers." C47/37/1.

"Trial of unnamed men arrested for an enterprise." C81/1529/20.

"Warrants made under the Great Seal: for trial." C81/1392/1.

"William Catesby, attained: Northamptonshire: 22 August 1487–21; August 1488." C 142/23/72.

Society of Antiquaries of London

Howard, John (1430–1485), 1st Duke of Norfolk. Household accounts: 1481–1491. MSS 76–77.

Suffolk Records Office

"Notice Relating to Demolition of Gipping Hall, Suffolk: Notice Concerns Sale of Materials with Details of Lots: 1874." HD 367.

West Sussex Registry Office

"Notes from the Duke of Norfolk's Records Relating to the Manor of Shillinglee in Kirdford: 1438–1583." SHILLINGLEE/3/1.

Index

Page numbers in ***bold italics*** indicate pages with illustrations.

Alcock, John, Dean of Westminster 140
Anlaby family cartulary 80
Anne, Duchess of Britany 67
Anne of York 125
Argentine, John 66, 91

Bacon, Francis 83–84
Battle of Barnet *51*
Battle of Bosworth ***38***, 39–42
Battle of Tewksbury *52*
Beaufort, Margaret 20, 33, 34, 35, 169–170; murder of princes 100–101
The Bloody or Garden Tower 74, ***189***, ***195***
Bodies in the Tower 93–95
Bold, Thomas 144
Bourchier, Thomas, Archbishop of Canterbury 12, 135–137
Brackenbury, Sir Robert 22, 41, 44, 77, 116, 150–151
Bray, Sir Reginald 168
Bridget of York 125
Buck, Sir George 106–107

Catesby, William 37, 152–154
Catherine of York 125
Caxton, William 58
Cecily of York 124–125
Cely letter 78
Colchester Oath book 79
Collingbourne, William 168–169
Courtenay, Peter 179–180
Croyland chronicler 77–78

Darcey, Lady Elizabeth 144
Davison, Dr. John 144

Davy William 188
de Commynes, Phillipe 81
de Rochfort, Guillaume 80–81
Devereux, Walter, Lord Ferrers 141–142

Edward IV 8, ***9;*** children 70–71
Edward V 8, 12, 22, 60–61, 71–73, 91; escape from the Tower, 20, 119; monarchy 67–70
Edward of Middleham, Prince of Wales 20, 33, 37
Elizabeth of York 35, 123–124

Fabyan, Robert 76–77
Fogge, Sir John 138–139

Giles, John 144
Grafton, Adam 144
Grey, Sir Richard 10, 18
Grey, Thomas, Marquess of Dorset 11, 36, 125–126

Haute, Sir Richard 10, 142–143
Hill, Richard 178
Howard, John, 1st Duke of Norfolk 26, 157

Ightham Mote ***142***
Ireland, Stephen 186–188

Life expectancy 55–56, 91
Lovell, Sir Francis 104, 120, 154–156
Ludlow castle 62

Index

Mancini, Domonic 8, 75–76
Margaret of York and Burgundy 104, 106, 127–128
Middelton Collection, King list 80
Middleham castle **35**, **36**
Millyng, Thomas, Abbot of Westminster 138
Molinet, Jean 81–82
More, Sir Thomas 82–83
Mortimer, Anne 67
Morton, John 16, 24, 25, 166–168; murder of princes 101

Nesfield, John 159
Neville, Anne 37, 122

October Rebellion 46–47, 119

Parliamentary Rolle 18
Powderham castle **179**
Precontract 17

Ratcliffe, Sir Richard 37, 156–157
Ricart, Robert 79–80
Richard III 8, 10–12, 16, 20, 22, 26, 42–45, 61–63, 91, 122; attempted rescue attempt of the princes 20, 119; murder of princes 96–98
Rous Rolle 81
Royal Council 8
Russe, Richard 186
Russell, John, Bishop of Lincoln 13, 157–158

St. Leger, Thomas 26
Scott, Sir John 139

Shaa, Sir Edmund 158–159
Shaa, Ralph 16
Shore, Jane 16
Simnel, Lambert 107–109
Smith, John 189
Stafford, Henry, Duke of Buckingham 10, 18, 20, 25, 26, 47–48, 176–177; murder of princes 98–99
Stanley, William, Lord Hastings 8, 15
Stillington, Robert, Bishop of Bath and Wells 16, 137–138
Stonor, Sir William 177–178
Storey, Edward, Bishop of Chicester 140–141

Titulus Regius 19, 33
Tower of London **183**, **184**, **185**, **186**, **190**, **193**, **194**
Tudor, Henry 18, 25, 26, 34, **41**, 165–166; invasion 38–39, murder of princes 99–100
Tyrell, Sir John 103, 151–152

Vaughn, Sir Thomas 10, 18
Vergil, Polydore 59, 82

Warbeck, Perkin 110–112, 120
Welles, Avice 144
White Tower **187**
Wydeville, Anthony, Earl Rivers 10, 18, 66
Wydeville, Sir Edward 12, 13, 34
Wydeville, Elizabeth 8, **10**, 11, 16, 35, 48, 103, 122

www.ingramcontent.com/pod-product-compliance
Ingram Content Group UK Ltd.
Pitfield, Milton Keynes, MK11 3LW, UK
UKHW041939140426
5217IPUK00014B/560